THE WYCLIFFE
EXEGETICAL
COMMENTARY

Kenneth Barker, General Editor

PHILIPPIANS

Moisés Silva

MOODY PRESS

CHICAGO

All Scripture quotations, unless otherwise noted, are the author's translation.

Library of Congress Cataloging in Publication Data

Silva, Moisés.
    Philippians / by Moisés Silva.
       p.   cm. — (Wycliffe exegetical commentary)
    Includes bibliographical references and indexes.
    ISBN 0-8024-9260-6
    1. Bible. N.T. Philippians—Commentaries. I. Bible. N.T.
Philippians. 1988. II. Title. III. Series.
BS2705.3.S5 1988
227'.607—dc19

    88-8438
    CIP

1 2 3 4 5 6 7 8 Printing/AK/Year 93 92 91 90 89

Printed in the United States of America

A mis queridos padres

THE WYCLIFFE EXEGETICAL COMMENTARY

The Wycliffe Exegetical Commentary provides a scholarly, thorough analysis of every passage in every book of Scripture. Written especially for the informed layman, student, and scholar, all exegesis and exposition is based on the original languages of the Bible books. Translations used are those of the authors. Textual criticism and word study are included where appropriate.

This in-depth commentary also includes extended excursuses on important topics of theological, historical, and archaeological interest.

The text is interpreted according to a historical, critical, grammatical hermeneutic and propounds a conservative, evangelical theology. But you will not get a narrow view of problem passages. This commentary interacts with a range of major views, both evangelical and nonevangelical.

Leading conservative scholars from many denominations have contributed. These scholars represent a cross-section of respected evangelical seminaries and colleges.

General Editor
Ken Barker (B.A., Northwestern College; Th.M., Dallas Theological Seminary; Ph.D., Dropsie College for Hebrew and Cognate Learning) is academic dean and professor of Old Testament literature and exegesis at Capital Bible Seminary, Lanham, Maryland.

Old Testament Coordinator
Richard Patterson (A.B., Wheaton College; M.Div., Northwest Baptist Theological Seminary; Th.M., Talbot Theological Seminary; M.A., Ph.D., University of California—Los Angeles) is chairman of the department of biblical studies and professor of semitic languages and literatures at Liberty University, Lynchburg, Virginia.

New Testament Coordinator
Moisés Silva (B.A., Bob Jones University; Ph.D., University of Manchester, England; B.D., Th.M., Westminster Theological Seminary) is chairman of the New Testament department and professor of New Testament at Westminster Theological Seminary in Philadelphia. He has writen *Biblical Words and Their Meaning* and *Has the Church Misread the Bible?*

PHILIPPIANS

When Paul set sail for what is now Europe, his first port of call was the Roman colony of Philippi. This became the site of the first Christian congregation in Europe. Though they were faithful providers and great encouragers for Paul on his long missionary journeys, the church was not without its problems.

The time came, while he was imprisoned in Rome, for Paul to send a message of love and rebuke to the church at Philippi. Moisés Silva says, "The difficult task that was before the apostle would draw from him, under divine inspiration, a message full of comfort and joy, rebuke and encouragement, doctrine and exhortation. Quite beyond Paul's own powers of anticipation, the letter he was about to dictate would speak to the hearts of countless believers for many centuries to come."

About the author
Moisés Silva (B.A., Bob Jones University; Ph.D., University of Manchester, England; B.D., Th.M., Westminster Theological Seminary) is chairman of the New Testament department and professor of New Testament at Westminster Theological Seminary in Philadelphia. He has written *Biblical Words and Their Meaning* and *Has the Church Misread the Bible?*

Table of Contents

General Editor's Introduction

John Wycliffe (c. 1320-1384) is widely known as "the Morning Star of the Reformation." One of the reasons for that reputation was his great concern for the translation, sufficiency, and understanding of Holy Scripture. Since that is also one of the chief concerns of this commentary series, it is appropriate that it be named after him.

The key descriptive term in the series title, however, is *Exegetical.* While the various areas of biblical criticism receive at least brief treatment, the principal emphasis of the commentary is exegesis. By exegesis we mean the application of generally accepted hermeneutical principles to the original (Hebrew, Aramaic, and Greek) biblical text with a view to unfolding (lit. "leading out," Gk. *exēgeomai*) its correct, contextual meaning. The method followed is commonly referred to as grammatico-historical exegesis. A more complete designation would be the grammatical-historical-literary-theological method.

To facilitate the reader's most effective use of the *Wycliffe Exegetical Commentary (WEC)*, it will be helpful to delineate here some of its policies and practices:

1. This is a commentary on the Hebrew, Aramaic, and Greek texts of the Bible, not some English translation. Consequently Hebrew, Aramaic, and Greek words and phrases appear in their original scripts, but with English transliterations and translations pro-

vided at their first occurrence. After that, transliterations alone normally suffice. However, only the original scripts are employed in the Additional Notes and footnote discussions, since scholars and specialists would be the ones most interested in that more technical material (e.g., word studies, grammatical or syntactical points, etymologies, textual variants in the original languages, specialized bibliographies, etc.). Unless otherwise indicated, all Scripture translations are those of the authors of the individual volumes.

2. *WEC* stresses the development of the argument of a given book and its central theme(s). An attempt has been made to show how each section of a book fits together with the preceding and following sections. We do not want the reader to become so preoccupied with the trees (analysis) that he fails to see the forest (synthesis).

3. Some flexibility has been allowed in the introductions to the books of the Bible—and even in the exegetical approach—in order to reflect the strengths and interests of the various commentators as well as the nature and purpose of the material.

4. Most of the abbreviations and transliterations follow the guidelines of the *Journal of Biblical Literature (JBL)*. Usually the only abbreviations listed are those not found in *JBL*.

5. Asterisks in either the Translation or the Exegesis and Exposition section refer the reader to discussions of text-critical problems in the Additional Notes section, though these are not the only kinds of discussions one will encounter in the Additional Notes sections (see above, under 1).

I wish to express my gratitude to Moody Press for inviting me to edit this entire series and particularly to Dana Gould and Garry Knussman for their assistance. Special thanks go to Richard Patterson (Old Testament editor) and Moisés Silva (New Testament editor). Grateful acknowledgment is also given to all the contributors of the individual volumes; they are to be commended especially for their cooperation and patience with the editors. All of us trust and pray that *WEC* will be used by God to advance the cause of a more exegetically-based, and so more accurate, biblical interpretation and biblical theology. In other words, we hope that this series will be an example of "correctly handling [lit. 'cutting straight,' Gk. *orthotomeō*] the Word of truth" (2 Tim. 2:15).

Paul's parting words to the Ephesian elders seem apropos here: "Now I commit you to God and to the word of his grace, which can build you up and give you an inheritance among all those who are sanctified" (Acts 20:32, *NIV*).

Kenneth L. Barker
General Editor

Preface

The distinctive features of the Wycliffe Exegetical Commentary series have made it possible for me to put into practice a few ideas about commentary writing that I have entertained for some time. I am grateful to the Moody Press editorial staff for allowing me the flexibility to pursue these individual interests, and the user of this volume may benefit from knowing what they are.

Traditionally, exegetical commentaries have been treated primarily as reference works, to be consulted for information on a few verses or even on isolated words and phrases. Since no commentator can anticipate all of the questions that may occur to Bible readers, students often experience disappointment that the commentaries do not address these questions specifically. More seriously, the verse-by-verse approach of the typical commentary, in spite of its obvious advantages, can become a hindrance to faithful exposition whenever it leads to an atomistic handling of the text—treating problems in relative isolation from each other at the expense of the main teaching of the passage.

My attempt in this volume has been to focus exclusively on the thrust of the text itself, to ask continually what is *distinctive* to Philippians, to determine how each passage contributes to the argument of the letter as a whole, to avoid being distracted by extraneous problems, and to communicate clearly the results of my research by means of uncluttered exposition. Others will have to evaluate to what extent I have been successful in this endeavor, but at least they will know what are the criteria that have guided my work. According to the guidelines for the series, each section of the commentary consists of the following three parts:

Translation. Because of the widespread use of the *NASB* and the *NIV* in evangelical circles, I have assumed that users of this commentary have access to both. My translation of Philippians does not attempt to compete with them—it certainly makes no claim to being either literal (for which the *NASB* is valuable) or literate (a fine *NIV* quality). Instead, I have attempted a full rendering, largely a paraphrase, that seeks to summarize the results of the exegesis. I have used brackets generously to include interpretive material. Brackets are also used occasionally for alternate renderings and for questionable textual readings (the latter are marked with an asterisk and discussed along with other variants in the Additional Notes).

Exegesis and Exposition. Hoping to meet the goals mentioned above, I have chosen to write "exegetical essays" on carefully defined units of thought. These essays, of course, do not overlook detailed problems of text, language, and interpretation; it is simply that the problems are discussed only to the extent that they have a bearing on the thrust of the passage being considered. The exposition, therefore, is not designed to provide quick answers; rather, it is designed to be read in blocks—the larger the block, the better. Some hardy souls may even wish to read through the whole exposition and thus benefit the most from the distinctive concerns of the commentary. In any case, the reader is strongly encouraged to look carefully at the introductory comments of a section before attempting to evaluate the interpretation of a particular word or clause.

Additional Notes. This section preserves some of the benefits of verse-by-verse exegesis, namely, ease of reference and attention to details that are of lesser importance for understanding the passage. Sometimes, however, these notes include discussions that, while hardly unimportant, would have unnecessarily cluttered the exposition. In these cases, the essays contain a summary of the argumentation and a reference to the additional material.

I am grateful to the general editor, Kenneth L. Barker, and to John S. Feinberg, who first invited me to contribute to this series eight years ago, for reading through an early draft of the commentary and giving useful advice. Richard B. Gaffin, Jr., from whom I learned to regard the apostle Paul as theologian, also read and evaluated the typescript; his encouragement is greatly appreciated.

Billie Goodenough and Dorothy Krieke initially transcribed this commentary from a hopeless handwritten draft; their faithful and careful work made much easier the process of revision. Dan G. McCartney ran a few GRAMCORD programs related to the text of Philippians; I also benefitted from his advice on several exegetical problems. My student assistant Christopher N. Mount offered invaluable help in the last stages of the project.

Finally, I feel I must offer my apologies to my wife and children—especially to John, who often had to give up playing his drums so that his dad could work on the computer—for bearing the brunt of this long undertaking.

Writing a biblical commentary can be a humbling experience, and doubly so when the text being commented upon touches as intensely as Philippians does on the doctrine of sanctification (manifested especially by humility!). Who is sufficient for these things?

Abbreviations

The following abbreviations supplement the list adopted by the *Journal of Biblical Literature:*

BDR	Blass-Debrunner-Rehkopf, *Grammatik des neutestamentlichen Griechisch*
Hwth.	Hawthorne
HF	Hodges-Farstad, *The Greek New Testament According to the Majority Text*
JETS	*Journal of the Evangelical Theological Society*
Ltf.	Lightfoot
MM	Moulton-Milligan, *Vocabulary of the New Testament*
NA	E. Nestle and K. Aland, *NT Graece*, 26th ed.
NASB	*New American Standard Bible*
NBE	*Nueva Biblia Española*
NIDNTT	*New International Dictionary of New Testament Theology*
NIV	*New International Version*
Rob.	A. T. Robertson, *A Grammar of the Greek New Testament*
s.v.	sub voce (under the word)
TrinJ	*Trinity Journal*
v.l.	varia lectio (variant reading)
WBC	Word Biblical Commentary
WW	Wordsworth-White, *Novum Testamentum Domini nostri Iesu Christi*

Commentaries

The following list, though by no means exhaustive, is intended as a fairly comprehensive guide to major commentaries on Philippians, not all of which have been consulted in the preparation of this volume. The list also serves as a complement to Hwth.'s bibliography, which includes some commentaries not listed here. Asterisked items are those through which I have worked systematically or which have otherwise played an important role in the writing of this commentary; for an evaluation of these items, see Introduction: Exegetical History. To avoid excessive footnoting, the volumes here are referred to in the text by author's last name only (occasionally, if there is the possibility of confusion, page numbers are also given).

From the Ancient Period to the Seventeenth Century

Ambrosiaster (Ambrosus Mediolanensis). *In Epistolam B. Pauli ad Philippenses. PL* 17:426–44.

*Calvin, John. *The Epistles of Paul the Apostle to the Galatians, Ephesians, Philippians and Colossians*. Translated by T. H. L. Parker. Grand Rapids: Eerdmans, 1965.

*Chrysostom (Joannes Chrysostomus). *In Epistolam ad Philippenses commentarius. PG* 62:177–298. Translated in *NPNF*, 1st ser., 13:173–255.

Erasmus, Desiderius. *Opera omnia.* 10 vols. Reprint. London: Gregg, 1962. *Annotations,* vol. 6; *Paraphrases,* vol. 7.

Herveus Burgidolensis Monachus. *In Epistolam ad Philippenses. PL* 181:1279–1314.

Lapide, Cornelius à. *Commentarii in Scripturam Sacram,* vol. 9. Lugduni: Pelagaud, 1864.

Marius Victorinus. *Victorini in Epistolam Pauli ad Philippenses liber unicus* (commentary begins at Phil. 1:15). *PL* 8:1197–1256.

Oecumenius Triccae. *Pauli Apostoli ad Philippenses Epistola. PG* 118:1260–1326.

Pelagius. *Pelagius's Expositions of Thirteen Epistles of St. Paul.* Edited by Alexander Souter. 2 vols. Cambridge: The University Press, 1922–26.

Theodore of Mopsuestia. *Theodori Episcopi Mopsuestem in Epistolas B. Pauli commentarii.* Edited by H. B. Swete. Cambridge: The University Press, 1880.

Theodoret (Theodoretus Cyrensis). *Interpretatio Epistolae ad Philippenses. PG* 82:558–90.

Theophylact (Theophylactus Bulgariae). *Commentarius in Epistolam ad Philippenses. PG* 124:1139–1204.

*Thomas Aquinas. *Commentary on Saint Paul's First Letter to the Thessalonians and the Letter to the Philippians.* Albany, N.Y.: Magi, 1969.

The Modern Period

Alford, Henry. *The Greek Testament.* 4 vols. 1845–60. Reprint. Chicago: Moody, 1958.

Barth, Gerhard. *Der Brief an die Philipper.* Zürcher Bibelkommentar NT 9. Zürich: Theologischer Verlag, 1979.

Barth, Karl. *The Epistle to the Philippians.* Richmond: John Knox, 1962.

Beare, F. W. *The Epistle to the Philippians.* (HNTC.) New York: Harper & Bros., 1959.

Bengel, Johann Albert. *Gnomon Novi Testamenti.* 1742. 3d ed. Tübingen: Sumtibus Ludov. Frid. Fues., 1855.

Bonnard, P. *L'épître de saint Paul aux Philippiens et l'épître aux Colossiens.* (CNT 10.) Neuchâtel: Delachaux et Niestlé, 1950.

Boor, Werner de. *Die Briefe des Paulus an die Philipper und an die Kolosser, erklärt.* 2d ed. Wuppertaler Studienbibel. Wuppertal: Brockhaus, 1962.

Bruce, F. F. *Philippians.* Good News Commentary. San Francisco: Harper & Row, 1983.

Caird, G. B. *Paul's Letters from Prison.* New Clarendon Bible. Oxford: The University Press, 1976.

*Collange, Jean-François. *The Epistle of Saint Paul to the Philippians.* (CNT 10a.) London: Epworth, 1979.

Dibelius, Martin. *An die Thessalonischer I II. An die Philipper.* 2d ed. (HNT 11.) Tübinger: J. C. B. Mohr, 1925.

Eadie, John. *A Commentary on the Greek Text of the Epistle of Paul to the Philippians.* London: Richard Griffin, 1859.

Ellicott, C. J. *Commentaries, Critical and Grammatical, on the Epistles of St. Paul, with Revised Translations.* Andover: Warren F. Draper, 1872.

Ernst, J. *Die Briefe an die Philipper, an Philemon, an die Kolosser, und an die Epheser.* (RNT.) Regensburg: Pustet, 1974.

Ewald, P. *Der Brief des Paulus an die Philipper.* 4th ed. Revised by G. Wohlenberg. T. Zahn's Kommentar zum Neuen Testament. Leipzig: Deichert, 1923.

Friedrich, G. *Der Brief an die Philipper.* (NTD 8.) Göttingen: Vandenhoeck & Ruprecht, 1962.

*Gnilka, Joachim. *Der Philipperbrief.* (HTKNT 10/3.) Freiburg: Herder, 1976.

Greijdanus, S. *De Brief van den Apostel Paulus aan de gemeente te Philippi.* Kommentaar op het Nieuwe Testament. Amsterdam: A. van Bottenburg, 1937.

Haupt, E. *Die Gefangenschaftsbriefe.* (MeyerK.) Göttingen: Vandenhoeck & Ruprecht, 1902.

*Hawthorne, Gerald F. (Hwth.) *Philippians.* Word Biblical Commentary, vol. 43. Waco, Tex.: Word, 1983.

Hendriksen, William. *Philippians.* New Testament Commentary. Grand Rapids: Baker, 1962.

Hengel, W. S. van. *Commentarius perpetuus in Epistulam Pauli ad Philippenses.* Lugduni: J. Luchtmans, 1838.

Heriban, Josef. *Retto φρονεῖν e κένωσις. Studio esegetico su Fil 2, 1-5.6-11.* Biblioteca di scienze religiose 51. Rome: LAS, 1983. (Though not a commentary, this work deals extensively with the epistle as a whole.)

Johnstone, Robert. *Lectures Exegetical and Practical on the Epistle of Paul to the Philippians.* 1875. Reprint. Grand Rapids: Baker, 1955. (Includes careful notes on the Greek text.)

Kennedy, H. A. A. "The Epistle to the Philippians." In *Expositor's Greek Testament,* edited by W. R. Nicoll. 5 vols. 1897–1910. Grand Rapids: Eerdmans, 1976.

Kent, Homer A., Jr. "Philippians." In *The Expositor's Bible Commen-*

tary, edited by Frank E. Gaebelein, vol. 11. Grand Rapids: Zondervan, 1978.

Klijn, A. F. J. _De Brief van Paulus aan de Filippenzen._ De predikking van het Niewe Testament. Nijkerk: G. F. Callenbach, 1969.

Klöpper, Albert. _Der Brief des Apostels Paulus an die Philipper erlautert._ Gotha: F. A. Perthes, 1893.

*Lightfoot, J. B. (Ltf.) _St. Paul's Epistle to the Philippians._ 1868. Reprint. Grand Rapids: Zondervan, 1965.

Lipsius, R. A. _Hand-Commentar zum Neuen Testament_ 2/2, 2d ed. Freiburg: J. C. B. Mohr, 1892.

*Lohmeyer, Ernst. _Der Brief an die Philipper, an die Kolosser und an Philemon._ (MeyerK.) Göttingen: Vandenhoeck & Ruprecht, 1930. _Beiheft_ by Werner Schmauch, 1983.

Martin, Ralph P. _Philippians._ (NCB.) Grand Rapids: Eerdmans, 1980. (This volume is to be distinguished from Martin's earlier contribution to the Tyndale series.)

Matter, H. M. _De Brief van Paulus aan de Philippenzen en de Brief aan Philémon._ Commentaar op het Nieuwe Testament. Kampen: J. H. Kok, 1965.

Metzger, Bruce M. _A Textual Commentary on the Greek New Testament._ New York: United Bible Societies, 1971.

*Meyer, H. A. W. _Critical and Exegetical Handbook to the Epistles to the Philippians and Colossians, and to Philemon._ (MeyerK.) 1847–48. Reprint. New York: Funk & Wagnalls, 1885.

Michael, J. H. _The Epistle to the Philippians._ (MNTC.) London: Hodder & Stoughton, 1928.

Motyer, Alex. _The Message of Philippians: Jesus Our Joy._ The Bible Speaks Today. Downers Grove, Ill.: InterVarsity, 1984. (In my opinion, the finest popularization available.)

Müller, Jac. J. _The Epistles of Paul to the Philippians and to Philemon._ (NICNT.) Grand Rapids: Eerdmans, 1955.

Rilliet, Albert. _Commentaire sur l'épître de l'apôtre Paul aux Philippiens._ Genève: V. Beroud, 1841.

Schenk, Wolfgang. _Die Philipperbrief des Paulus. Kommentar._ Stuttgart: W. Kohlhammer, 1984.

Turrado, Lorenzo. _Biblia Comentada,_ vol. 6. Madrid: Biblioteca de Autores Cristianos, 1965.

*Vincent, Marvin R. _Critical and Exegetical Commentary on the Epistles to the Philippians and to Philemon._ (ICC.) Edinburgh: T. & T. Clark, 1897.

Weiss, Bernhard. _Der Philipper-Brief ausgelegt und die Geschichte seiner Auslegung kritisch dargestellt._ Berlin: W. Herz, 1859. (This work is not to be confused with his later, shorter commentaries on the NT.)

Wiesinger, Augustus. In H. Olshausen's *Biblical Commentary on the New Testament*, vol. 5. New York: Sheldon, Blakeman, & Co., 1858.

Introduction to the Commentary

The primary purpose of this introductory chapter is to help the reader approach exegetical problems in the epistle to the Philippians by providing a broad interpretive framework. No textual detail ought to be interpreted in isolation from the larger context of which it is a part, yet it would be tiresome and impractical to review such broader concerns at every relevant point in the commentary. This chapter should therefore be regarded as an intrinsic part of the exposition.

On the other hand, this chapter represents, for the most part, conclusions drawn from the exegesis. The summary that follows, therefore, is deliberately brief and seldom accompanied by substantive argumentation. The reader is referred to the relevant sections in the commentary itself for further detail.

HISTORICAL CONTEXT

When we insist that exegesis, to be valid, must pay attention to the context, we usually mean the literary context—and, in particular, the material that immediately precedes and follows the passage in question. We are seldom aware, however, that the life-setting of the document is just as important for proper interpretation.[1] The epistle

---

1. Cf. Moisés Silva, *Biblical Words and Their Meaning: An Introduction to Lexical Semantics* (Grand Rapids: Zondervan, 1983), chap. 6, esp. pp. 144–

to the Philippians did not appear out of a time-space vacuum; it was written by a historical person to a historical church in a particular historical period, and every effort must be made to identify those historical features as precisely as possible.

A number of those features are not in dispute. The document was certainly written by Paul of Tarsus[2] to a Christian church in the city of Philippi, province of Macedonia. This church had been founded by Paul himself in the early 50s of the first century (Acts 16). At the time of writing, in the late 50s or early 60s, Paul was in prison, and he had just received a monetary gift from the Philippians through their emissary, Epaphroditus.

These facts, though important, are few. Beyond them, there is wide disagreement among students of the epistle. Before we consider the areas of dispute, however, it may be helpful to summarize the viewpoint that serves, tentatively, as the basis for this commentary.

RECONSTRUCTION OF EVENTS

In A.D. 51 Paul, in obedience to a vision, made the momentous decision of leaving the Middle Eastern setting of Asia Minor. With Silas, Timothy, and Luke, he set sail for what we now call Europe. His first stop was the Roman colony of Philippi, a city of considerable importance in the ancient world. Meeting a group of faithful Jewish women, he proclaimed the Christian gospel, found a receptive audience, and established his first Christian congregation in Europe. (See Acts 16:1–15.)

Young Timothy appears to have played a significant role in this work, and a natural bond was created between him and the Philippians. Among the first believers who struggled along with Paul in his ministry were several women—Lydia, Euodia, and Syntyche—along with an important figure named Clement, and other laborers. Paul's experiences in that city were not all pleasant; they included conflict and imprisonment. Even

---

47. This book, incidentally, formulates and defends several principles and methods that have played an important part in the writing of the present commentary. Rather than repeat the argumentation, I shall refer to the book when appropriate.
2. There have been sporadic, but completely unsuccessful, attempts at disproving the authenticity of this letter. See especially F. C. Baur, *Paul, the Apostle of Jesus Christ*, 2 vols. (London: Williams & Norgate, 1875), chap. 5. It is sobering to see this brilliant scholar arguing with great power and erudition for a viewpoint that the vast majority of subsequent writers (including some otherwise regarded as "radical") consider to have no foundation whatever.

his jailer was converted, however, and presumably joined the congregation (Acts 16:16–34; Phil. 2:19–22; 4:2–3).

Having been asked by the authorities to go away, Paul left Luke in charge of the congregation and headed west toward Thessalonica. During the three weeks of difficult ministry in this city, Paul several times received material assistance and thus spiritual encouragement from the believers in Philippi. Forced to flee, Paul went on to Berea, then to Athens, and finally to Corinth, where he stayed for a full eighteen months before returning to Antioch. During his prolonged stay in Corinth he again received assistance from the Philippian church (Acts 16:35–18:22; 2 Cor. 11:7–9; Phil. 4:15–16).

Eventually, perhaps a year later, Paul set out on another trip (the so-called third missionary journey), a major purpose of which was the raising of money from among his Gentile churches to meet the needs of the poor Jewish church in Jerusalem and Judea (Acts 18:23; Rom. 15:25–26; 1 Cor. 16:1–4; 2 Cor. 9:1–2, 12–23). There was a theological as well as a practical reason behind this effort. Paul's emphasis on the gospel of grace entailed accepting Christian Gentiles without their being required to fulfill any Jewish ceremonies (cf. Gal. 5:2–6). This approach raised a few eyebrows in some Jewish circles, created serious tensions even among moderate groups, and provoked furious opposition elsewhere (cf. Acts 15:1–5; Gal. 2:1–16).

The Judaizers, as members of this last group were known, began a campaign of their own, designed to lead Paul's converts to accept circumcision and the law as essential complements to their Christian confession (e.g., Gal. 1:6–9; 3:1–5; 5:7–10; 6:12–13). Because many perceived Paul's missionary work to be an abandonment of his Jewish heritage, the apostle felt constrained to clarify his position. The bringing in of the Gentiles through faith apart from works was not a contradiction but a fulfillment of the Scriptures (e.g., Rom. 3:21, 29–31; 4:9–16). To show in a very concrete way that his work did not entail separation from the Jewish Christian church, Paul determined to raise a significant contribution motivated by love; after all, the Gentile churches owed at least this much to the Jews (Rom. 15:26–27).

As Paul traveled through Macedonia during this third journey (Acts 20:1–2), he would surely have warned the Philippians of the Judaizing threat (cf. below, the exegesis of Phil. 3:1), which had created havoc in Galatia and would no doubt spread to Philippi. Because the Philippians were in financial straits, and because they had already shown great generosity on several occasions, Paul was not intending to request that they contribute to this present project. As soon as they heard of it, however, they insisted on having a share; indeed, their poverty welled up in magnanimity—and they gave their very hearts (2 Cor. 8:1–5).

Paul completed his project and eventually brought the offering to Jerusalem (Acts 21:17–19; Rom. 15:25–32). Jewish opponents, however, managed to get him imprisoned, and for two years he awaited his fate in Caesarea (Acts 21:27–24:27). During this time the Philippians felt a responsibility to help Paul, but their own difficult circumstances, along with uncertainty about Paul's status, prevented them (Phil. 4:10). At last the apostle appealed to the emperor himself, and in the year 59 or 60, under guard, he sailed for Rome (Acts 25:10-12; 27:1). Word of this turn of events must have spread quickly through the Gentile churches, and the Philippians determined to have a share in Paul's struggles as soon as they had the necessary information.

The apostle's experience in Rome was mixed. He found opportunities to proclaim and defend the gospel among Jews, and his message spread through the praetorian guard and beyond; moreover, his boldness encouraged many Roman Christians to speak God's Word (Acts 28:16-31; Phil. 1:12-14). But his imprisonment was also a time of affliction, filled with uncertainties, needs, and discouragement. Adding to his anguish was the presence of Jewish Christians who sympathized with many of the Judaizers' concerns. Rejecting the distinctive elements of Paul's preaching, these men were engaged in the proclamation of the gospel. Though they did not embrace the more objectionable elements of the Galatian heresy, their motivation was not pure; they aimed to undermine the work of the apostle for the sake of their own advancement (see the exegesis of Phil. 1:15-17).

Within a few months of Paul's arrival in Rome, the Philippians had become aware of his worsened situation. They therefore mounted their efforts and raised a large monetary gift (Phil. 4:18). The Philippians themselves, however, were undergoing some serious difficulties. Opponents of the Christian community were causing great alarm in the congregation, and the Judaizing threat was beginning to make itself felt (Phil. 1:27-30; 3:2, 18-19). Physical needs were producing anxiety among the members, who had begun to wonder whether their Christian faith was capable of sustaining them (Phil. 4:6, 19). All of those factors combined to create disagreements, distrust, and a poisonous spirit of self-seeking (Phil. 2:1-4). The leadership of the church, particularly in the persons of Euodia and Syntyche, had fallen into the sin of dissension, and the general health of the church had deteriorated considerably (Phil. 2:14-16; 4:2-3).

Conscious of how much they were in need of spiritual help and guidance, they dispatched Epaphroditus with the gift and asked Paul to keep him as his assistant but to send their beloved Timothy back to Philippi. On the way to Rome, Epaphroditus fell gravely ill and was unable to fulfill his mission speedily. A report of this setback reached Philippi, causing great consternation. Eventually, however, God spared Epaphroditus, who, at the risk of his life, continued on to Rome. By the time Epaphroditus reached Rome, Paul had been in prison perhaps for one year. The Philippians' offering therefore was truly a God-given blessing, and the apostle was at a loss how to express his thanks to a church that had given so sacrificially. The news of the problems in Philippi required immediate attention, but their request that Timothy be sent to them could not be granted. More and more people had deserted Paul, and Timothy alone could minister to him in this dark hour (Phil. 2:19-30).

Aware that the Philippians would be deeply disappointed to see Epaphroditus rather than Timothy return, Paul was faced with a serious challenge. How would he cushion this inevitable disappointment? Might Epaphroditus become the object of undeserved criticism? How could he convey his great joy for the church's continual participation in his apostolic ministry while at the same time rebuking them unambiguously for their grave lapse in sanctification? Would he be able to express his heart-felt thanks for their costly offering and yet discourage them from doing it again? And how would he report truthfully his own troubles without intensifying their spirit of discontent? How to help them in this great hour of their need!

The very difficulty of the task that was before the apostle would draw from him, under divine inspiration, a message full of comfort and joy, rebuke and encouragement, doctrine and exhortation. Quite beyond Paul's own powers of anticipation, the letter he was about to dictate would speak to the hearts of countless believers for many centuries to come.

PROVENANCE

The most controversial element in this reconstruction is, no doubt, the place of writing. That Paul was in Rome when he wrote Philippians is the traditional view, but in modern times strong arguments have been set forth in favor of Caesarea and Ephesus (less commonly Corinth). This is a matter of some consequence for exegesis. A different geographical (and therefore chronological) setting will, for example, affect our identification of Paul's opponents, and

5

hardly anything is more important to understand a polemical passage than to know what the writer is polemicizing against.

One important factor supporting the traditional view is precisely the fact that it is the only tradition that has survived. Whereas every other argument consists of inferences drawn from internal evidence, early tradition provides external attestation—presumably less ambiguous and therefore more "objective." Most scholars would probably recognize, in principle, the wisdom of an old rule-of-thumb: go along with the external evidence if internal considerations are at least compatible with it. (To put it differently, we should not dismiss external attestation unless the internal evidence against it is very clear and persuasive.)

Unfortunately, the external evidence in favor of a Roman provenance is not all that strong. We cannot even be sure that it really qualifies as "external" evidence, because the earliest statements may themselves have been inferences drawn from the text of Philippians![3] Given these circumstances, it is not fair to demand that alternate theories be supported by *conclusive* arguments; internal considerations that merely tip the scales may be sufficient reason to adopt a different view.

A common argument against the traditional view stresses the geographical distance between Rome and Philippi. Since the epistle assumes that several communications have already taken place between Paul and the Philippians, many scholars argue that the evidence does not allow for all the time required to complete the necessary travels.[4] If, on the other hand, Paul wrote this letter from

---

3. The tradition for a Roman imprisonment can be traced as far back as the second century (in the Marcionite Prologues attached to Vulgate MSS.), but the basis for that tradition cannot be ascertained.
4. See especially George S. Duncan, *St. Paul's Ephesian Ministry: A Reconstruction* (London: Hodder and Stoughton, 1929), pp. 80–82, building on Adolf Deissmann's work. Our best estimates are that a trip between Philippi and Rome would have taken four to seven weeks (though one must also allow for the time necessary to find an adequate envoy). For the evidence, see Ltf. (p. 38), who argued for one month. William M. Ramsay, whose mastery of these details was second to none, wrote the article "Roads and Travels (in NT)" for *HDB* 5:375–402. According to his data, in addition to the two days required to cross the Adriatic, the trip entailed some 740 miles. Traveling on foot, a courier could be expected to cover 15–20 miles per day. At the slower rate, therefore, the trip would require a total of 52 days; at the faster rate, 39 days. One must leave open the possibility, however, that at least part of the journey might have been covered by carriage, which could halve the time. Imperial couriers averaged 50 miles per day (Ramsay, p. 387; cf. *The Oxford Classical Dictionary*, ed. N. G. L. Hammond and H. H. Scullard, 2d ed. [Oxford: Clarendon, 1970], p. 869; cf. also p. 1090).

Ephesus during the third missionary journey, the length of travel could be dramatically reduced. In my opinion, commentators have greatly overestimated the weight that can be placed on this argument. The reconstruction suggested above makes clear that only three communications are required:

- The Philippians hear that Paul is imprisoned in Rome. (It may well be, however, that the Philippians became aware of the circumstances even before Paul actually reached Rome.)
- Paul receives a gift through Epaphroditus.
- The Philippians receive news that Epaphroditus has fallen ill. (However, if this incident took place during the journey, the distance involved would be reduced considerably.[5])

It is quite possible to fit those three journeys into a period of four to six months. But even if we allow a very generous two months for *each* of these journeys, far less than a year is necessary to account for them (and nothing in the data requires us to say that less than a year must have elapsed from Paul's arrival in Rome to his writing of Philippians). It is very difficult to understand why this argument against a Roman origin continues to be taken seriously. The matter should be dropped from any further consideration. If we do so, however, then the *only* clear argument against the traditional view disappears. In other words, all other available internal evidence is at the very least *compatible* with a Roman imprisonment as the context for Philippians.

This conclusion affects how we evaluate alternate views. A competing theory, even though it may be plausible, can hardly be accepted simply on the grounds that the traditional position is deficient; rather, a persuasive *positive* case must be made for the new one. The case for an *Ephesian* origin rests on the relative geographical proximity of Ephesus to Philippi, but we have already suggested that the issue of distance is a pseudo-problem. The Ephesian theory, in any case, labors under two serious disadvantages: we have no positive evidence either for an imprisonment of Paul in Ephesus or for the presence of a praetorian guard in a senatorial province (see Additional Notes to 1:13). To be sure, no one disputes the likelihood that

---

5. Some would argue, on the basis of Phil. 2:26, that a fourth communication is required for Epaphroditus to know that the Philippians were worried about him. As several writers have pointed out, however, 2:26 may simply reflect a natural inference on Epaphroditus's part. If we should insist that this communication is required, we should allow for the possibility that it might have reached Epaphroditus long before he arrived in Rome.

Paul may have been imprisoned during his lengthy stay in that city; and the possibility that a praetorian guard could have been stationed in Ephesus must be left open. One must wonder, however, how much weight can be placed on a theory that builds possibility upon likelihood.[6]

Some other scholars—uncomfortable with both the Roman and the Ephesian theory—opt for a *Caesarean* origin. This theory cannot appeal to the long distance separating Rome from Philippi, since Caesarea is not any closer; it can, however, build on the unquestioned fact that Paul spent two years imprisoned in this Palestinian port city. Moreover, one can argue with some plausibility that the presence of an imperial palace in Caesarea accounts for Paul's reference to the praetorian guard. The question is then whether we can identify any positive evidence that would lead us to *favor* this theory over that of a Roman origin. No such evidence is forthcoming. The argument rests completely on the ability of some scholars to construct a Caesarean setting that makes sense out of the data in Philippians.[7] The line of reasoning is plausible and may be correct—it certainly cannot be disproved. But it cannot be said to hold a *higher* status of credibility than the Roman theory.

In short, a Roman setting fits the data at least as well as competing views, and it has the added (though admittedly weak) advantage of being supported by some early tradition. Since alternative theories are based on plausible, but not compelling, arguments, we are left without a reason to abandon the traditional view. I shall, therefore, in this commentary assume a Roman origin for Philippians and allow it to serve us as a *tentative* framework for the discussion of exegetical problems, such as the identification of Paul's opponents. On the other hand, it remains little more than a theory, and any exegetical conclusions that lean heavily on it must be regarded as methodologically weak or even invalid.

---

6. In addition to the issues discussed here, many secondary arguments for and against the various options can be advanced. Hwth. and Martin can be profitably consulted for these. Note also Aldo Moda, "La Lettera a Filippesi e gli ultimi anni di Paolo prigioniero," *BeO* 27 (1985): 17–30, which pays special attention to the Corinthian theory set forth by S. Dockx.
7. This view, which goes back to the eighteenth century, has been adopted by, among others, Lohmeyer and Hwth. For an extensive argumentation, see J. J. Gunther, *Paul: Messenger and Exile* (Valley Forge, Pa.: Judson, 1972), chap. 4, esp. pp. 98–107; Gunther's discussion depends heavily on arguments from silence.

PAUL'S OPPONENTS

Apart from the question of the place of origin, other debatable issues regarding the historical context of Philippians are best treated as they come up in the text itself, since the exegesis of the text is our primary tool for resolving such problems. Only one additional question requires preliminary discussion at this point, and that is the identification of the opponents to whom Paul alludes in the letter. The relevant passages are 1:15-17; 1:27-28; 3:2; and 3:18-19 (though we also detect hints of this problem in 2:14-16 and 3:12-16).

It would be possible to see a distinct group of opponents in each of those four passages. Only the first one refers specifically to individuals with whom Paul himself was having to deal while he was in prison: they were "brethren" who preached the gospel with the impure motive of harming the apostle. The warning in 1:27-28 could reflect opposition from Gentiles. The reference in 3:2 is clearly to legalists, whether we regard them as unbelieving Jews or as Christian Judaizers. Finally, the "enemies of the cross" described in 3:18-19 sound like morally loose teachers (libertines or, more specifically, antinomians).

Such a wide diversity of references is unlikely, and most scholars detect no more than two or three distinct groups. The present commentary is rather unusual (though hardly unique) in arguing that all of the passages in question refer to groups that shared some fundamental concerns. Although it is obvious that Paul's attitude as he writes 1:15-17 is quite different from that which he reflects in 3:2, and that therefore the two groups must certainly be distinguished in *some* way, there is much to be said for the view that both groups objected to Paul on the same or very similar grounds. My thesis is:

— that 3:2 describes Judaizers such as are explicitly opposed in Galatians;
— that just as the Judaizing heresy, strange as it may sound, led to antinomianism and perfectionism in Galatia (cf. Gal. 5:13-21; 6:1?), so it may have happened in Philippi;[8]
— that such a front of opposition easily accounts for the words in 1:28-29 and so there is no need to postulate yet another group (though nothing prevents us from thinking that the Philippian believers did suffer persecution from Gentiles);

---

8. I argue at 3:18–19, however, that this passage need not be interpreted as a description of antinomianism.

— that the conduct of the "brethren" described in 1:15-17 cannot be accounted for satisfactorily unless they had some disagreements of *substance* with the apostle, and our knowledge of conflicts in the early church suggests strongly that they may have objected to some of the distinctive features of Paul's preaching to the Gentiles.

Scholars rarely point out that among Jewish Christians in the early church one surely could have found the whole range of possible responses to Paul's preaching—from full sympathy to minor reservations, then on to explicit opposition and even vicious hostility. The reservations, whether minor or major, would, of course, have focused on where the line was to be drawn regarding the status of, and requirements for, Gentile Christians. The desire to draw that line tightly would often, but not always, reflect theological opposition to the gospel of grace. It is not difficult to imagine how, in any early Christian community, unworthy and jealous leaders might have capitalized on these conflicts—without *necessarily* preaching a message of works righteousness—to advance their own cause at the expense of Paul's reputation.

A Roman setting is naturally compatible with this description. The epistle to the Romans makes clear that Christians in Rome were aware of and concerned about the Judaizers' attacks on the integrity of Paul's gospel. Some of those believers may indeed have been disposed to raise the very objections that Paul addresses in Romans (e.g., 3:1, 5; 6:1, 15; 9:6, 19). On the other hand, we have no evidence that the full-blown Judaizing heresy had yet manifested itself in the capital of the Empire; Paul therefore, as he described his opponents in Rome (Phil. 1:15-17), would have seen no need to utter the anathema of Gal. 1:8-9.

On the other hand, an extreme form of Jewish Christianity was very likely making its presence felt in Macedonia by the late 50s. Most commentators, quite rightly in my opinion, see this heresy reflected in Phil. 3:2. What is not so clear is whether the same or a very different kind of opposition forms the background for the second part of that chapter. The evidence is ambiguous, and I refer the reader to the exegesis of 3:12 and 3:17-19 for the details. While a definitive conclusion is not within our reach, I shall argue that chapter 3 of Philippians is a coherent passage and that there are no insuperable objections to identifying "the enemies of the cross" (3:18) as heterodox Jewish Christians or their disciples.

LITERARY CONTEXT

In the broadest sense, the literary context of Philippians consists of the whole range of ancient literature that is part of Paul's cultural milieu. Different scholars, depending on their interests and expertise, may legitimately appeal to a wide variety of parallels in expounding this epistle. Naturally, those writings closest to the thought of the apostle (contemporary Christian documents, that is, the NT) are bound to be particularly helpful. Our primary source, however, is the Pauline corpus itself. And while one runs the danger of blunting the distinctiveness of Philippians by appealing to the rest of the epistles, it would be a grave mistake to treat this letter in isolation from the rest. Accordingly, the present commentary makes abundant use of parallels in the Pauline writings to interpret the Philippians text.

In the present section, of course, we cannot attempt to summarize the Pauline corpus. Our purpose here is rather to look at the text of Philippians as a whole with a view to identifying patterns and distinctive emphases in the letter. I am, therefore, using the term *literary* to include not only the narrower concerns of literary criticism but also linguistic traits, argumentation, and even the distinctive theological teaching of Philippians.

LANGUAGE AND STYLE

The easiest, but also the most superficial, method of profiling the linguistic character of a writing is by presenting statistics based on the writer's vocabulary. We can very quickly, for example, count those words that occur that are unique to Philippians.[9] The total comes to forty different words, a proportionately higher number than average: Galatians and Ephesians, which are longer, contain thirty-one and thirty-five, respectively. Four of these *hapax legomena*, however, are proper names (Euodia, Clement, Syntyche, Philippians), and many others are derivatives of otherwise common terms.[10]

---

9. My statistics come from Kurt Aland, ed., *Vollständige Konkordanz zum griechischen Neuen Testament* (Berlin and New York: W. de Gruyter, 1978–83), esp. Band 2: Spezialübersichten.
10. E.g., ἀγνῶς, ἐξανάστασις, ὀκταήμερος, συμμιμητής. Some significant *hapax legomena* are found in the Christological poem of 2:6–11: ἁρπαγμός, καταχθόνιος, ὑπερυψόω. Also interesting are such terms as πολίτευμα (see comments on 3:20), μυέομαι (4:12), κατατομή (3:2), παραβολεύομαι (2:30), σκύβαλον (3:8). The word ἔπαινος is hardly a *hapax*, yet it appears to be used in a unique sense in 4:8.

11

We learn a little more about the lexical distinctiveness of Philippians, however, by noticing certain terms, not uncommon in themselves, that appear with disproportionate frequency in this letter. The term δέσμιος (*desmios*, "prisoner") occurs four times in Philippians; otherwise in Paul only once in Colossians and once in 2 Timothy. The verb ἡγέομαι (*hēgeomai*, "regard, consider") occurs six times; otherwise only once in 2 Corinthians, 1 Thessalonians, 2 Thessalonians, twice in 1 Timothy. Very noticeable is the frequency of "joy" terminology, namely, the verb χαίρω (*chairō*) and the noun χαρά (*chara*): these terms occur fourteen times (3.5 times per chapter) in Philippians, while the total for the rest of Paul's letters is thirty-six times (less than 0.5 times per chapter). Most significant of all are the ten occurrences of φρονέω (*phroneō*, "think"), otherwise used only thirteen times in Paul, nine times in Romans; this striking characteristic will come up for discussion below under Distinctive Teaching.

One question that arises generally in the Pauline corpus, but pointedly in Philippians, is whether the apostle intends clear semantic distinctions when similar terms are grouped together.[11] Many commentators, persuaded that Paul could not be guilty of redundancy, look for these distinctions and emphasize them. It is unfortunate, however, that the term *redundancy* continues to be viewed in a purely negative light. Linguists, drawing on the work of communication engineers, have long recognized that redundancy is a built-in feature of every language and that it aids, rather than hinders, the process of communication.

Though Paul is certainly not thoughtless in his choice of vocabulary, this commentary will argue that lexical distinctions are often neutralized in specific contexts and that many variations result from a need for stylistic reinforcement rather than from a desire to make an additional substantive point. Even some of the controversial terms in the Christ-hymn, I believe, are better understood if we resist sharp distinctions among them (see comments on 2:6-8). What is true of individual lexical items may also be reflected in longer linguistic

---

11. E.g., εὐχαριστέω, μνεία, δέησις (two times) in 1:3–4; ἄμεμπτοι, ἀκέραιοι, ἄμωμα in 2:15; λαμβάνω, καταλαμβάνω, τελειόω (passive) in 3:12. For further comments see Silva, *Biblical Words*, pp. 151–56. One of the distinctive and valuable traits of Schenk's recent commentary is his recognition that "contextual synonymy" is found time and time again in the text of Philippians. We should keep in mind that ambiguity is a regular (and even necessary) feature of human language, and that a high view of inspiration does not at all require us to interpret the biblical language in an unnatural way (e.g., by attributing to it artificial precision).

units, such as the emotive phrases in 2:1, which Ltf. (p. 67) perceptively described as a "tautology of earnestness."

Syntactical questions too must be treated in accordance with the common functions of natural languages. The assumption that Paul's syntax must always be rigorously logical contradicts this principle, and it comes to grief at a few points in this letter (see Additional Notes on 1:27). Grammatical irregularities are exceptional, however, and we dare not use them to justify a sloppy approach to the text.

One specific syntactical question that requires comment is that of tense (or better, *aspectual*) distinctions. The viewpoint adopted in this commentary is that the significance of such distinctions for biblical interpretation has been greatly overestimated by most commentators, particularly conservative writers. Aspectual choices are usually restricted by factors of a grammatical or contextual nature, and so only seldom do they reflect a conscious semantic motivation (so probably 3:7-8, though even this passage is controverted). In short, no reasonable Greek author, when wishing to make a substantive point, is likely to have depended on his readers' ability to interpret subtle syntactical distinctions.[12] Decisions regarding the use of grammatical aspect in Philippians sometimes involve textual variants (as in 1:9), but they also come up elsewhere (e.g., see Additional Notes on 1:21).

The description of an author's style cannot be limited to the level of words and sentences, and in recent decades linguists have given increasing attention to the paragraph as a basic unit of language. This new approach, usually referred to as *discourse analysis,* has led to a renewed concern for the textual coherence of biblical writings.[13] Such a concern, however, overlaps with the task of identifying the structure of a writer's argument. In the case of Philippians, that task is complicated by challenges to the literary unity of the letter, a question to which we must now turn our attention.

---

12. For a defense of this approach, see my forthcoming book, *God, Language, and Scripture: Using Linguistics in Biblical Interpretation* (Grand Rapids: Zondervan).

13. This subdiscipline still lacks a standardized terminology and has not been fully integrated into the more traditional approaches. For a brief and clear introduction, see Johannes P. Louw, *Semantics of New Testament Greek* (Semeia Studies; Philadelphia: Fortress, 1982), esp. chap. 10. I have not considered it advisable to attempt a full-scale analysis of Philippians along these lines, since a considerable amount of space would be taken up defining specialized terms and explaining the method.

13

LITERARY INTEGRITY

Our discussion of the historical context of Philippians assumed that the letter is an integral whole and that therefore our reconstructed occasion applies to it in its totality. In the current state of scholarship, however, that is a big assumption indeed. Many important commentators, for example, believe that the tone of chapter 3 is incompatible with the rest of the epistle; this section (including perhaps the opening verses of chapter 4) is widely regarded as a separate letter written to the Philippians specifically to combat the heretical forces they were facing. Some of those scholars also find it difficult to believe that Paul would wait till the end of his letter (4:10-20) to thank the Philippians for their gift; thus it is thought that this passage represents yet a third missive (chronologically the first?) occasioned simply by the arrival of that offering.

In spite of its relative popularity, this literary reconstruction labors under enormous difficulties. In the first place, no external textual evidence can be adduced in its favor. The textual attestation for Philippians is rich and early. One document, P[46], brings us to the early third or even late second century, yet neither this nor any other MS., to say nothing of early patristic allusions, gives any indication that the letter ever circulated in a different form from that which we have.[14] One can argue, of course, that someone simply brought these three letters together prior to their being circulated. Anything is possible. The question is whether it is *likely* that absolutely no trace of such a process would have been preserved.

In the second place, proponents of this view may be reasonably asked to provide a motive that would have led to such a literary process. Here again we cannot be satisfied with speculating what possibly may have led someone to edit three separate letters of Paul into one. If we are expected to accept a literary reconstruction for which no external evidence exists, we may rightfully ask for a demonstration of *probability*. Do we know (say, from statements by the church Fathers) that any early Christian attempted to merge separate apostolic writings into one, or even that anyone thought such an attempt would be useful?

In the third place, the theory is unable to account for the alleged

---

14. When writing to the Philippians in the second century, Polycarp tells them that Paul "wrote letters [ἐπιστολάς] to them" (*Phil.* 3). A few scholars, without success, have tried to use this passage as evidence against the integrity of Philippians. Ltf.'s discussion (pp. 138–42) adequately deals with this question.

redactor's method of working. The strongest evidence for the theory is the abruptness of 3:1-2, but this is a two-edged sword: what would lead an editor to incorporate a separate document at such an awkward point? Again, why would a redactor append the note of thanks at the end, where it seems to be out of place? Editorial revisions are normally undertaken with a view to attenuating, not aggravating, literary problems and inconsistencies. (See also the introductory comments to 3:1.)

Supporting the literary integrity of the letter are some interesting features, such as the striking verbal parallels between chapter 3 and earlier sections (cf. esp. 2:6-11 with 3:7-11). Particularly significant is the coherence achieved by beginning and ending the main body of the epistle with similar phraseology (see comments at 1:27-28 and 3:20–4:1). These and many other traits have caught the attention of recent scholars interested in discourse analysis and rhetorical criticism, disciplines that focus on the question of literary consistency.

The most important contribution in this field is a very fine article by Garland that has, in my opinion, changed the complexion of the contemporary debate.[15] Though various aspects of his literary interpretation are debatable, he has clearly demonstrated, by the use of internal evidence, that the unity of the letter is on a sure footing and, more important, that such evidence is *incompatible* with any view of literary fragmentation. Further details are best discussed at the relevant points in the commentary itself. What needs to be stressed here is that the only kind of evidence brought forth against the unity of Philippians is now being proved to be not merely ambiguous, which would be sufficient reason to reject the theory in the absence of other evidence, but clearly supportive of the opposite viewpoint.

At any rate, the letter deserves to be understood in the only form in which it has come down to us. One need not succumb to some of the faddish elements of "canonical criticism" to recognize the significance of that principle. It affects not only the question of literary unity, but also the way we approach passages that may reflect Paul's use of preexisting materials. This issue comes up in connection with 3:20-21 and especially with the *Carmen Christi*, 2:6-11. As will be

---

15. David E. Garland, "The Composition and Literary Unity of Philippians: Some Neglected Factors," *NovT* 27 (1985): 141–73. Other recent articles along similar lines include William J. Dalton, "The Integrity of Philippians," *Bib* 60 (1979): 97–102; Ronald Russell, "Pauline Letter Structure in Philippians," *JETS* 25 (1982): 295–306; Robert C. Swift, "The Theme and Structure of Philippians," *BSac* 141 (1984): 234–54.

argued in the exegesis of those two passages, the responsibility of a commentator is to make sense of the text in the context in which it is found, not on the basis of a setting that is no longer extant.

LITERARY STRUCTURE

The arguments that support the unity of Philippians also provide a basis for understanding its structure. Admittedly, the epistle is not easy to outline, and commentators have failed to reach a consensus. An effort must be made, nevertheless, to trace the flow of the argument as carefully as possible. Exegesis depends heavily on contextual information, since the meaning of a particular proposition is largely determined by its place in the larger argument: What has led to this proposition? How does it advance the argument? What does it lead to? An outline should be no mere table of contents, but an interpretive summary of the document. And while the effort should be made to approximate the original author's conception (assuming he had self-consciously constructed an outline), the success of an outline is to be gauged primarily by whether or not it communicates clearly *the interpreter's* understanding of the letter.[16]

Certain portions of Philippians can be clearly identified as discrete sections. For example, no one doubts that the first two verses constitute the salutation and that vv. 3-11 conform to the Pauline pattern of opening a letter with a thanksgiving. There is also wide agreement that the section that begins at 1:12 concludes at 1:26, a view supported by the likelihood that Paul uses the rhetorical technique of *inclusio* (or inclusion), that is, the bracketing of the passage by beginning and ending it with the same term, in this case προκοπή (*prokopē*, "progress," found nowhere else in the NT). Other clear units are 2:5-11; 2:19-30; 3:1–4:1 (though the precise beginning and end are disputed); and 4:10-20. But are we able to relate these units to one another as parts of larger sections?

To begin with, we could point out that the body of the letter (as distinct from its opening and closing) extends from 1:12 to 4:20, but this observation, while accurate, is minimally helpful. More interest-

---

16. Helpful discussions regarding the structure of Philippians can be found in the articles mentioned in n. 15. By applying rhetorical categories to Philippians, Duane F. Watson has attempted a new (but to my mind not fully persuasive) arrangement consisting of *exordium*, 1:3–26; *narratio*, 1:27–30; *probatio*, 2:1–3:21; and *peroratio*, 4:1–20. See, "A Rhetorical Analysis of Philippians and Its Implications for the Unity Question," *NovT* 30 (1988):57–88.

ing and significant is the possibility of *inclusio* bracketing the section from 1:27 to 4:3.[17] If so, that material could be viewed as the true body of the letter, in which the Philippians are exhorted to stand and struggle together as they exercise their Christian citizenship. While there is no doubt some validity in this approach, a different analysis is needed if we wish to bring out the diversity of material in that large section.

One important clue is the distinctive character of 1:12-26. This passage is unusual in that Paul does not normally give details about his personal circumstances at this early point in the letter (the closest parallel is 2 Cor. 1:8-11, 15-17; cf. Rom. 1:13-15). I shall argue in the commentary that the peculiar relationship between Paul and the Philippians, and in particular their support of his missionary work, made it appropriate for the apostle to give an account of his present conditions at the very beginning of the letter. The section ends with a vague allusion to his plans, a topic that he takes up again and develops in 2:19-30. A useful outline should in some way indicate the connection between these two passages.

Now while a new section begins at 1:27, commentators are unable to agree beyond that point. Since 1:30 seems to mark the end of a paragraph, should we begin a completely new section with 2:1? Or does the new section begin with v. 5? or v. 12? or v. 19? One of the most important structural points made in this commentary is that all of that material, from 1:27 to 2:18, belongs together and constitutes the heart of the epistle. It would be a mistake, however, to draw too sharp a line between this section and the one that follows. Indeed, vv. 19-30 fulfill a double purpose: they resume the report of 1:12-26, but they also, more subtly, reinforce the exhortations of 1:27–2:8 by setting up Timothy and Epaphroditus as examples to be followed. I have therefore treated 1:27–2:30 as a self-contained major section while making it clear that its last subsection (2:19-30) has a different character from what precedes it.

As for chapter 3, we must leave open the possibility that Paul had not intended, initially, to deal with the matters covered there—after

---

17. Notice the triad πολιτεύεσθε . . . στήκετε . . . συναθλοῦντες in 1:27 reflected in πολίτευμα . . . στήκετε . . . συνήθλησαν in 3:20; 4:1, 3. In my opinion, however, 4:2 begins a new section that consists of specific exhortations. Moreover, stressing the conceptual unity of 1:27–4:3 obscures the abruptness of chap. 3; as will be argued in the commentary, a concern to preserve the integrity of the epistle should not lead to a minimizing of this feature.

all, it would have meant repeating instructions that the Philippians were familiar with (cf. comments on 3:1). The seriousness of the Judaizing threat, however, suggested that he should take nothing for granted, and so he decided to extend the letter. This is a possible, though admittedly speculative, explanation for the abruptness of the passage. At any rate, 3:1 (or possibly 3:2) begins a wholly new section that ends at 4:1 (possibly at 4:3). With 4:2 the concluding exhortations begin. Then at v. 10, for reasons discussed fully in the commentary, Paul finally gets around to thanking the Philippians for the offering they sent with Epaphroditus.

The resulting outline, on the basis of which the chapters of the commentary have been divided, is as follows:

I. Opening 1:1-11
   A. Salutation 1:1-2
   B. Thanksgiving 1:3-8
   C. Prayer 1:9-11
II. Paul's Missionary Report 1:12-26
   A. Paul's Circumstances 1:12-17
   B. Paul's Attitude 1:18-26
III. A Call to Sanctification 1:27–2:30
   A. Christian Citizenship 1:27–2:4
   B. Christian Humility 2:5-11
   C. Christian Obedience 2:12-18
   D. Resumption of Paul's Missionary Report 2:19-30
IV. Doctrinal Polemics 3:1–4:1
   A. Judaizers as the Context for Theology 3:1-6
   B. The Essence of Pauline Theology 3:7-11
   C. Practical Theology 3:12–4:1
V. Final Concerns 4:2-23
   A. Exhortations 4:2-9
   B. A Word of Thanks 4:10-20
   C. Closing 4:21-23

DISTINCTIVE TEACHING

Considerations of a document's literary context cannot be limited to formal questions such as style and structure. While these are not merely preliminaries to "the real thing" (they are very much part of the whole substance), our primary interest is of course the content communicated through them. The discussion of structure has already, and necessarily, touched on the content of Philippians, but we need to identify more directly the letter's teaching (the whole), against which we can more accurately interpret its individual propositions (the parts). Inevitably, the discussion becomes a theological exercise.

Now in our attempt to interpret a biblical book, hardly any issue is more important than that of its *distinctiveness*. For believers who take seriously the divine inspiration—and therefore the unity—of Scripture, biblical study should focus very sharply on this basic question: Why did God see fit to include this or that document in the NT canon? Let us consider then what it is that Philippians contributes to our understanding of the gospel. What is its specific "canonical function"?

Two factors, unfortunately, have hindered students in this endeavor. In the first place, the strong emphasis of the epistle on the subject of rejoicing, along with the obvious affection that united the apostle with the Philippian church, have led many readers to think of that church as a model congregation with relatively few and minor problems. This feature also lends a very practical and personal tone to the letter, so that we tend to downplay its doctrinal content. The influential commentator J. B. Lightfoot, in fact, argued that it was precisely that feature that distinguishes Philippians from the theologically charged letter of Paul to the Galatians.[18]

The second factor pulls in quite a different direction. I refer here to the *Carmen Christi* (2:6-11). While no one is likely to deny the very great importance of this passage, perhaps we need to ask if excessive attention has been paid to it at the expense of obscuring some other important features of the letter. This matter has been complicated, of course, by the tendency in contemporary scholarship to focus primarily on the (pre-Pauline) origins of this hymn, with the result that the passage has been isolated from its literary context. In any case, many of us have been conditioned to think of Christology as the primary teaching of Philippians, even though this doctrine is quite secondary to Paul's main concern.

As the outline delineated above makes clear, 2:6-11 is but one paragraph in a larger section that may be considered the heart of the epistle. The pervasive theme in this section is Christian sanctification, as reflected in the commands to behave in a manner worthy of

---

18. "As we lay down the Epistle to the Galatians and take up the Epistle to the Philippians, we cannot fail to be struck by the contrast. We have passed at once from the most dogmatic to the least dogmatic of the Apostle's letters, and the transition is instructive" (from Ltf.'s preface). See also below on Exegetical History.

the gospel (1:27), to obey (2:12), to become blameless (2:15). More specifically, Paul focuses on the need for Christian unity, which in turn calls for selflessness and humility (1:27; 2:1-4). Right in the middle of this discussion Paul appeals to the selfless act of Jesus Christ, who made Himself nothing, but who was then exalted by the Father. And so the point of the *Carmen Christi* is not primarily to make a statement regarding the nature of Christ's Person (ontology), but to impress on the Philippians the pattern to which they must be conformed.

Now the Christian's duty to grow in holiness requires the right attitude, singleness of purpose, and mental concentration. Paul's concern with this matter is reflected in the striking frequency of the verb φρονέω (*phroneō*, lit. "think") in Philippians. This peculiarity has often been mentioned by commentators but seldom developed.[19] Moreover, the English reader can easily miss it because the verb, which can be used in a variety of contexts, requires more than one rendering.

As early as 1:7, for example, Paul sets the tone by telling the Philippians that he, as their model (cf. 3:17; 4:9), "thinks rightly" about them, that is, has the proper frame of mind or attitude toward them. The verb is used twice in 2:2 (also in 4:2) to stress the unity of mind that should characterize the congregation, and then again in v. 5 to exhort them to imitate Jesus' own attitude. In chapter 3, proper thinking (v. 15, two times) is set against the earthly thinking of the enemies of the cross (v. 19). In 4:10, finally, Paul uses the verb twice to encourage the Philippians by acknowledging that they already have shown a commendable attitude.

That these facts are significant is further impressed on the reader by other comparable terminology, such as ἡγέομαι (*hēgeomai*, "consider, regard," which appears in the important contexts of 2:3, 6 and 3:8), σκοπέω (*skopeō*, "notice, consider," 2:4; 3:17), and λογίζομαι (*logizomai*, "reckon, consider," 3:13; 4:8). Moreover, we find in Philippians an abundance of "knowledge" terminology, esp. in 1:9-11 and 3:8-10. All of these references include, but are not restricted to, purely intellectual concerns. The main point is expressed by Paul elsewhere with military and athletic imagery (1:27, 30; 3:12-14; 4:1, 3). The focus on the mind, therefore, has much to do with mental determination.

---

19. This weakness has now been remedied by Jozef Heriban, *Retto φρονεῖν e κένωσις. Studio esegetico su Fil 2, 1–5, 6–11* (Biblioteca di scienze religiose 51; Rome: LAS, 1983).

As suggested in the discussion of the letter's historical context, the Philippians were facing great adversity, had lost their sense of Christian joy, and were tempted to abandon their struggle.[20] Accordingly, this letter places great weight on the need to stand fast and persevere. It is remarkable that this note of perseverance has not played a more significant role in the interpretation of Philippians. Most readers tend to view the Philippian church in the best possible light, but the text makes clear that these believers were experiencing severe spiritual problems. Many of them, apparently, had lost confidence in their ability to maintain their Christian confession. Paul encourages them to stand fast and contend (1:27-28; 4:1), to run their race without looking back (3:13-15), to take seriously their awesome responsibility of working out their salvation (2:12).

Such an emphasis on spiritual effort may appear to minimize the doctrine of grace. Remarkably, it is in Philippians more than in any other letter that Paul stresses our complete dependence on God for sanctification. That note is sounded triumphantly as early as 1:6 and is applied forcefully in 2:13, but it is also reflected throughout the letter (see comments on 1:19-20; 3:12; 4:13, 19). The twin truths of human responsibility and divine sovereignty thus turn out to provide the theological underpinnings for the teaching of Philippians.[21]

TRANSMISSION

Though we normally use the term *context* in reference only to the original setting of an author and of the immediate readers, responsible exegetes understand that we have no direct access to that setting. The documents we study have acquired, so to speak, many new settings in the course of history, including our own contemporary context.[22] Consciously or not, we all read Philippians through the spectacles provided by that history. Only by paying some attention to the

---

20. On the importance of determining the situation of the Philippian church for proper interpretation, see especially Berthold Mengel, *Studien zum Philipperbrief* (WUNT 2/8; Tübingen: J. C. B. Mohr, 1982), which surveys the history of research on this question (with emphasis on the work of W. H. Schinz) and relates it to the issue of the letter's integrity.
21. Most contemporary commentators would dispute my theological reading of Philippians. The matter will be treated at the appropriate points in the exegesis.
22. Cf. Silva, *Biblical Words*, pp. 147–48. I have also touched briefly on some of the problems connected with the notion of contextualization in *Has the Church Misread the Bible? The History of Interpretation in the Light of Current Issues* (Grand Rapids: Zondervan, 1987), chap. 5.

transmission of the letter can we determine to what extent those spectacles have clarified or distorted the text.

TEXTUAL HISTORY[23]

Understandably, the study of textual criticism focuses on the original form of a document. The student must remember, however, that textual variants are not to be regarded as isolated options contemporary with the document. On the contrary, their proper evaluation depends on our ability to understand their place in the historical transmission of the text.[24] Moreover, that transmission has its own independent value, even when it does not aid us in establishing the original form. Textual changes often reflect patterns of interpretation; textual history thus flows over into exegetical history.

From the point of view of an exegetical commentary, the need for a coherent summary of textual transmission becomes especially pressing. The Additional Notes sections in this volume comment on some forty variants.[25] Unfortunately, the treatment of textual problems as they come up in the text means that the variants tend to be treated in isolation from each other. The user of this commentary will be in a much better position to assess individual variants if we can summarize the nature of the variations as a whole.

The best source for this purpose is the 26th edition of NA, which lists many more variants than *UBSGNT*. Even the larger number, of course, represents only a portion of the available evidence; the editor,

---

23. Since text-critical discussions are of value only to readers familiar with the Greek language, this section dispenses with the use of transliteration. I became aware of James D. Price's article, "A Computer-Aided Textual Commentary on the Book of Philippians," *Grace Theological Journal* 8 (1987):253–90. My initial reaction is one of partial skepticism, but I have not been able to give to this material the attention it deserves.
24. From a narrower perspective than I am using here, Hort pointedly formulated this principle in the well-known statement: "all trustworthy restoration of corrupted texts is founded on the study of their history." See B. F. Westcott and F. J. A. Hort, *The New Testament in the Original Greek: Introduction, Appendix* (Cambridge and London: Macmillan, 1881), p. 40. That statement is contrasted with the treatment of readings or even whole documents "independently of each other" (p. 39).
25. These variants were not chosen systematically according to a strict set of criteria. Some were chosen because they affect directly the exegesis of the text; others because they shed light on the general transmission of the text; still others because of their intrinsic interest. I have assumed that the reader has access to NA and that no useful purpose is served by trying to reproduce the information found there (and in *UBSGNT*).

Kurt Aland, has had to do a great deal of preliminary sifting of the material to produce this handy text, and those students who depend on it are in effect trusting the editor's judgment for a very large number of decisions. In my opinion, Aland's principles and procedure are generally valid and well-executed. The resulting work is a magnificent edition that can serve us well as a starting point.

If we exclude four conjectures (1:7; 2:1, 6, 16) and two interpretive problems (1:25 and 4:3; συνεπισκόποις in 1:1 probably belongs here as well), we come up with approximately 112 variations.[26] The categories of omissions, additions, and grammatical alterations are fairly evenly divided and constitute more than 70 of the variations. Almost 20 of the variants are simple changes of one word for another (such as θεός for κύριος, δέ for καί, etc.) and 6 or 7 are transpositions, leaving another dozen or so that are not easily classified. A list of the passages, with more detailed categories, will prove helpful (question marks alert the reader to passages that could be placed in more than one category):

Omissions
    article—1:5, 17; 2:9; 3:10 (two times), 14
    preposition—1:7, 23, 24; 3:11; 4:16
    conjunction—1:18?, 23; 2:4, 12?; 3:7, 8, 12; 4:15
    other (may include art./prep./conj.)—1:30; 2:4, 30; 3:3, 12; 4:1
Additions
    article—1:10; 2:3, 13, 30; 3:1, 8
    preposition—none
    conjunction—1:4, 28; 2:5; 4:18
    other—1:3, 8, 15?; 2:24, 26; 3:6, 8, 12, 16, 18, 21; 4:1, 3?, 8, 13, 23
Grammatical changes
    case etc.—1:8, 11, 28; 2:1 (three times), 4 (two times), 7, 27; 3:3, 6, 11;
       4:10, 16
    verbal endings—1:9, 22, 24, 27; 2:4, 5, 11, 14?, 15, 16; 4:19
Word substitutions
    divine name—1:3; 2:19, 30; 3:14?; 4:7 (two times)
    prep./conj.—1:18, 19, 22?; 3:13, 14
    other—1:17; 2:2, 15 (two times), 30?; 4:7
Transpositions—1:6, 16-17, 28; 2:21, 26; 3:7; 4:3?
Miscellaneous—1:11, 20, 23, 25; 2:3 (two times); 3:14 (two times), 21;
    4:21

---

26. The word *approximately*, even in places where I do not use it explicitly, applies to most counts, since a few variations can be interpreted in more than one way. Note also that more than one variation may be included by Aland under one sign; conversely, variations listed separately may at times be closely related (so that they could be regarded as a variation unit).

Ideally, this summary of information should include the whole Pauline corpus and be more rigorously classified. Even in this limited form, however, the data can be of considerable help. Decisions on individual variants should be preceded by an examination of other variants in the same category. A reading that appears strong when evaluated in isolation may prove suspect once we discover it reflects a certain pattern of scribal activity (e.g., see Additional Notes to 3:10 on the omission of the articles).

An additional consideration is that, generally speaking, individual MSS. tend to align themselves according to certain text-types. As is well known, the reconstructed text that appears in both NA and *UBSGNT* corresponds very closely to the Alexandrian text-type found in such important witnesses as P⁴⁶ and codices Vaticanus, Sinaiticus, and Alexandrinus. When all or most of these MSS. agree on a reading, NA rejects it very rarely (cf. however the addition of ἰδεῖν at 2:26 and the bracketing of the articles at 3:10). How do the other text-types differ from this one?

The "Western" Text,[27] represented primarily by the Greek codices D, F, and G (and sometimes supported by witnesses to a different text-type), contains approximately:

nine omissions—1:5, 7, 17, 23; 2:4 (two times), 9; 3:12 (two times)
seven additions—1:3, 4, 14; 2:5; 3:6, 12, 16
nine word substitutions—1:11, 20, 23; 2:3?, 15 (two times), 19; 3:14; 4:7

Other kinds of variants are found at 1:8, 11 (μοι in F and G); 2:11; 4:10, 19. Not all of those, however, should be regarded as *distinctively* "Western" readings (on the other hand, NA does not include all of the variants that may be so regarded). Worthy of note is the large proportion of variants that involve a change in the divine names (1:3, 11, 14; 2:19; 3:6, 12, 14).

The Byzantine (or Majority) Text is that form found in the majority of surviving Greek MSS., which were produced in the Middle Ages. Distinctively Byzantine readings can sometimes be found in very ancient witnesses and may certainly be original (though the combina-

---

27. The term "Western" simply reflects conventional use. The geographical element is misleading, while the integrity of the text-type is questioned, especially by Kurt and Barbara Aland, *The Text of the New Testament: An Introduction to the Critical Editions and to the Theory and Practice of Modern Textual Criticism* (Grand Rapids: Eerdmans, 1987), chap. 2. Even a superficial look at the textual apparatus, however, shows clearly that there is an alignment of D with F and G, less frequently with the Latin tradition.

tion or pattern of readings that constitutes the Byzantine text-type is demonstrably late). The following Byzantine variants are included in NA, except for those with asterisks, which are listed in HF.

> five omissions—1:5, 8, 18; 2:5, 9
> six additions—2:13; 2:30; 3:8, 16, 21; 4:13
> five word substitutions—1:17, 25; 2:15, 30; 3:14
> seven transpositions—1:1*, 8, 16-17, 28; 2:21, 27*; 4:3*

Other variants are found at 1:11, 27, 28; 2:4 (two times), 5, 15*; 3:6, 10*, 11; 4:19*.

In addition to the material we have surveyed so far, it is very helpful to focus on a few selected witnesses and examine them in greater detail, noting even insignificant variations that would normally not be included in a critical edition of the Greek NT. The accompanying chart summarizes the results of my own collation of the Majority Text and the MSS. listed;[28] it indicates, under each category, the number of times a given MS. *departs from the NA text.* In other words, the NA text is here treated, provisionally, as if it were identical with the autograph. My assumption, which would be disputed by some, is that the NA text is sufficiently reliable to permit us to identify *patterns* that represent accurately the document's early textual history.

Among several interesting facts, we should note that, while the *total* number of omissions and additions do not reveal clear patterns, the picture changes considerably once we segregate small "grammatical" words (conjunctions, articles, and prepositions, but also pronouns). On every column, except for the Majority Text, the omission of such words clearly exceeds the number of insertions. Scribal mistakes in these circumstances were common. We should therefore not place too much weight on the fact that important MSS. or text-types support minor omissions. In particular, it seems unnecessary for the NA text to include brackets at such points as 1:23, 24; 2:4; 3:10. (I am less sure about 3:7, 12.)

---

28. That material was first presented as a paper entitled "The Text of Philippians: Its Early History in the Light of *UBSGNT₃*," SBL Annual Meeting, New York, 1982. Because the collation is exhaustive rather than carefully selected, the data cannot be used to draw inferences regarding text-types (e.g., the fact that the total number of variants for Sinaiticus, the Majority Text, and P[46] are respectively 38, 43, and 63 hardly means that the former two are closely related). With regard to the implications of the material for the principle that the shorter reading is preferable, see my article, "Internal Evidence in the Text-Critical Use of the Septuagint," in *La Septuaginta en la investigación comtemporánea,* ed. N. Fernández Marcos (Madrid: C.S.I.C., 1985), pp. 151–67.

Philippians: Tentative Collation Against $UBSGNT_3$ (=NA_{26})

	A	B	ℵ	Maj.	P[46]	D	G
Morphology							
prefixes	1	1	1	1	3	2	2
case endings	1	2	2	5	6	6	7
verbal changes	2	4	4	4	3	9	11
Total	4	7	7	10	12	17	20
Conjunctions							
omitted	2	3	4	3	6	9	7
added	0	0	1	2	5	3	5
altered	0	1	1	0	3	3	5
Total	2	4	6	5	14	15	17
Articles							
omitted	2	4	2	2	5	6	5
added	1	2	2	3	3	2	4
altered	0	0	0	1	0	1	3
Total	3	6	4	6	8	9	12
Prepositions							
omitted	2	0	2	0	3	4	3
added	0	0	0	0	1	0	1
altered	0	2	0	1	0	0	1
Total	2	2	2	1	4	4	5
Pronouns							
omitted	0	1	1	0	3	2	1
added	1	1	0	0	1	1	2
altered	1	1	1	1	1	3	3
Total	2	3	2	1	5	6	6
Single Words							
omitted	0	0	0	0	1	1	2
added	5	0	2	3	2	5	6
synonym	2	0	1	3	2	3	3
altered	1	1	3	0	4	2	16
Total	8	1	6	6	9	11	27
Divine Names & Titles							
omitted	0	1	1	0	2	1	2
added	1	1	2	1	0	1	5
transposed	2	1	1	3	1	2	4
altered	2	0	1	0	0	4	4
Total	5	3	5	4	3	8	15

(continued)

	A	B	ℵ	Maj.	P[46]	D	G
Phrases							
omitted	1	0	2	0	4	1	2
shortened	0	0	1	2	0	3	1
added	1	0	1	2	3	3	4
expanded	0	0	1	2	1	2	2
word order	0	2	1	4	0	5	9
Total	2	2	6	10	8	14	18
Total of variants	28	28	38	43	63	84	120
Omissions							
conj./art./prep./pron.	6	8	9	5	17	21	16
all others	1	1	3	0	7	3	6
Total	7	9	12	5	24	24	22
Additions							
conj./art./prep./pron.	2	3	3	5	10	6	12
all others	7	1	5	6	5	9	15
Total	9	4	8	11	15	15	27

This commentary pays special attention to the readings of P[46]. Not only is it the oldest extant MS. of the Pauline epistles; the basic character of its text is widely recognized as of the greatest importance. At the same time, its scribe was not particularly careful (sloppy omissions, for example, are frequent, but these are easily recognized), and his tendencies are most instructive with regard to scribal activity.[29] Moreover, this document contains a number of fascinating readings that deserve careful attention (see especially at 1:11 and 3:12).[30]

---

29. For an excellent analysis, see James R. Royse, "Scribal Habits in Early Greek New Testament Papyri" (Th.D. diss., Graduate Theological Union, 1981), chap. 3. Working on the basis of the document's singular readings, he has identified 167 instances of omissions (pp. 254–60), many of them longer than one word. On the basis of ligature forms and other scribal characteristics, Young Kyu Kim has recently sought to push back the date of this document; see "Palaeographical Dating of P[46] to the Later First Century", *Bib* 69 (1988): 248–57.
30. In my evaluation of the textual data I have been aided by the research of some of my previous students. H. Breidenthal, D. M. Cahill, and L. M. Ovenden provided analyses of P[46]. W. Arndt examined the text used by Origen. I was particularly helped by a very thorough analysis of the Vulgate (and related Latin witnesses) prepared by T. Uehara.

EXEGETICAL HISTORY

The common practice of listing commentators who side with one interpretation or another, though it has certain advantages, can be very misleading. For example, a particular commentator may have nuanced his position in a way that sets it apart from the views of others included on the same list. Even if the exegetical conclusion is the same, the various commentators have possibly reached their decision in different ways. In some cases, the conclusion does not cohere with the broader interpretive framework adopted by a particular writer (and possibly preferred by the reader) and should perhaps be rejected for that reason.

The point is that we cannot properly evaluate a writer's position on some individual exegetical question if we are ignorant of that writer's own context. In other words, commentators have themselves become part of the exegetical tradition that needs to be interpreted. What follows is a very modest attempt to minimize our problem by giving a critical summary of selected commentators who have been particularly influential and who are referred to with some frequency in this commentary.[31]

Chrysostom. References to Philippians abound in the writings of the Fathers.[32] Substantive expositions of the whole epistle, however, are not numerous, and most of these (including those by Theodore of

---

31. It should be clear from these introductory comments that I am not offering here a history of the interpretation of Philippians. In the first place, such a history would require the examination of numerous writers who have not necessarily written expositions of the letter but who have used it in the formulation of theology and for other purposes. Moreover, my treatment does not survey primarily the exegetical conclusions of commentators but rather their characteristic approach, their general strengths and weaknesses, and so forth.

32. For an exhaustive listing through the third century, see *Biblia patristica, Index des citations et allusions bibliques dans la littérature patristique.* 3 vols. (Paris: Centre National de la Recherche Scientifique, 1975–80). Cf. also, among others, R. A. Krupp, *Saint John Chrysostom: A Scripture Index* (Lanham, Md.: University Press of America, 1984). One important source for the early interpretation of the NT is Karl Staab, *Pauluskommentare aus der griechischen Kirche aus Ketenenhandschriften gesammelt und herausgegeben* (NTAbh 15; Münster: Aschendorftschen, 1933), esp. pp. 621–30 (Photius). For a very fine study of Marius Victorinus, Ambrosiaster, and Pelagius (plus Jerome and Augustine, who however did not comment on Philippians), see Alexander Souter, *The Earliest Commentaries on the Epistles of Paul: A Study* (Oxford: Clarendon, 1927); however, Souter gives relatively little attention to exegetical method. Finally, note the valuable synthesis by M. F. Wiles, *The Divine Apostle: The Interpretation of St. Paul's Epistles in the Early Church* (Cambridge: Cambridge U., 1967).

Mopsuestia, Theodoret, Ambrosiaster, and Pelagius) consist of rather brief comments on the text. Chrysostom's homilies on Philippians, though not precisely in commentary form, constitute the most significant patristic exposition of this letter. Some of the material, particularly toward the end of each homily, where he seeks to relate the exposition to the needs of his congregation, has little exegetical value.[33] At other times, as in his discussion of the *Carmen Christi*, he allows heretical opinion to set the agenda for his exposition.

In general, however, Chrysostom shows genuine sensitivity to the historical meaning of the text. He is alert to possible ambiguities in the apostle's language, for example, and knows how to deal with those and comparable problems concisely and clearly. He is also quite capable in assessing the theological import of the text, though we may want to dissent here and there, especially in his formulation of works vis-à-vis divine grace (e.g., at 1:29, where he says that if Paul ascribes virtues entirely to God, that is because "the greatest part" comes from Him; a similar concern is reflected at 2:13).

Strange as it may sound, Chrysostom, along with other Greek Fathers, can be particularly helpful when he does *not* offer an opinion on an exegetical problem. As a native Greek speaker, his innate sense of the language—but not necessarily his conscious reflection on it— provides an important bridge between the modern commentator and the Pauline writings (with the qualification that Paul's Greek was of course not identical to Chrysostom's). Educated speakers are notoriously unreliable in analyzing their own language. If Chrysostom weighs two competing interpretations, his conclusion should be valued as an important opinion and no more. If, on the other hand, he fails to address a linguistic problem because he does not appear to perceive a possible ambiguity, his silence is of the greatest value in helping us determine how Paul's first readers were likely to have interpreted the text.[34]

---

33. In this connection cf. M. F. Wiles, "Theodore of Mopsuestia as Representative of the Antiochene School," in *The Cambridge History of the Bible*, ed. P. R. Ackroyd et al. (Cambridge: Cambridge U.), 1:490.

34. A good illustration of this principle is the grammatical ambiguity at 1:7. The arguments in favor of the interpretation "you have me in your heart" are powerful but not conclusive. The fact that Chrysostom (along with other Greek Fathers), without any apparent awareness of a difficulty, takes the clause to mean "I have you in my heart" finally swayed me to reject the alternate view—though it was not easy. Incidentally, though Broadus's translation of Chrysostom in *NPNF* is dependable, consulting the original is essential when dealing with some of these issues.

Aquinas. Greek medieval writers, such as Theophylact and Oe-cumenius, were strongly influenced by Chrysostom, though their commentaries have some independent value as well. Several expositors in the Latin tradition also deserve attention, but I have chosen to comment on Aquinas for some important reasons. Modern exegesis, to be sure, has little to learn from Aquinas's exposition of Philippians (it has in fact played a very small role in the writing of the present commentary), but that is not to say that the exposition is of poor quality. On the contrary, it is quite excellent. To the extent that we may use the term *grammatico-historical* for works prior to the modern period, Aquinas's commentary is deserving of that adjective, because only seldom does he allow extra-biblical preoccupations to displace the meaning of the original (e.g., at 4:15, which he interprets as grounds for the pope to "take from one church to help another").

Moreover, the most characteristic feature of his approach is the abundance of biblical quotations used to throw light on the text. Aquinas's commentary, in effect, is one of the best illustrations of an exegete allowing the Bible to be its own interpreter. One might wish for a larger proportion of specifically Pauline parallels (Paul's distinctiveness tends to dissolve in the ocean of biblical citations), but only occasionally are his citations ill-chosen. Assuming a Protestant stance, one may be pleasingly surprised even by Aquinas's theological reflections. Though it would not be difficult to find disagreeable features in them, the dominant tone is unobjectionable. In fact, building as he does on an Augustinian foundation, his emphasis on God's (predestinating) grace shows through at key points (e.g., at 1:11; 2:13; 4:3).

For anyone who views Scholasticism in a purely negative light, Aquinas's exegesis can be an excellent antidote. Given his stature and influence in the late medieval period, this brief piece of work stands as something of a milestone in the long history of expositions on Philippians. Nevertheless, the commentary is not based on the Greek text and Aquinas is often unaware of important interpretive questions that affect our understanding of the epistle as a whole.[35]

---

35. For a very thorough study of Aquinas's exegesis, see Thomas Domanyi, *Der Römerbriefkommentar des Thomas von Aquina, Ein Beitrag zur Untersuchung seiner Auslegungsmethoden*, Besler und Berner Studien zur historischen und systematischen Theologie 39 (Bern: Peter Lang, 1979), esp. chaps. 4–5 on literary and historical method. For the medieval material more generally, consult Robert E. McNally, *The Bible in the Early Middle Ages* (1959; reprint, Atlanta: Scholars Press, 1986), esp. the fine introduction and the listing of Philippians commentaries on p. 112.

Calvin. We need not rehearse here the developments that took place during the Renaissance period in the critical study of ancient documents. Some writers, such as Erasmus and Lefèvre, produced useful paraphrases and annotations on the Pauline epistles that influenced the course of NT exegesis.[36] By common consent, however, it is John Calvin's commentaries that mark a new epoch in the exposition of Scripture.

Calvin combined, in an unusual way, a commitment to the humanistic study of the classics with unswerving devotion to the final authority of Scripture; but he also combined his faith in the distinctive tenets of the Protestant Reformation with a high regard for church tradition. In addition, Calvin was a student of Chrysostom, whose brevity in exposition he regarded as a model of commentary writing. All of those fine features, and more, are clearly displayed in his commentary on Philippians.

The work is not without its faults, of course. Occasionally he is distracted by his own opponents (e.g., at 2:11), and a few of his exegetical ideas, being based on the limited knowledge available in his day, are no longer tenable (e.g., in attributing an active meaning to the passive εὑρεθῶ, *heurethō*, "be found," 3:9). But the total effect of his commentary is consistently positive; indeed, one often wonders how a work of this character could have been written prior to the modern period. For example, Calvin's regard for Scripture might easily have led him (as it leads many even today) to press the force of Paul's language beyond what it can bear. Instead, we find him exercising commendable restraint and sensitivity when dealing with problem passages (cf. Additional Notes to 1:27).

Like Aquinas, moreover, Calvin possessed a powerfully synthetic mind that enabled him to expound Philippians with an eye to the teaching of Scripture as a whole. Yet, it would be very unfortunate to assume that he allowed an abstract theological system to impose itself upon the text. Any fair reading of his work on Philippians must recognize that its theological richness was not imported from outside the Bible but arose from a responsible handling of the text.

Meyer. It is not possible to draw a sharp line that divides the

---

36. Cf. Erika Rummel, *Erasmus' Annotations on the New Testament: From Philologist to Theologian* (Toronto: U. of Toronto, 1986); Philip Edgcumbe Hughes, *Lefèvre: Pioneer of Ecclesiastical Renewal in France* (Grand Rapids: Eerdmans, 1984), esp. pp. 69–73 on Phil 1:6 and 2:12–13. The best discussion of Calvin's exegesis is T. H. L. Parker, *Calvin's New Testament Commentaries* (Grand Rapids: Eerdmans, 1971).

modern, "scientific" period from everything that preceded it. We can identify a stage, however, when the intensive textual work of several generations begins to bear fruit in a dramatic way.[37] The commentaries of H. A. W. Meyer were not the first to exemplify a "scientific" approach to the NT text, but the erudition, finesse, and magnitude of his work made the "Meyer series" the lodestar for commentators during the second half of the nineteenth century and the early decades of the twentieth.

Meyer's greatest strength was his ability to perceive problems and to ask questions that would not occur to most of us. There is hardly a grammatical or exegetical issue that he fails to consider and carefully weigh after cataloguing the whole range of opinion on the subject. Unfortunately, this approach sometimes leads to unnecessarily complicated discussions, to a merciless dissection of textual details, and to a measure of overconfidence regarding the validity of his conclusions. Meyer's series is the paragon of encyclopedic commentaries that manage, unwittingly, to obscure the broad and weightier teaching of Scripture. Perhaps for that reason (and because of its age) Meyer's work is seldom quoted nowadays. That, too, is unfortunate. The serious student of the Greek NT, even today, can always learn something from this master.

Lightfoot. German scholarship, as represented primarily by Meyer, was imported to English territory by several British scholars, most notably Henry Alford.[38] But the Anglo-Saxon world was to produce a master of its own. As unpretentious as Meyer was pedantic, and as lucid as Meyer was cryptic—but not one whit inferior in erudition—J. B. Lightfoot would break new ground with his extraordinary commentaries on the shorter epistles of Paul.

Lightfoot is often credited (or blamed) for helping students of Paul realize that there was more to the apostle than polemics and doctrine. As already pointed out (cf. above, n. 18), he sets Philippians over against Galatians; he further argues that Philippians reveals "the normal type of the Apostle's teaching." The substance of the gospel, he concludes, "is neither a dogmatic system nor an ethical code, but a Person and a life." We do no justice to Lightfoot if we infer

---

37. Some of the most influential works preceding that stage include the brief but incisive expositions of Bengel in the eighteenth century and the early nineteenth-century commentary by van Hengel, which Lightfoot valued highly.
38. Other important British figures include the erudite Ellicott and the more homiletical Eadie.

from these words that he regarded doctrine as unimportant. In the same preface he states: "Dogmatic forms are the buttresses on the scaffold-pole of the building, not the building itself."

It is still true, however, that Lightfoot minimizes somewhat the theological import of Philippians. Interestingly, that factor may have something to do with the fact that his commentary on this letter is not as highly valued as his *Galatians,* even by scholars for whom theology is not a great priority. But that comment must not be misunderstood. If his commentary on Philippians is a notch lower in quality than his commentary on Galatians, it is still several notches higher than any other English commentary on Philippians. Vincent's contribution to the International Critical Commentary series, though hardly a work to be despised, only highlights the contrast between Lightfoot and those who have followed him.

Lohmeyer. Meyer's Philippians commentary for his series went through four editions (1847–74). It was then revised by A. H. Franke in 1886, but this edition did not make an impact. A more thorough and important revision—really a new work—was produced by E. Haupt (1897 and 1902). Yet another edition was assigned to Ernst Lohmeyer, whose commentary appeared in 1930. A scholar of the highest caliber who had already published a ground-breaking monograph on the *Carmen Christi,*[39] Lohmeyer set a new agenda for the exegesis of Philippians.

Lohmeyer's style and approach were vastly different from those of his predecessors. Grammatical questions were relegated to the footnotes, while the commentary itself became more accessible, even to nonscholars. Most notably, Lohmeyer set himself to prove a bold thesis regarding the purpose and character of Philippians. Using the tools honed by the history of religions approach, he argued that the whole epistle could be understood as a tractate on martyrdom. His position is best summarized by reproducing his outline of the body of the letter:

> Paul's Martyrdom (1:12-26)
> The Community's Martyrdom (1:27–2:16)
> Helpers in Martyrdom (2:17-30)
> Dangers in Martyrdom (3:1-21)
> Last Admonitions in Martyrdom (4:1-9)

---

39. See below the exegesis of 2:6–8. Other important German commentators prior to Lohmeyer include B. Weiss (whose impressive work I regret having used in only a cursory way), Ewald (for the Zahn series), Lipsius, Klöpper, and Dibelius.

In spite of its many valuable insights, the commentary leaves the distinct impression that the text is being adjusted to fit a thesis. Accordingly, Lohmeyer's broad interpretation of the letter has not been adopted by recent exegetes.

Contemporary Works. No major German commentary on Philippians appeared for several decades. Then the Roman Catholic scholar J. Gnilka contributed a substantive and highly praised volume on Philippians to the Herder series. A novelty of this commentary is the decision to treat the text as consisting of two distinct letters of Paul. Apart from that feature, the exegesis reflects a relatively cautious approach.

Not many French works since Rilliet's in the last century have had a significant impact on scholarship. Bonnard's commentary, which appeared almost thirty years ago, was well received, but its successor in the same series has been more influential. This is the work of J. -F. Collange, who distinguishes three different letters in the text of Philippians. His exposition is clear and reveals the thought of an independent mind.[40]

The first major English commentary on the Greek text of Philippians since Vincent is the contribution to the Word Biblical Commentary series by the evangelical scholar G. F. Hawthorne. Distinguishing this work are the carefully compiled bibliographies, close attention to the original language, and a refreshing balance between conservative and innovative elements. Because Hawthorne's work will be readily accessible to most readers of the present commentary, I have deliberately avoided duplicating his effort (for example, by repeating bibliographic lists). For the same reason, it has seemed wise to engage him quite frequently, particularly where my approach presents an alternative way of dealing with the text.[41]

Finally, special attention needs to be given to the recent and extraordinary commentary by W. Schenk, which came into my hands after I had completed an initial draft of the present volume. This work is the first thorough application of modern linguistics to the exegesis of a NT book. And although the linguistics idea may appear

---

40. Commentaries written in other European languages have not had a significant effect on the mainstream of scholarship. We should note, however, Greijdanus's 1937 commentary, a substantive piece that regretfully I used only sporadically. More recent Dutch works, and written at a more popular level, are the commentaries by Matter and Klijn. Though not a commentary, the important Italian monograph by Heriban (see above, n. 19) will no doubt have considerable impact in future scholarship.

41. For a more detailed evaluation, see my review in *WTJ* 46 (1984): 413–16.

dull to many readers, there is nothing dull about this commentary. In fact, Schenk has such a fertile mind and forceful style that any other commentary looks dull beside his. Some readers may be initially put off by the terminology, but Schenk uses a fairly limited number of technical terms and his exposition is at any rate sparklingly clear.

Schenk's penetrating discussions have at many points confirmed my judgment, usually on similar grounds (e.g., note his insistence on contextual synonymy); at many other points he has challenged my conclusions. His work no doubt deserves more attention than I have given to it. Unhappily, Schenk seems unable to keep his ideas in check. For example, while it is useful to note the correspondence between "being confident of this" (1:6) and "this I pray" (1:9), one must question the judgment of describing the two verbs as contextually identical. Similarly, his grammatical understanding of 1:22 (with καί, *kai*, interpreted as introducing an apodosis, after the analogy of v. 21) is simply impossible. It is also unfortunate that Schenk conveys a certain arrogance. I do not refer to a personal quality, but to disciplinary cocksureness, as though linguistics is the great panacea. One can only hope that readers of his commentary will not be put off by that tone and so miss the rich exegetical fare that he has to offer.

1
Opening (1:1–11)

All of the NT epistles that bear Paul's name exhibit certain common structural traits, one of which is the natural inclusion of an introductory paragraph clearly set off from the body of the letter. This paragraph normally consists of a standard salutation, immediately followed by a thanksgiving.

Some variations occur. For example, Paul expands the salutations in Romans, Galatians, and Titus by the inclusion of material that anticipates important themes developed in those letters. Again, on five occasions—2 Corinthians, Galatians, Ephesians, 1 Timothy, and Titus—he omits a thanksgiving and therefore appears to move from the salutation right into the body of the letter, though one could argue that the benedictions in 2 Cor. 1:3-7 and Eph. 1:3-14 parallel the thanksgivings in the other letters. (As for Galatians, the rebuke in 1:6-10 takes on special significance when one realizes that it corresponds structurally to the section where the reader expects a warm word of thanksgiving to God.)

It is not always pointed out, however, that Philippians and Colossians differ from the other epistles by the inclusion of a substantive prayer of intercession following the thanksgiving (Phil. 1:9-11; Col. 1:9-12). To be sure, the distinction between petition and thanksgiving should not be pressed, since Paul can move from one to the other very easily, as in Rom. 1:8-10 and Philem. 4-6 (and may not the assurance

in 1 Cor. 1:8 also be understood as an expression of Paul's prayer?).
Moreover, the prayer in 2 Thess. 1:11-12, though somewhat removed
from the thanksgiving in vv. 3-4, certainly parallels Phil. 1:9-11 and
Col. 1:9-12.

In spite of these qualifications, Philippians and Colossians correspond to each other so closely, both structurally and conceptually,
that the relationship deserves special attention. The exposition that
follows, therefore, divides the introduction into three sections: salutation (vv. 1-2), thanksgiving (vv. 3-8), and petition (vv. 9-11).

A. SALUTATION (1:1-2)

Translation

**[From] Paul and Timothy, servants of *Christ Jesus, to all in
Philippi, including overseers and deacons, who are holy through
their union with Christ Jesus: Grace and peace to you from God our
Father and our Lord Jesus Christ.**

Exegesis and Exposition

The standard opening in the letters of the Hellenistic period consisted of three words: name of sender (nominative case), name of
addressee (dative case), and the infinitive χαίρειν (*chairein*, usually
translated "greeting").[1] Variations were minor: inversion of sender
and addressee, further identification of the sender, and strengthening
of the greeting (e.g., by adding the infinitive ἐρρῶσθαι, *errōsthai*,
"good health").

Paul follows the convention in general yet imparts his own distinctiveness by changing *chairein* to the cognate χάρις (*charis*,
"grace"), which calls attention to the very essence of the Christian
message; by adding εἰρήνη (*eirēnē*, "peace"), a reminder of the rich
themes of spiritual welfare evoked by the Hebrew equivalent, שלום
(*šālôm*); and by specifying the true source of our well-being, "God our
Father and the Lord Jesus Christ." (First and 2 Timothy add ἔλεος,
eleos, "mercy"; further, Colossians and 1 Thessalonians vary slightly
from this format.)

---

1. Cf. the collection by A. S. Hunt and C. C. Edgar, eds., *Select Papyri* (LCL;
   New York: Putnam's, 1932), 1:268–395. For a brief and clear synthesis of
   Greek epistolography, see David E. Aune, ed., *Greco-Roman Literature and
   the New Testament: Selected Forms and Genres* (SBLSBS 21; Atlanta: Scholars Press, 1988), esp. chap. 5 by John L. White. For a detailed study of
   openings and closings, see Franz Schnider and Werner Stenger, *Studien
   zum neutestamentlichen Briefformular* (NTTS 11; Leiden: Brill, 1987).

It is also instructive, however, to note certain variations that turn up when we compare the greetings in Paul's epistles. First, Paul includes Timothy as one of the senders. This feature is also found in 2 Corinthians, Colossians, and Philemon, while 1-2 Thessalonians include Silvanus (Silas) as well as Timothy (1 Corinthians mentions Sosthenes; Galatians has "all the brethren who are with me").

Although commentators are correct in pointing out that this feature does not indicate coauthorship, it would be a mistake to ignore or downplay its significance. Not only was Timothy actively involved in the evangelization of Macedonia and Achaia (Acts 16-18), he also appears to have provided special support for Paul during the latter's imprisonment (Phil. 2:20-22), a factor that accounts for Timothy's inclusion in the salutations of Colossians and Philemon. There is also good reason to believe (see comments on 2:19-30) that the Philippians had a strong attachment to Timothy. This faithful minister, therefore, constituted a link that bonded the apostle with his Macedonian congregation; it would have been surprising had his name been omitted.

It should further be noted that the inclusion of Timothy's name was more than a friendly or sentimental gesture. Paul, though self-conscious of his unique apostolic authority, did not intend to monopolize the attention of his converts; and his teachings, while distinctive in emphasis ("my gospel," Rom. 2:16; 16:25; 2 Tim. 2:8), were hardly idiosyncratic in substance. We may then recognize that the apostle, by joining Timothy's name to his, calls upon his coworker as a corroborating witness of the truths he expounds; Timothy, in turn, lends his influence and authority to Paul's words, which he commends as an expression of his own thoughts.

Second, notice the omission of ἀπόστολος (*apostolos*, "apostle"). It is intriguing to find that of the four epistles in which Paul does not introduce himself as an apostle, three were addressed to Macedonian churches: Philippians and 1-2 Thessalonians (the fourth is Philemon, where the delicacy of the occasion, as seen especially in vv. 17-20, accounts for this feature). In view of the early date of 1-2 Thessalonians (and assuming a later date for Galatians), we may consider the possibility that Paul had not yet found it necessary to emphasize his apostolic authority, which began to suffer systematic challenges during the third missionary journey.[2] On the other hand, we should note

---

2. So also Vincent Perkin, "Some Comments on the Pauline Prescripts," *Irish Biblical Studies* 8 (1986): 92–99, esp. p. 99.

1 Thess. 2:7-8, 17-20, and 3:1-10, passages that suggest a special and mutual affection bonding Paul with the believers in Thessalonica.

However we explain the absence of *apostolos* in 1-2 Thessalonians, its absence in Philippians is generally understood as evidence of the warm relationship existing between Paul and the saints in Philippi. Not only was there no need to remind the Philippians of Paul's authority, Paul may have even considered such a reminder inappropriate in view of the character of this epistle as, at least in part, a thank-you note.

Third, Paul identifies himself and Timothy as δοῦλοι (*douloi*, "servants" or "slaves"). This designation, although common in Paul, occurs in the salutation of only two other letters, Romans and Titus. Here it takes on special significance precisely because it replaces *apostolos*. In view of the prominence that Philippians gives to the subject of humility, we can hardly doubt that Paul is here exploiting the word's reference to lowly service rather than its sense of privileged position.[3]

I find it somewhat misleading, however, to say that "the word has pejorative force here."[4] Since "the foolishness of God is wiser than men, and the weakness of God is stronger than men" (1 Cor. 1:25), the humility that appears contemptible to unbelievers receives God's praise. Moreover, the truth that He who was rich "became poor" by taking the form of a *doulos* (2 Cor. 8:9; Phil. 2:7) injects into this word, paradoxically, an undeniable dignity. Thus, quite apart from the Hebrew OT use of עבד (*'ebed*, "servant") with reference to the prophetic office, the Greek *doulos* in Christian parlance is not an insult, but the highest commendation possible.

It has often been pointed out that this passage is the only instance in the Pauline letters in which the apostle shares the title *doulos* with anyone else. Hwth. puts great emphasis on this fact: he calls it "a

---

3. Contra Martin G. Sass, "Zur Bedeutung von δοῦλος bei Paulus," *ZNW* 40 (1941): 24–32, and others who emphasize the OT background of עבד יהוה (*'ebed yhwh*, "Servant of the Lord") with its nuances of divinely given authority. Schenk makes the valid point that δοῦλος occupies the same lexical field as διάκονος (with ἀπόστολος being a more specific term), but that fact is not sufficient reason to set aside the sociological nuance of "slave," much less to water down its meaning with the translation *Mitarbeiter* ("colleagues").

4. So Collange; similarly, E. Best calls it "the derogatory sense of ordinary speech" (see "Bishops and Deacons: Philippians 1,1" *SE* 4 [1968]: 371–76, esp. p. 375).

radical departure from Paul's standard procedure" and argues that Paul was here willing to share "his otherwise carefully and jealously guarded uniqueness" to teach the Philippians a lesson in humility (pp. 3-4). This remark seems to me an overstatement, since Paul clearly had no reservations about using the term σύνδουλος (*syndoulos*, "fellow-servant") with reference to Epaphras and Tychicus (Col. 1:7; 4:7; Hwth. accepts the Pauline authorship of Colossians); but I would not wish to deny that an element of humility is indeed present here.

Fourth, we should note the unique reference to ἐπισκόποις καὶ διακόνοις (*episkopois kai diakonois*, "overseers and deacons"). As is well known, the pastoral epistles, and 1 Timothy 3 in particular, stress the importance of these two church offices, though this factor is interpreted by large segments of current scholarship as evidence of late date. Outside the pastorals, the word *episkopos* and the related term πρεσβύτερος (*presbyteros*, "elder") do not occur at all in the Pauline corpus. Clearly, the presence of *episkopois* and *diakonois* here requires some explanation.

One suggestion is to understand these titles as functional (describing activity) rather than official in some technical sense. However, though Paul can certainly refer to church workers without specifying an office (cf. Rom. 12:8; Gal. 6:6; 1 Thess. 5:12), here he must have "in view individual members of the congregation who are unequivocally characterised by the designation. . . . Otherwise the addition has no meaning."[5] It seems clear that "at the time of the epistle there are thus two co-ordinated offices."[6]

But whether or not we accept the official status of these individuals, we must still ask why they are singled out. E. Best links the mention of these officers with the omission of *apostolos;* he assumes that a letter from Philippi to Paul had been signed with the words, "from all the saints with the bishops and deacons," suggesting a distinction between believers and officers. "Paul writes back to them but in so doing he very quietly rebukes them by the omission of his own title of 'apostle.' "[7] This view, however, is at bottom speculative; moreover, the irony suggested by Best is so subtle that the original readers (like most commentators since) would most likely have missed it altogether.

---

5. K. Beyer, "ἐπίσκοπος," *TDNT*, 2:616.
6. K. Beyer, "διάκονος," ibid., 2:89.
7. Best, "Bishops and Deacons," p. 374.

Collange argues plausibly that Paul begins by applying "gentleness and persuasion"; the titles show his regard for them and thus prepare the way for the rebukes and criticisms that occur in the body of the letter. If Collange's view should prove unsatisfactory, the best alternative is the common interpretation (from Chrysostom to Martin) that Paul singles out the church officers as those primarily responsible for raising the offering delivered to Paul.

Additional Notes

1:1 Χριστοῦ 'Ιησοῦ: The Majority Text, accompanied by some versional and patristic evidence (see Tischendorf) transposes the names to 'Ιησοῦ Χριστοῦ, an order that "predominates decidedly only in the Thessalonian Epistles" (Vincent).

πᾶσιν: Ltf. (on 1:4) speaks of the "studied repetition of the word 'all' in this epistle" (cf. 1:2, 4, 7 [two times], 8, 25; 2:17; 4:21) and finds it "impossible" not to link this fact with Paul's emphasis on unity. Since Rom. 1:17 is the only other salutation that addresses the congregation in this fashion (1 Cor. 1:2 and 2 Cor. 1:1 are not exactly parallel), Ltf.'s point seems reasonable.

ἁγίοις: Paul uses this word approximately forty times to describe Christians collectively, and because it occurs in most of the salutations, we need not look for any special significance in its use here. One should note, however, that this Pauline trait is hardly a trivial mannerism. Quite the contrary, it reflects in a striking way one of Paul's most fundamental conceptions, the believer's definitive sanctification (see the exegesis on 3:10).

σὺν ἐπισκόποις: The suggestion that these two Greek words should be read as one, "fellow-bishops," can be traced back as early as Chrysostom (though this is disputed by Ltf., p. 96 n. 2); and his contemporary, Theodore of Mopsuestia, appears to reject it.[8] Metzger, who attributes this view to "dogmatic or ecclesiastical interests," rejects it on two grounds: first, "the construction would be imperfect, the συν- having no appropriate reference" (but does not this remark beg the question at issue, namely, whether Paul regarded himself as an ἐπίσκοπος?);[9] second, "the letter is obviously intended for the whole community" (but would the disputed reading neces-

---

8. See the helpful note in H. B. Swete, ed., *Theodori Episcopi Mopsuestem in epistolas B. Pauli comentarii* (Cambridge: The University Press, 1880), 1:198–99.

9. Beyer, incidentally, greatly overstates the point when he describes this view as "not grammatically possible" (*TDNT*, 2:616, n. 22). Schenk, who gives an unnecessarily involved discussion of σύν (whether it is inclusive or additive), regards the phrase as a non-Pauline interpolation.

sarily exclude the church as a whole?). Although those two arguments appear inconclusive, Metzger and virtually all commentators are probably correct in rejecting this reading. Paul never calls himself an ἐπίσκοπος, so that the burden of proof would seem to rest on those who might see a self-reference in συν-. More important, σύν occurs in the salutations in 1-2 Corinthians, where its force is clearly "with."

1:2 ἀπὸ θεοῦ πατρὸς ἡμῶν καὶ κυρίου ᾽Ιησοῦ Χριστοῦ: Even though Vincent is correct in stressing the need "to distinguish between ideas which unconsciously underlie particular expressions, and the same ideas used with a definite conscious dogmatic purpose," so that the present (and common) conjoining of God and Christ is not unequivocal proof that Paul believed in the deity of Christ—it would be unhelpful to ignore the ease and naturalness with which Paul appears to regard his Lord as on the same level with the Father. Vincent himself agrees that the expression "may be allowed to point to that doctrine which he elsewhere asserts."

B. THANKSGIVING (1:3-8)

Just as in Rom. 1:8, where Paul first expresses his gratitude, giving also a briefly stated reason for it, and then proceeds to expand on that reason in vv. 9-12 (including an expression of his desire to see them), so also here in Philippians we may analyze the thanksgiving as consisting of an initial statement (1:3-5) followed by an expansion (vv. 6-8, which include an expression of his love, "I long for all of you"). Modern editions of the Greek NT, it is true, usually indicate a more significant grammatical pause between vv. 6 and 7 than between vv. 5 and 6, with a full pause between vv. 7 and 8 (cf. also Gnilka, who believes the thanksgiving comes to an end in v. 6). In Greek, however, the distinction between clauses and sentences admits of very few hard-and-fast rules, and one need not insist that the clause of v. 7, though it is introduced by καθώς (*kathōs*, "even as"), should be regarded as more independent than the participial clause of v. 6. (See Additional Notes on v. 5.) At any rate, my division of this section between vv. 5 and 6 depends not on syntactical or grammatical considerations but on the conceptual shift that seems to occur at that point.

1. INITIAL STATEMENT (1:3-5)

Translation

*I thank my God every time I remember you [*or*, for your every remembrance of me]—yes, always, in every prayer of mine on behalf

of all of you; and it is with joy that I make my prayer because of your participation in the work of the gospel from *the beginning of your faith until this very moment.

Exegesis and Exposition

The syntax of these verses is particularly difficult to unravel. Is the main verb εὐχαριστῶ (*eucharistō*, "I thank") to be linked with the prepositional phrase that follows immediately, ἐπὶ πάσῃ τῇ μνείᾳ ὑμῶν (*epi pasę tę mneią hymōn*, lit. "upon every remembrance of you")? Should we instead link it with the prepositional phrase in v. 5, ἐπὶ τῇ κοινωνίᾳ ὑμῶν (*epi tę koinōnią hymōn*, "because of your participation"), so that the intervening words from *epi* in v. 3 to the end of v. 4 should be enclosed within dashes? Again, should πάντοτε (*pantote*, "always," v. 4) be construed with what precedes or with what follows? Similarly, is μετὰ χαρᾶς (*meta charas*, "with joy") part of the preceding or the subsequent clause? Several other questions could be asked, pushing the combined number of possibilities to a staggering total. (See the Additional Notes for the most likely possibilities and for a discussion of the more substantive problem regarding the syntax of *epi pasę tę mneią hymōn*.)

Attempting to answer all those questions can be a profitable linguistic exercise, though from Paul's perspective we should perhaps regard them as pseudo-questions. The point is that all of the syntactical combinations yield the same sense. (The only possible substantive issue is whether δέησιν [*deēsin*, "petition, prayer," v. 4] can be used with reference to thanksgiving, as would be the case if construed with what follows, or only with reference to petition. See Additional Notes.) The freedom of Greek word order has the advantage of providing the writer with a great variety of expressive resources; it also has the disadvantage of creating considerable ambiguity. A Greek writer, however, could foresee the potential for equivocation and guard against it. In the present sentence the ambiguities, touching no matter of substance, probably did not even occur to Paul.

One may wish to ask how it is possible for such a sentence *not* to create a semantic problem. The simple answer is repetition. Paul makes reference to his praying in four different clauses with the words *eucharistō, mneia,* and *deēsis* (two times); thus, whether we construe *pantote* with one or another of these words, the force of the statement is the same. The exegetical value of this rather obvious point is that it calls attention to a distinctive element in this thanksgiving: Paul is not being thoughtlessly repetitive but deliberately emphatic (cf. Introduction: Language and Style). While we find some ambiguity of construction in other thanksgivings (Colossians, 1 Thessalonians, Philemon), those are not nearly as complicated as the present passage. It is the intensity of Paul's emotion that accounts for the syntax; it also accounts for the fourfold recurrence of *pas* (in the forms *pasę* [two times], *pantote*, and *pantōn*), for the apparent emphasis on joy (*meta charas*), and for the forcefulness of subsequent expressions ("from the first day"; "being persuaded").

In v. 5, however, we encounter a syntactical ambiguity of greater significance: How shall we construe "from the first day until now"? We have three basic options, each of which yields a different sense. Most versions and commentators construe this clause with the first part of the verse, *tę koinōnią hymōn* ("your participation"); from the very beginning the Philippians have been participating in the work of the gospel. An alternative view is to take the clause as the emphatic beginning of a new thought altogether ("I have been persuaded from the first day until now that . . ."), but Meyer correctly points out that this construction tends to shift attention away from the clear concern of the passage, namely, the Philippians' conduct.

The third option is to see a reference to Paul's own prayers; he has been thanking God from the very beginning. This interpretation, which implies a linking of the clause with the end of v. 4 (less likely with *eucharistō*, as Bengel suggests), fits nicely with Paul's emphasis on the intensity of his prayer. Moreover, it could be argued that it yields a smoother syntax: if the clause were to modify *tē koinōnią*, as in the first interpretation, one would expect the repetition of the article before ἀπό (*apo*, "from"). In fact, however, the absence of the article before an attributive is not unusual.[10]

In support of the first and common interpretation is the good rule-of-thumb that we should prefer a natural connection—such as taking together linguistic units that are close to one another—unless we have weighty reasons for doing otherwise. Most important, however, is the consideration that in v. 5 Paul has shifted attention from the *fact* of his prayer of thanksgiving to the *reason* for it. Meyer perceptively emphasizes that the constancy of the Philippians' commitment to the gospel "is the very thing which not only supplies the motive for the apostle's thankfulness, but forms also the ground of his just confidence for the future." My paraphrase above adopts this usual understanding of v. 5 and further assumes that the only necessary pause is in the middle of v. 4.

---

10. BDF §272.

We may proceed to ask whether the present thanksgiving differs in any substantive way from those found in the other letters. Two matters come up for attention: the explicit note of joy and the reference to the Philippians' participation in the gospel.

Although the very mention of thanksgiving in his epistles is clear evidence of Paul's joy, only the introductions to Philippians and Philemon (see Philem. 7) contain the word *chara*. One might not want to make too much of this factor if we had no other indications of its significance. But we do. In fact, Paul here announces one of the most obvious themes in the epistle—joy in the midst of adversity (see Introduction: Distinctive Teaching). Quite clearly, the Philippians are troubled by Paul's circumstances and Paul wishes at the very opening of the letter to allay their concerns by assuring them of his deep, personal contentment. Yet, we should note that the apostle's joyful response to his adversity arises not from a consideration of personal well-being but from the recognition that his apostolic ministry is bearing fruit, as he makes clear in v. 12. (Conversely, his greatest fear consisted in the possibility that his ministry might come to naught; see comments on 2:16.)

What needs particular emphasis is that Paul's overflowing gratefulness focuses on a *concrete* expression of the Philippians' care for him as a minister of the gospel. In other thanksgiving sections (see esp. Rom. 1:18 and 1 Thess. 1:8) Paul commends believers for contributing to the advance of the faith, but the term *koinōnia* is included only here and in Philem. 6. Although the word may have the general meaning of "communion" or "fellowship" in this passage,[11] such renderings as "participation" (*NASB*) and "partnership" (*NIV*) more accurately bring out the *activity* of the Philippians in promoting the work of the gospel.

Can we be more specific as to what that activity entailed? Although G. Panikulam may be correct in stating that this expression indicates "the entire response the Philippians gave to the good news

---

11. BAGD (p. 439) translate *"close relationship w. the gospel."* With regard to the force of εὐαγγέλιον see Peter T. O'Brien, "The Importance of the Gospel in Philippians," in *God Who Is Rich in Mercy: Essays Presented to Dr. D. B. Knox*, ed. P. T. O'Brien and David G. Peterson (Homebush West, NSW: Lancer, 1986), pp. 213–33. He argues that out of nine occurrences of this noun in Philippians, eight denote activity (*nomen actionis* = proclamation); the exception is the first instance of the word at 1:27, which has in view the content of the gospel message. It seems to me misleading to take the usage in 1:5 as a quasi-personification (p. 217, following Gnilka).

they received,"[12] it seems unreasonable to deny that the Philippians' financial contributions, understood as concrete evidence of the genuineness of that response, must have been "foremost in the Apostle's mind" (Ltf.). When speaking of the Macedonians' contribution to the Jerusalem saints (Rom. 15:26; 2 Cor. 8:4; cf. 9:13) Paul uses the same noun, *koinōnia*, with the preposition *eis*, though the construction is not exactly parallel.[13] Moreover, Paul uses the verbal form *koinōneō* with reference to financial contribution in Rom. 12:13; Gal. 6:6; and esp. Phil. 4:15, a passage strangely ignored by Panikulam and others in spite of the additional parallel to 1:5 in the phrase "from the beginning of the gospel." (Remarkably, Schenk appeals to 4:15 as evidence that *koinōnia* must have an active meaning, yet he denies a reference to the offering. The only explanation for this move must be his conviction that 4:10 ff. constitute a different document.)

In summary, Paul's thanksgiving in this letter is distinguished by emphatic repetitions and emotional intensity. The apostle's joyful gratitude flows from an appreciation of his converts' consistent support of his ministry and care for his needs, from the very beginnings of their Christian experience to the most recent contribution, which in effect occasioned the present letter. Yet Paul is careful to interpret their gifts, not as intended for him personally (contrast μοι, *moi*, "to me," 4:15), but rather for the advance of the gospel.

Additional Notes

1:3 εὐχαριστῶ: Most commentators prefer to construe this verb with v. 5, in which case one needs to take v. 4 (or at least the second part of v. 4; cf. Ltf.) as more or less parenthetical. This understanding, though defensible, creates a slight awkwardness, namely, the use of

---

12. George Panikulam, *Koinōnia in the New Testament: A Dynamic Expression of Christian Life* (AnBib 85; Rome: Biblical Institute Press, 1979), p. 85, following Gnilka. J. H. Schütz, *Paul and the Anatomy of Apostolic Authority* (SNTSMS 26; Cambridge: Cambridge U., 1975), p. 49, referring to Lohmeyer but without any real basis, thinks "it is contradictory to the tenor of the entire thanksgiving to tie it to this particular mundane transaction." Peter T. O'Brien, whose work *Introductory Thanksgivings in the Letters of Paul* (NovTSup 49; Leiden: Brill, 1977) contains one of the finest exegetical treatments of Phil. 1:3–11, argues for a reference here to the offering, but not exclusively (pp. 23–25). Note also his very useful article, "The Fellowship Theme in Philippians," *RTR* 37 (1978): 9–18.
13. I would venture to explain the construction in Phil. 1:5 as an ellipsis for ἐπὶ τῇ κοινωνίᾳ ὑμῶν τῆς διακονίας τῆς εἰς τὸ εὐαγγέλιον, in conformity with 2 Cor. 8:4.

ἐπί in two different senses within the same grammatical construction (that is, two prepositional phrases ruled by the same verb). It appears more natural to take vv. 3-4a (up to ὑμῶν) as the main clause, with vv. 4b-5 as a subordinate, participial clause. Meyer (on v. 5) objects that in this case "the specification of the ground for thanks would be entirely wanting," but this comment overlooks how easy it is for Paul to shift or readjust his thought in the middle of a sentence. In other words, his desire to bring in the note of joy leads Paul to a reiteration of the initial thought of thanksgiving, only that now (at the end of v. 4—see Additional Notes, 1:4) he uses the broader notion expressed by δέησις.

The addition of ἐγὼ μέν (preceding εὐχαριστῶ) by the "Western" tradition led some older scholars to draw the inference that Paul had just received a communication from the Philippians in which they apologized for the smallness of their gift. Paul's response is, "As for me, I am most thankful." For an extensive discussion of this variant, see especially Greijdanus.

ἐπὶ πάσῃ τῇ μνείᾳ ὑμῶν (lit. "in all the [i.e., my] remembrance of you"): It has been suggested that this construction is a subjective genitive, yielding the translation, "for all your remembrance [of me]." The suggestion is most intriguing and is supported by the immediate context, where Paul has in view the Philippians' concern for him (cf. also 4:10). If so, it would mean that ἐπί is used in the same causal sense both times (vv. 3 and 5) and that the two prepositional clauses are parallel and interpret each other.

In spite of its attractiveness, however, this interpretation conflicts with the broader context of Paul's epistolary style. Paul uses μνεία in the thanksgivings of Romans, 1 Thessalonians (also the verb μνημονεύω), Philemon, and 2 Timothy; in all of those cases, the reference is to Paul's remembrance of his addressees. Given the somewhat formal and stereotyped character of those opening sections, it seems much preferable to take the Philippians construction as an objective genitive.

Moreover, ἐπί is used "temporally" in the parallel passages in Romans, 1 Thessalonians, and Philemon. It is true that in those passages the construction is different (ἐπὶ τῶν προσευχῶν), but we should keep in mind that in this kind of context μνεία and προσευχή seem to occupy the same semantic field, and BAGD prefers the meaning "mention" for μνεία here (though Ltf. argues cogently that this meaning should be reserved for instances in which the noun is coupled with ποιέομαι). Notice further the suggestive parallel phrase ἐπὶ πάσῃ τῇ θλίψει ἡμῶν in 2 Cor. 1:4 and 1 Thess. 3:7. The *NIV* is probably correct in translating, "every time I remember you."[14]

1:4 ὑπὲρ πάντων ὑμῶν: In the parallel passages Paul uses the preposition περί. The use of ὑπέρ for περί is not unusual in Paul,[15] but could its presence here be due to its proximity with δεήσει (even if the sense "petition" is not prominent in this passage)? If so, ὑπὲρ πάντων ὑμῶν should be connected with what immediately precedes and only indirectly with εὐχαριστῶ (contra Ltf.). On the significance of πάντων see Additional Notes on 1:1.

μετὰ χαρᾶς τὴν δέησιν ποιούμενος: The article τὴν would seem to indicate a reference to the previously mentioned δεήσει, and this factor suggests strongly that μετὰ χαρᾶς begins a new clause (contra *NASB*) and is emphatic.

The word δέησις may be used in a broad sense as a synonym for προσευχή (cf. also εὐχή) or in a narrow sense as a synonym of αἴτημα ("request"; cf. also ἱκετηρία, "supplication," in Heb. 5:7). In the second sense it contrasts with εὐχαριστία ("thanksgiving"), and this factor has led most commentators to deny that the beginning of v. 5 (= the ground of thanksgiving) should be construed with δέησιν ποιούμενος. Such a construction, however, seems preferable because of the likelihood that δέησις is being used in its more general sense, whereby the semantic contrast with εὐχαριστία is neutralized—indeed, the notion of "thanksgiving" is thereby included in that of "prayer." (Does not the emphasis on joy seem more easily associated with the idea of thanksgiving than with that of petition?[16]) Note that

---

14. For a detailed argument in favor of the causal interpretation, see O'Brien, *Thanksgivings*, pp. 41–46 (building on the work of Schubert). On p. 43 he tells us he has not found one instance (in or outside the NT) where εὐχαριστῶ ἐπί has a temporal force. Strictly speaking, however, it would be imprecise to describe the use even here as temporal (note my quotation marks above). The preposition ἐπί probably preserves its "local" sense. It is simply that the idea conveyed by the whole is naturally translated with a temporal English clause. Incidentally, because of the position of the article (cf. BDF § 275.3), Meyer argues for the following sense: "my remembrance of you *in its entire tenor and compass* is mingled with thankfulness towards God" (similarly most commentators). I view this approach as an instance of overinterpretation and would suggest that Paul uses this construction here primarily because it lends some emphasis to his statement.
15. BDF § 231.1.
16. Indeed, Schenk (who stresses the verbal similarity with 4:6) argues that Paul intends a substantive connection, not just a pun, between εὐχαριστῶ

ἔντευξις, which normally means "petition," seems to be used of thanksgiving in 1 Tim. 4:5 (cf. BAGD).

1:5 ἐπί (here "because, in view of"): This preposition is used to express the grounds of thanksgiving only here and in 1 Cor. 1:4; normally Paul uses a causal participle (Col. 1:4; 1 Thess. 1:3; Philem. 5) or ὅτι (Rom. 1:8; 1 Cor. 1:5 [?]; 2 Thess. 1:3).

τῆς πρώτης ἡμέρας: This phrase corresponds to ἐν ἀρχῇ τοῦ εὐαγγελίου (lit. "in the beginning of the gospel," Phil. 4:15). Ltf. points out that the article τῆς, omitted by most MSS., is unnecessary with numerals; however, its attestation (see NA) is early and strong.

Several editors place a comma at the end of both v. 5 and v. 6; Kennedy uses a colon both times; Wettstein has a period at the end of v. 5 and a colon at the end of v. 6. We may defend the latter punctuation by noting that even in English a careful stylist may deliberately, and for special effect, allow a subordinate clause to stand by itself in spite of the usual aversion to sentence fragments. (Would the conception of a "sentence fragment" have been meaningful to an ancient Greek writer?)

2. EXPANSION (1:6-8)

Translation

Moreover, I am confident of this truth: the One who began a good work in you will bring it to completion at the day of *Christ Jesus. And indeed it is right that I should feel this way about all of you—for I hold you dear in my heart [*or,* because you hold me dear in your heart], since you all have participated with me in the grace of my apostolic ministry, both when I have been in chains and when I have defended and confirmed the gospel. Truly God is *my witness how I long for all of you with the intense love of Christ Jesus.

Exegesis and Exposition

In v. 6 Paul gives us a further, but closely related, reason for his joyful sense of gratitude—his assurance that God's work cannot be

---

and χαρά: "The prayer of thanks is an expression of joy to God for what He has done." Nevertheless, Schenk affirms that δέησις = intercession (though he certainly understands the principle of neutralization). Kent goes too far, however, in construing v. 5 with μετὰ χαρᾶς; this connection is grammatically inexact, though it usefully calls attention to the emphatic position of the phrase. For the LXX background to the semantic field of prayer, see the useful (though somewhat superficial) summary by Mario Cimosa, *Il vocabulario di preghiera nel Pentateuco greco dei LXX* (Quaderni di "Salesianum" 10; Roma: LAS, 1985).

thwarted. Theologians who speak of salvation as being God's from beginning to end are not using mere rhetoric, for this is precisely Paul's conception as he addresses the Philippians regarding their share in the gospel: "Do not misunderstand my commendation; it was not you who began this work, but God, and He will complete it" (cf. the qualification in Gal. 4:9).

This paraphrase overstates the contrast between vv. 5 and 6, but it helps us to focus on a point often ignored by commentators yet fundamental to this epistle, namely, the tension that exists between the believers' accountability for their own spiritual conduct and their need to rely totally on God's grace in order to meet that obligation ("the paradox of all religion," says Ltf.; cf. also Chrysostom's suggestive comments on v. 6). Some will no doubt object to this construction as an attempt to introduce modern categories of systematic theology (human responsibility and divine sovereignty) into a Pauline statement that is motivated by different concerns. My comments on 2:12-13, however, will seek to show that no reasonable exegesis of that passage can dispense with these categories, for they are thoroughly Pauline (granted that our precise *formulation* of them may not correspond exactly to that of the apostle).

Apart from a consideration of 2:12-13, it may still be asked whether we are justified in seeing these theological concerns in the passage before us. Martin, for example (following Collange), argues that the apostle "is supplying a theological undergirding" for his troubled readers by alluding to God's good work of creation, which will surely be brought to consummation. It is true that Paul's language here is reminiscent of Gen. 1:2, LXX,[17] that elsewhere Paul cites God's creation of light as analogous to spiritual enlightenment (2 Cor. 4:6), and that the correspondence between creation and redemption is a fundamental biblical motif (Gnilka in particular appeals to such passages as Isa. 41:4; 44:6; 48:12-13).

On the other hand, it should be noted that Gen. 2:2 speaks of God's having already completed His work on the sixth day, and this lack of conceptual correspondence with Paul's main point (future consummation) should weigh more heavily than linguistic correspondences. Moreover, the linguistic correspondence is only partial: even the word for "good" in LXX, καλόν (*kalon*), is missing here. Why would Paul have used the synonym ἀγαθόν (*agathon*) if he meant to refer to the Genesis description of God's good work? Finally, Paul

---

17. συνετέλησεν ὁ θεὸς...τὰ ἔργα αὐτοῦ ("God finished His work").

himself elsewhere uses the contrast between beginning and completing (see passages discussed below) with regard to the activity of believers. A deliberate allusion to Genesis, therefore, is at best possible, and then only in a secondary and indirect way. Even if we accept such an allusion, that fact would hardly exclude a reference to the Philippians' Christian activity, as the following discussion should make clear.

Paul uses the verb ἐπιτελέω (*epiteleō*, "complete") six other times. One of those speaks of the need for "perfecting holiness in the fear of God" (2 Cor. 7:1). Four (Rom. 15:28; 2 Cor. 8:6, 11 [two times]) occur in the context of finishing the task of raising an offering for the saints in Jerusalem (see Introduction: Historical Context).[18] A closer parallel thought is Gal. 3:3, which contains the only other occurrence of ἐνάρχομαι (*enarchomai*, "begin") in Paul: "Having begun [*enarxamenoi*] by means of the Spirit, are you now finishing [*epiteleisthe*] by means of the flesh?" The Galatians as well as the Philippians had begun their life of faith not with their own strength but with God's through the Spirit. The Galatians were in terrible danger of perverting and thereby destroying that life (Gal. 5:5) by trying to bring it to perfection with the works of the flesh. The Philippians, while not in the same precarious position, also needed to hear that their growth in sanctification, already evident through their participation in the gospel, was really God's work, and He would not fail to bring it to perfection.

No sooner has Paul made clear that God is the author of their salvation than he shifts focus again in v. 7, where he commends them (not God) for their constancy in supporting Paul whatever the circumstances. Of course, God is the only grounds of our confidence, but the apostle claims no insight into God's secret counsel. His assurance that the Philippians will persevere to the end arises from the external, visible evidence that their lives provided.[19]

The evidence is so clear, in fact, that it would have been wrong for

---

18. The 2 Corinthians passage is particularly intriguing because there Paul twice (vv. 6 and 10) contrasts ἐπιτελέω with προενάρχομαι (Phil. 1:6 uses ἐνάρχομαι). However, although the allusion to a material contribution is certainly present in Phil. 1:6, Paul can hardly mean that the Philippians must raise yet another offering for the Last Day.

19. Because that evidence was frighteningly small in the case of the Galatians, Paul would not presume on the genuineness of their faith so as to exclude the possibility of their perdition (4:11, 20; 5:4). Even in that setting, however, the apostle could give an expression of confidence (5:10).

Paul to doubt their future: καθώς ἐστιν δίκαιον ἐμοὶ τοῦτο φρονεῖν (*kathōs estin dikaion emoi touto phronein*, lit. "even as it is right for me to think this"). A similar expression occurs in 2 Thess. 1:3 (*kathōs axion estin*, "as it is proper"), but a more striking parallel is found in Heb. 6:9-10: in that passage the author, after considering the awesome possibility of destruction (v. 8), moves on to express his confidence (πεπείσμεθα, *pepeismetha*) in the genuineness of their salvation, a confidence based on previous evidence: "For God is not unjust [*adikos*] to forget your work [*ergou*]."

What Paul had expressed in v. 5 with the expression *tę koinōniạ hymōn eis to euangelion* takes a somewhat different form here in v. 7, συγκοινωνούς μου τῆς χάριτος (*synkoinōnous mou tēs charitos*, "partakers of grace with me," or more likely "of my grace"; cf. Lohmeyer's appeal to 4:14). What does this mean? The view that *charis* is yet one more reference to the Philippians' gift, while superficially attractive, does not yield a good sense in this verse (Paul and the Philippians were not coparticipants in their gift to him). The prevailing opinion is that the word here refers to "the absolute grace of God" (Vincent); according to Martin it "carries the meaning of God's strength made available to his people in their weakness," as in 2 Cor. 12:9.

This interpretation has the advantage of taking the construction in a natural way and may therefore be correct, but I do not find it fully convincing. In the first place, Paul characteristically uses *charis* in reference to his apostolic ministry (Rom. 1:5; cf. also 12:3; 15:15; 1 Cor. 3:10; Gal. 2:9), and it is that ministry that the present verse has in view: "the defense and confirmation of the gospel." Second, a general reference ("sharers in divine grace") does not do justice to the parallel expression in v. 5, which also has in view Paul's gospel ministry.[20] Third, commentators have strangely ignored the clear parallel in 1 Cor. 9:23, "And I do all things on account of the gospel [*euangelion*], that I may become a partaker [*synkoinōnos*] of it."

Without suggesting that *charis* = *euangelion*, we should recognize that the connection is very close; similarly, the meaning of *syn-*

---

20. The connection with v. 5 was stressed by Theodore, who also interprets χάρις with reference to Rom. 1:5. His resulting understanding of the verse, however, is different from the one presented here. Gordon D. Fee, *The First Epistle to the Corinthians* (NICNT; Grand Rapids: Eerdmans, 1987), p. 432, gives Phil. 1:9 as evidence that Paul in 1 Cor. 9:23 means the benefits rather than the work of the gospel, but he does not exegete the Philippians passage. Note also Schütz, *Paul*, p. 52.

koinōnos here approaches that of *synergos* ("fellow-worker"; cf. 4:3; 1 Thess. 3:2). The apostle has in view, therefore, not divine grace in general but the Philippians' specific identification with, and support of, his gospel ministry. One must stress, however, that this ministry entails suffering (cf. the verb *echaristhē* in 1:29 and the linking of *synkoinōneō* with *thlipsis*, "affliction," in 4:14).

But we should also note carefully how that ministry is defined: the qualification—"both in my chains and in the defense and confirmation of the gospel"—is of special importance in grasping the reason Paul values so highly the support of the Philippians. If we take ἀπολογία καὶ βεβαιώσει (*apologia kai bebaiōsei*) in their technical sense, "legal defense and proof," then Paul would be referring to activity coordinate and linked with his imprisonment (so Hwth. and many others; cf. Acts 25:16; 2 Tim. 4:16). But it seems much preferable to see a contrast between the two prepositional phrases, in which case the words in question (which, contra Vincent, may well constitute a hendiadys) would retain their general sense: "You have supported me *not only* during those times when I have been able to set forth openly *the defense that confirms* the gospel, but even during this period of confinement" (cf. Acts 22:1; 1 Cor. 9:3; 2 Cor. 7:11; 1 Pet. 3:15; see also notes on 1:16). The Philippians, who had no way of knowing that this confinement had opened new avenues for the spread of the gospel (vv. 12-14), had shown their constancy and commitment to the apostolic ministry by supporting Paul even when, to the best of their knowledge, he was not "producing."

Finally, we may note in this passage the intensity of Paul's personal affection for the Philippian congregation. The apostle first introduces this emotional note at a point that jars the expected logical progression of the sentence: "I have good reason to be confident that God will preserve you, because I have you in my heart." The awkwardness of this clause has led some to translate, "because you have me in your heart" (see Additional Notes). This move is unnecessary, however, for both sides of this mutual affection are explicit and prominent in the passage.

Verse 8 in particular reveals the depth of Paul's feeling. Note, first, that this verse is an oath ("God is my witness"), something not altogether unusual for Paul (see Rom. 1:9; 2 Cor. 1:23; Gal. 1:20; and esp. 1 Thess. 2:5, 10, in an epistle that rivals Philippians in emotional intensity). Second, though the emphatic verb ἐπιποθέω (*epipotheō*, "to long for") is elsewhere used by Paul with ἰδεῖν (*idein*, from *horaō*, "to see") of his desire to see the recipients (Rom. 1:11; 1 Thess. 3:6; 2

Tim. 1:4), only here does he speak directly of longing for individuals (cf. 2:26 and 2 Cor. 9:14). Third, Paul uses the most expressive term available to indicate the source of human emotion, σπλάγχνα (*splanchna,* "entrails"; cf. 2:1; 2 Cor. 6:12; 7:15; Col. 3:12; and esp. Philem. 7, 12, 20), used here by metonymy of the affection itself; moreover, the use of that term with the qualifying genitive, "of Christ Jesus," is unique to this passage (but cf. Philem. 20) and adds pathos to an already powerful statement.

Additional Notes

1:6 πεποιθώς: The position is emphatic as common with Paul (cf. Alford). Schenk takes his structural approach to an extreme when he views this participle as synonymous ("Kontextidentisch") with προσεύχομαι in v. 9.

αὐτὸ τοῦτο: Appealing to 2 Pet. 1:5, Meyer argues for an adverbial use here, referring to the previous verse rather than to what follows. We may paraphrase: "being persuaded, for this very reason [viz., your constancy], that God will preserve you." This construction would fit nicely with the exposition above; moreover, it could be supported with appeal to τοῦτο αὐτό in 2 Cor. 2:3 (cf. BAGD, p. 123A, but see *NASB*). Ltf. dismisses this idea on the basis of word order and most commentators follow him; indeed, the use of αὐτὸ τοῦτο elsewhere in Paul (2 Cor. 7:11; Gal. 2:10; and several instances of εἰς αὐτὸ τοῦτο) does not support an adverbial force here. The matter cannot be solved conclusively (1:25 does not really help us); Meyer's construction should be regarded as plausible but not probable. (Cf. also Ewald's discussion.)

ἐν ὑμῖν (lit. "in you"): This construction often means "among you, in your midst," a rendering preferred by Martin. Meyer objects that the ὑπὲρ πάντων ὑμῶν of v. 7 suggests that Paul is expressing "a confidence felt in respect to all individuals." This passage alone does not help us resolve the ambiguity, though the parallel in 2:13 (see my comments there) strongly supports Meyer.

ἄχρι ἡμέρας Χριστοῦ Ἰησοῦ: The literal *NASB* rendering, "until the day of Christ Jesus," is awkward, for the English speaker anticipates "at"; *NIV* preserves "until" and smooths out the sentence by rendering the verb ἐπιτελέσει, "will carry it on to completion," possibly the best solution (the *NEB* uses the preposition "by"). See further the comments on v. 10.

Many important witnesses have the transposition Ἰησοῦ Χριστοῦ, but the reading adopted in the NA text is extremely early

(P[46]) and has wide geographic attestation (B D lat); it also fits the pattern of the later epistles (see note on 1:1). In spite of Sinaiticus even Tischendorf adopts this text.

1:7 φρονεῖν: On the significance of this word see Introduction: Distinctive Teaching.

διὰ τὸ ἔχειν με ἐν τῇ καρδίᾳ ὑμᾶς ("because I have you in my [lit. the] heart"): Earlier commentators suggested taking με as object and ὑμᾶς as subject: "because you have me in your heart." This rendering yields a smoother connection with the first part of the verse; that is, the Philippians' love and care for Paul is the reason (διά) he is justified to feel confident. In fact, however, we may see the reason as resting "not on the act of remembering but on the thing remembered" (Ltf.; no one would want to argue on the basis of Rom. 6:17 that Paul was thankful that the Romans had been servants of sin— such grammatically imprecise constructions are natural and common).

Since Meyer's time, moreover, virtually all commentators have argued that the accusative closest to the infinitive is normally to be taken as subject; usually, no evidence is given, and Winer[21] emphasizes that only the context can be decisive, but we may note the evidence of 2 Cor. 2:13; 8:6. (In his summary of the evidence Hwth. does not mention these two important verses because he limited his research to phrases where the preposition διά occurs. As for the occurrences he lists, his analysis of them seems to me to need sharper focus.) Of particular importance is the fact that Chrysostom, a Greek speaker himself who often weighs alternate positions (see Introduc-

---

21. G. B. Winer, *A Treatise on the Grammar of New Testament Greek,* 3d ed., trans. W. F. Moulton (Edinburgh: T. & T. Clark, 1882), p. 414n. Thorough GRAMCORD searches produced several instances where the accusative closest to the infinitive is the subject: Luke 2:27; 11:18; 24:51; Acts 4:2; 21:21 (plus the 2 Corinthians passages mentioned above). The only break in the pattern comes from the NT writer whose word-order patterns are the least regular: Heb. 5:12 (but here the τινα can be interpreted as an interrogative). I do not consider Luke 19:11 an exception, because one of the accusatives is not a person. An Ibycus search of the LXX (limited to the infinitive endings -ειν and -σαι with an accusative personal pronoun in the context) yielded a large number of instances in which the pronoun closest to the infinitive is the subject (e.g., Gen. 32:20; Exod. 3:12; Lev. 23:43; Deut. 4:37; 2 Kgdms. 21:2; 3 Kgdms. 8:53; Tob. BA 6:16; Bar. 4:6; Jer. 2:17, 19; Ezek. 16:52; 20:41–42; 44:7). I found very few breaks in the pattern: Gen. 4:15; Ps. 69:2; Zech. 8:14. (Searches in other Hellenistic writings, such as Epictetus and Plutarch, were not productive.) Ambiguous instances should no doubt be interpreted according to the usual pattern.

tion: Exegetical History), takes με as subject and shows no awareness of the alternate possibility (similarly Theodore).

συγκοινωνούς . . . ὄντας (lit. "being fellow-sharers): The participle is probably causal (cf. *NASB* "since" and *NIV* "for"), though Lenski prefers to take the participial construction as in apposition ("you all as being joint-fellowshippers of my grace"). The difference is minimal.

1:8 μου: MSS. containing a "Western" text, supported by a few other witnesses, have the dative μοι (cf. Old Latin and Vulgate *mihi*). Curiously, P⁴⁶ and one Old Latin MS. (a, which belongs to the 9th cent.) omit the pronoun; if the omission is original, it would account for the variation, but accidental omissions in P⁴⁶ are not uncommon (see Introduction: Textual History). The addition of *estin* is certainly a secondary smoothing of the text.

C. PRAYER (1:9-11)

Translation

Now this is what I am praying for: that your love may *abound more and more in knowledge and in total discernment, so that you may approve the things that really matter and thus show yourselves pure and blameless for the day of Christ, that is, filled with the fruit of right conduct that comes through Jesus Christ *to the glory and praise of God.

Exegesis and Exposition

The καί (*kai*, "and") of v. 9 should probably be viewed as resumptive, picking up the reference to Paul's prayer in v. 4. As already pointed out (see the beginning of the previous section), Philippians and Colossians are characterized by a substantive intercessory prayer that follows immediately upon the thanksgiving. The similarities, however, go beyond matters of structure: some striking lexical correspondences are also present, as the following chart demonstrates.

Phil. 1:9, 11	Col. 1:9-11
proseuchomai	*proseuchomenoi*
I pray	praying
perisseuę en epignōsei	*auxanomenoi tę epignōsei tou theou*
abound in knowledge	growing in the knowledge of God
kai pasę aisthēsei	*en pasę sophią kai synesei*
and in all discernment	in all wisdom and understanding

peplērōmenoi   plērōthēte
  being filled   you may be filled
karpon dikaiosynēs   karpophorountes
  fruit of righteousness   bearing fruit
eis doxan kai epainon theou   kata to kratos tēs doxēs autou
  to the glory and praise of God   according to the power of his
                                          glory
ergon agathon (v. 6)   en panti ergǭ agathǭ
  a good work   in every good work

Distinctive of Colossians, in keeping with the primary concerns of that letter, is the abundance of cognitive terms. Distinctive of the prayer for the Philippians are the following elements.

Note first *its literary effect*. Paul achieves a stylistic crescendo by the logical progression of these verses. Already in v. 9 the words "still more and more" (ἔτι μᾶλλον καὶ μᾶλλον, *eti mallon kai mallon*) indicate something of the Philippians' present yet partial enjoyment of the graces Paul prays for. The subsequent clauses express, with progressive significance, three goals that the apostle sets before his readers. What we may call the immediate purpose is expressed at the beginning of v. 10 by the words, "so that you may test [*or* approve] the things that matter," while the final purpose is the believer's perfection: "in order that you may be pure and blameless for the day of Christ."

But there is a third and higher purpose, for Paul's ultimate goal focuses not on the believer but on God: "to the glory and praise of God" (v. 11). We may notice here a fundamental correspondence with the Lord's Prayer. By making the first petition the hallowing of God's name, our Lord taught us to place every other request within the framework of our desire to glorify God. This pervasive biblical principle (cf. the prayers of Moses and Hezekiah, Exod. 32:11-13 and 2 Kings 19:15-19) finds clear expression in Paul's theocentric view of the believer's sanctification.[22]

A second distinctive of the prayer consists in *the interweaving of knowledge and love*. While it is generally true—and certainly true in Colossians—that Paul's use of cognitive terms has a direct ethical bearing, this aspect comes out explicitly in the prayer for the Philippians. We may already have an indication of it in Paul's actual choice of terms at the end of v. 9, ἐν ἐπιγνώσει καὶ πάσῃ αἰσθήσει (*en epignōsei kai pasę aisthēsei*, "in real knowledge and all discernment"). Generally speaking, the English term *knowledge* has a broader reference

---

22. Cf. Ridderbos, *Paul*, pp. 258–65.

than *discernment* insofar as the latter indicates the practical application of knowledge. The relation between the two Greek terms (i.e., semantic overlap as well as distinction) corresponds fairly closely to that of the English terms.

Is the combination of *epignōsis* and *aisthēsis* in this passage one more example of "stylistic reinforcement" (see Introduction: Language and Style)? The term *aisthēsis* (also translated "insight, experience, perception") occurs only here in the NT, and it seems unlikely that Paul would choose a term that had such a specific sense if the purpose was only stylistic. The cognate term αἰσθητήρια (*aisthētēria*) is used of the moral faculties or senses in Heb. 5:14, a conceptually parallel passage: ". . . solid food is for adults, who by practice have their faculties trained to discern [*pros diakrisin*] good and evil." We have good reason, then, to believe that Paul chose *aisthēsis* to specify the practical outworkings of the knowledge in view.

Immediately following his use of this term Paul gives more explicit expression to the ethical concern: εἰς τὸ δοκιμάζειν ὑμᾶς τὰ διαφέροντα (*eis to dokimazein hymas ta diapheronta*, "so that you may approve the things that matter"; see Additional Notes for the translation). Paul uses this very phrase (*dokimazeis ta diapheronta*) in Rom. 2:18 with reference to the knowledge of a Jew who has been instructed in the law yet whose life is inconsistent. The sound judgment of which Paul speaks here, therefore, even though it is a step beyond mere knowledge of facts, might still fall short of Paul's full desire for the Philippians. Yet the apostle has already precluded such an inadequate understanding by the initial statement of his prayer: "that your love may abound."

The central focus of Paul's concern is *knowledge that cultivates love*. This emphasis is surely to be related to the Philippians' struggle over the problem of unity (see Introduction: Historical Context and Distinctive Teaching), and it prepares the readers for the more forceful words in 2:1-4. For the moment we should note the ease with which Paul intertwines knowledge and love. The apostle cares not for any (false) knowledge that fails to issue in love. But it is just as important to reflect that Paul does not view love as mindless. Quite the contrary: knowledge is the very way of love.

A third, and major, distinctive of the prayer in Philippians is its emphasis on *moral perfection at Christ's return*. Paul's ethical concerns reach full expression in the descriptive terms εἰλικρινεῖς (*eilikrineis*, "sincere"), ἀπρόσκοποι (*aproskopoi*, lit. "not stumbling"), and πεπληρωμένοι καρπὸν δικαιοσύνης (*peplērōmenoi karpon dikaiosynēs*, "filled with the fruit of righteousness"). The first term, *eilikrineis,* is not used elsewhere by Paul, but the sense of moral purity is well established in extrabiblical literature (cf. also 2 Pet. 3:1).

The term *aproskopoi* is more controversial because it can be taken in either a passive or an active sense. The former ("not stumbling, not suffering damage") leads to the common translation "blameless," which is consonant with the sense of *eilikrineis* (cf. also Acts 24:16, ἀπρόσκοπον συνείδησιν, *aproskopon syneidēsin,* "a clear conscience"). However, the only other occurrence of this adjective in Paul's letters has the active sense, "not causing to stumble," as in 1 Cor. 10:32, "Give no offense [*aproskopoi ginesthe*] to Jews or to Greeks or to the church of God" (cf. also *proskomma* in Rom. 14:13; 1 Cor. 8:9; *proskopē* in 2 Cor. 6:3). This latter meaning is consonant with Paul's broader concern for unity among the Philippians and may be appropriate here (cf. Vincent and Hwth.), though my subsequent comments regarding Christ's return will tend to favor the passive sense. The matter cannot be resolved with certainty.

Also ambiguous is the phrase "fruit of righteousness." The genitive *dikaiosynēs* can be understood as subjective (indicating origin: "fruit produced by righteousness"), as epexegetical ("fruit that is righteousness"), or as a Semitic-like genitive of quality ("righteous fruit"). Moreover, the word *dikaiosynē* itself may have a forensic force (justification = a legal judgment) or an ethical sense (righteous character or conduct).

In spite of these ambiguities, only two basic interpretations are likely. (1) If we take *dikaiosynē* in the forensic sense that is so characteristic of Paul, the genitive should be understood as subjective: "fruit that results from our justified state."[23] (2) If we choose the ethical meaning (cf. Rom. 6:13; 2 Cor. 6:7, 14; Eph. 5:9; several occurrences in the pastorals), the genitive should probably be viewed as epexegetical, "the fruit that consists in right conduct" (note that there is virtually no difference between such a force and the genitive of quality, "righteous fruit").

Can we decide between these two interpretations? Paul does not use this expression elsewhere (but cf. Heb. 12:11; James 3:18; and the commentaries). Other Pauline occurrences of *karpos* with the genitive are best interpreted as subjective genitives, but these are not de-

---

23. Martin suggests an epexegetical force ("fruit which consists of being rightly related to God"), but that makes poor sense. Schenk argues that δικαιοσύνης is an authorial genitive, therefore equivalent to διὰ Ἰησοῦ Χριστοῦ.

cisive.[24] A much better parallel is 2 Cor. 9:10, "the harvest of your righteousness" (τὰ γενήματα τῆς δικαιοσύνης ὑμῶν, *ta genēmata tēs dikaiosynēs hymōn*). Although the genitival construction here too is by itself ambiguous, one can hardly deny that Paul is alluding to Hos. 10:12, LXX, which clearly speaks of moral conduct.

The LXX, moreover, has other instances of *karpos dikaiosynēs* (Prov. 3:9; 11:30; Amos 6:12), in none of which a forensic notion seems to be present. These factors, combined with the specific context of Phil. 1:11, make an ethical interpretation almost certain. Furthermore, even if *dikaiosynē* here were interpreted as forensic, the ethical note would still be present in *karpos:* sanctification flowing out of justification. In short, whatever our understanding of the grammar, the fruit mentioned here must be described along the lines of the list in Gal. 5:22–23.

All told, it would appear that the object of Paul's prayer is the *total sanctification* of the Philippians; what they now have in part must be brought to full fruition εἰς ἡμέραν Χριστοῦ (*eis hēmeran Christou*). This phrase is best translated "for the day of Christ" (cf. Vincent). Rendering the preposition *eis* with "until" (so *NASB* and *NIV*, for example) might suggest that Paul is praying merely for a *continuation* of the sanctification the Philippians already enjoy, as though some Christians have arrived at their spiritual destination. Against such an inference we should note that it is not consonant with the emphasis Paul places on progression ("abound still more and more," v. 9). Moreover, we have an important parallel within the context of this passage, namely v. 6, which speaks of "the day of Jesus Christ" as the time of perfection (*epitelesei;* on the significance of *achri* see the Additional Notes for that verse).

An additional consideration is the thanksgiving in 1 Corinthians.[25] Several lexical features in Philippians are shared by 1 Corinthians (e.g., *pasē gnōsei* in 1:5; *bebaioō* in 1:6, 8; *koinōnia* in 1:9; further, v. 7 contains a specific reference to Christ's return). Particularly important, however, is 1 Cor. 1:8: "who will also confirm you

---

24. The important difference between these occurrences and Phil. 1:11 is that in the former occurrence the noun in the genitive is of quite a different character from δικαιοσύνη. In Phil. 1:22 it is ἔργου; in Gal. 5:22 it is a personal agent, πνεύματος; Eph. 5:9, φωτός, is closer, but an important textual variant is πνεύματος.
25. The parallel prayer in Colossians makes no explicit reference to the Lord's return, but note the prominent role this theme plays in 1 Thess. 1:10 and 2 Thess. 1:9–10.

blameless to the end on the day of our Lord Jesus Christ." The preposition "on" (Greek *en*) unambiguously expresses what is less clear
in the *eis* of Phil. 1:10. That which Paul has in view, both in 1 Corinthians and in Philippians, is the sanctified state of his readers *at* the
time of the Lord's return.

Now it is generally agreed that in the introductory sections of his
epistles Paul often anticipates themes that he will develop in the
body of the letter. It is not farfetched, for example, to see in 1 Cor.
1:4-9 a hint of Paul's concern with the perfectionism that was plag-
uing some of the Corinthian believers.[26] Even more clearly, Philippians addresses this issue in 3:12, "Not that I have already obtained
it, or have already become perfect, but I press on." Not surprisingly,
therefore, twice in his introduction (1:6, 10) Paul reminds the Philippians of the *partial* character of their sanctification. To be sure, believers may—no, must—be regarded as "pure and blameless" in this
life, and thus Paul's prayer is in effect a commandment that the
Philippians give evidence of their sanctification now. All the same,
the apostle is focusing, as he did when writing to the Thessalonians,
on the perfection of the sanctifying process, on his desire that God
will sanctify them "completely" (*holoteleis*) and preserve them
"without blame at [*en*] the coming of our Lord Jesus Christ" (1 Thess.
5:23).

Additional Notes

1:9 καὶ τοῦτο προσεύχομαι: We may relate the prayer to what
immediately precedes: "I long to see you, but since I am prevented by
my chains, I will minister to you through prayer" (cf. Martin). Alter-
natively, as suggested in the exposition above, we may understand it
as a resumption of v. 4: "I said that I was making prayer for you; here
is what I have been praying." These two ideas, of course, are not
mutually exclusive.

περισσεύῃ: This present subjunctive fits well with the progressive
element in the sentence (though it would be an overstatement to say
that the tense itself emphasizes that element), and this factor has
persuaded most critics that the variant aorist reading (περισσεύσῃ,
supported by few MSS., including B) is a corruption. Possibly so, but
Greek writers do not always use tenses as we might expect, and it is
difficult to explain how an aorist might have arisen if the present is
original. This variation, contrary to what is often thought, does not

---

26. Cf. F. F. Bruce, *1 and 2 Corinthians* (NCB; Greenwood, S.C.: Attic Press,
    1971), pp. 20f.

involve a substantive difference. We should incidentally note that this verb, as Hwth. rightly emphasizes, is characteristically Pauline and draws attention to the abundance of "the new age opened up by Christ."

ἐπιγνώσει: It is very difficult to come up with an adequate English equivalent for this term if we wish to distinguish it from the simple form γνῶσις, "knowledge." The *NASB* rendering, "real knowledge," tends to overload the Greek compound.[27] It should be noted that Paul uses γνῶσις fifteen times in the Corinthian correspondence, three times in Romans, four times in the prison and pastoral epistles; in contrast, ἐπίγνωσις does not occur in 1-2 Corinthians at all, occurs three times in Romans, twelve times in the prison and pastoral epistles. Assuming a traditional view of the chronology of the epistles, one could reasonably argue that Paul simply developed a preference for the compounded term and that this factor (not some substantive semantic difference between it and γνῶσις) accounts for its use here.

1:10 δοκιμάζειν . . . διαφέροντα: Both of the terms are polysemous and so four translations are possible—"test/approve the things that differ," "test/approve the things that are excellent."[28] "Approve what is best" is doubtless the correct idea here (similarly Rom. 2:18), though one must note that these terms were common in Hellenistic times, particularly in Stoic circles: Epictetus uses δοκιμάζω with φαντασία when expounding on our God-given ability to test external impressions (e.g., 1.20.7), whereas διαφέρω is especially common, and the derivative ἀδιάφορα ("things indifferent") is contrasted to both the good and the bad (e.g., 1.20.12). The early Fathers tended to see in Paul's statement a concern that believers be able to distinguish heresy. Johnstone, interestingly, sees here not a reference to the contrast between virtue and vice but to "the faculty of distinguishing Christian virtue from all counterfeits; of seeing, in an apparent conflict of duties, what present duty really is; . . . of avoiding moral pitfalls, however carefully covered over" (p. 42).

1:11 εἰς δόξαν καὶ ἔπαινον θεοῦ ("to the glory and praise of God"): One of the most striking variants of P[46] is found here, εἰς δόξαν θεοῦ καὶ ἔπαινον ἐμοί, "to the glory of God and my praise." Metzger, who

---

27. Such a rendering could be supported by an appeal to the arguments of Trench (*Synonyms*, 285) and Ltf. (on Col. 1:9).
28. Both terms are examples of a common kind of metonymy. English *prove*, which earlier meant "try, test," provides a close parallel to δοκιμάζω; similarly, the verb *distinguish* leads to the commendatory adjective *distinguished*.

describes this variant as "astonishing," considers it an early confla-
tion of the original reading with the reading of F and G, "to my glory
and praise" (supported by the Latin MS. g and by Ambrosiaster).
Ross agrees that P[46] gives us a conflate reading, but he argues that F
and G preserve the original because it easily explains the other variants: "At first sight it would seem outrageous that Paul should make
so egotistical a remark, so scribes would naturally alter the offensive
ἐμοί."[29]

Ross is quite right in stressing the difficulty, and therefore possible originality, of this reading and in pointing to 2 Cor. 1:14 and Phil.
2:16 as evidence that the concept may be compatible with Paul's
thought (see also 1 Thess. 2:19 and my comments on Phil. 2:16). It is
too much to suggest, however, that Paul could have used the theologically charged term δόξα in this particular construction; that is,
although the term by itself may be used of human beings (e.g., 1
Thess. 2:20), the reading of F and G would constitute a doxology
ascribed to Paul.

On the other hand, the term ἔπαινον is quite naturally applied to
human beings, as in Rom. 2:29; we should note in particular the
construction in 1 Pet. 2:14, εἰς . . . ἔπαινον . . . ἀγαθοποιῶν ("for the
praise of those who do right"). Indeed, there is much to be said for
the originality of the reading of P[46], which is perhaps reflected in
Latin MS. a (= D in WW: *in gloriam mihi et laudem Dei*, "to my glory
and God's praise"). If so, then the omission of θεοῦ in F and G could
be explained either as accidental or as a desire to avoid such a close
juxtaposition of God and Paul. In short, the reading of P[46] accounts
most easily for the history of the text, but one hesitates to adopt such
a jarring variant when it is found in this lone witness.

---

29. J. M. Ross, "Some Unnoticed Points in the Text of the New Testament,"
NovT 25 (1983): 59–72, esp. p. 70 (cf. also Hwth., p. 14).

2
Paul's Missionary Report (1:12–26)

We noticed in the previous chapter that the introductory section of Philippians, and particularly its intercessory prayer, contains certain traits that distinguish this letter from the other Pauline epistles. With 1:12 the apostle moves into the body of the letter,[1] and here again we meet a feature distinctive of Philippians, namely, a detailed account of Paul's current circumstances (see Introduction: Literary Structure).

In his other epistles, Paul covers this topic toward the end of the body, in connection with a so-called travelogue (see comments on 2:19–30). And even though 2 Cor. 1:8–11 parallels closely what we find in Philippians, the differences are important. First, in sharp contrast to the tone of the Corinthians passage, where Paul informs the readers of his grave difficulties ("we despaired even of life"), here the apostle immediately reassures the Philippians that, whatever they

---

1. The standard description is John L. White, *The Form and Function of the Body of the Greek Letter: A Study of the Letter-Body in the Non-Literary Papyri and in Paul the Apostle* (SBLDS 2; Missoula, Mont.: Scholars Press, 1972). See pp. 2–3 regarding the so-called disclosure formula; also p. 73 for his view that the body-opening in Philippians covers 1:12–18. That this paragraph extends to v. 26 seems much preferable. Schenk, for example, points out that προκοπή and the first person pronoun in vv. 12 and 25–26 provide the frame for the passage.

may have heard, his imprisonment has actually brought great blessing and joy. Second, the Philippians account is characterized by much more detail (somewhat comparable in this respect is Rom. 15:22–32), including both a description of Paul's circumstances (vv. 12–17) and a moving expression of his attitude toward the Philippian believers (vv. 18–26).

How do we explain the prominence that this matter receives in Philippians? Part of the answer is surely the mutual affection enjoyed by the apostle and this congregation. The saints in Philippi must have communicated to Paul their deep concern for his welfare (cf. 4:10), and the first item on his agenda is to put them at ease; not surprisingly, he returns to this topic at the very end of the letter (4:11, 13, 18). One must also view this passage specifically as a response to the Philippians' gift. The Philippians are in effect supporting Paul and they have a "right" to find out about his affairs; thus the apostle assures them that their effort is not wasted.

Modern readers may find these comments offensive. Does it not spoil the passage to bring in finances? Was not the love between Paul and the Philippians above such mundane considerations? Is it not out of character for Paul to play the part of a public relations man? These questions, I suspect, reflect false dichotomies: love versus material support; the first century versus our times; the apostles versus "normal" Christians. It is, of course, true that Paul's love for the Philippians would not have flagged if they had been unable to contribute. It is also true that in certain situations (e.g., 1 Cor. 9:1–8; 1 Thess. 2:9) Paul did not accept contributions and that even here in this letter (4:10–11) one detects a note of embarrassment over the Philippians' gift.

But these considerations should not prevent us from recognizing the importance that the apostle attached to such gifts as an expression of his converts' commitment to the gospel (see comment on 4:18). Moreover, all the cultural differences that separate us from the early church do not make void those fundamental traits that we have in common with them—the apostle, no less than modern missionaries, had to eat. Indeed, contemporary missionary letters look very much like Phil. 1:12–26. We make a very important *exegetical* point when we refer to this passage as Paul's missionary report.

A. PAUL'S CIRCUMSTANCES (1:12–17)

As I have already stressed, Paul wishes in this section to reassure the Philippians that his imprisonment has not suppressed the work of the gospel; indeed, the words προκοπὴν τοῦ εὐαγγελίου (*prokopēn tou euangeliou*, "progress of the gospel," v. 12) sound the keynote of the whole passage. Paul offers two pieces of evidence in support of his claim: the praetorian guard itself has become exposed to the Christian faith (v. 13), and other Christians have received encouragement to preach boldly (v. 14). Paul, however, does not overlook the reality of adversity, and so vv. 15–17 introduce a sour note by informing the Philippians (or confirming to them?) that the apostle has enemies who wish to bring affliction upon him.

1. THE UNFETTERED PROGRESS OF THE GOSPEL (1:12–14)

Translation

Now I want you to know, brothers, that my adversities [instead of damaging the faith as you fear] have rather turned out for the advance of the gospel. In the first place, all the members of the palace guard—and even the rest of the people here—have become aware that I bear my chains by virtue of my union with Christ. Moreover, the majority of the brothers, having gained confidence in the Lord as a result of my chains, are becoming exceedingly bold to speak the word *[of God] without fear.

Exegesis and Exposition

The introductory formula "Now I want you to know, brothers" (v. 12; see Additional Notes) calls the reader's special attention to the importance of what follows: though Paul may be in chains, "the word of God is not imprisoned" (2 Tim. 2:9). In this respect, though not in others, Paul's circumstances during his next (and final) imprisonment were to prove comparable: "The Lord stood by me and strengthened me, in order that through me the proclamation might be fulfilled and that all the Gentiles might hear it" (2 Tim. 4:17, and cf. comments below on 1:25).

The apostle, however, did not merely say that the gospel had continued to make progress *in spite* of adversity; rather, the adversity itself had turned out for the advancement of the gospel. Far from trying to evoke sympathy from his readers by expressing resignation, the apostle went out of his way to make sure that the Philippians did not grow overly concerned about him; indeed, he gave a glowing report of his ministry intended to produce joy in their hearts (v. 18). One should note, moreover, that implicit in this statement is a recognition of God's sovereign workings in the affairs of men, though the point may seem veiled by the impersonal ἐλήλυθεν (*elēlythen*, "come about"). Paul stressed the ironic turn of events: men may have intended to curtail his ministry with chains, but, in fact, his imprisonment had led both to the evangelization of pagans (v. 13) and to the edification of believers (leading in turn to even greater evangelism, v. 14). We must focus on those two items, because they constitute the evidence set forth by the apostle to demonstrate his claim.

First, the imprisonment had made it possible for the whole praetorian guard, and others, to be exposed to the faith. Paul expresses this thought in a peculiar way, ὥστε τοὺς δεσμούς μου φανεροὺς ἐν Χριστῷ γενέσθαι (hōste tous desmous mou phanerous en Christō genesthai). The clause may be rendered, "so that my chains in Christ have become manifest" (construing tous desmous mou with en Christō), meaning, "so that my imprisonment in the cause of Christ has become well known" (so NASB, with the words "the cause of" italicized). Paul's style, however, would not lead us to expect the predicate adjective phanerous separating two syntactically linked phrases. Generally, commentators agree on the construction, "so that my chains have become manifest in Christ"—a compressed and unusual expression meaning, "it has become clear . . . that I am in chains for Christ" (NIV). We may further ask why Paul did not express his thought with what may be considered a more predictable phrase, hyper Christou, "for the sake of Christ." The use of en Christō here reflects in a notable way Paul's conception of solidarity with Christ. We should see in this choice not a careless overuse of the phrase but Paul's recognition that he is sharing in Christ's sufferings (see comments on 3:10).

Second, Paul rejoiced because his imprisonment, instead of intimidating Christians, had actually encouraged most of them to become bolder witnesses. Here again the construction is ambiguous, but in this case commentators are divided, and their discussions (cf. Meyer and Vincent especially) seem unnecessarily confusing. The basic question is whether ἐν κυρίῳ (en kyriō, "in the Lord") should be construed with τῶν ἀδελφῶν (tōn adelphōn, "the brothers") or with πεποιθότας (pepoithotas, "trusting"). If we choose the former, we could translate with Alford: "Most of the brethren in the Lord, encouraged by [having confidence in] my bonds, are venturing more abundantly [than before] to speak the word of God" (cf. also NIV). If the latter: "Most of the brethren, trusting in the Lord because of my imprisonment, have far more courage to speak the word of God" (NASB). The arguments advanced for either interpretation are not decisive (see Additional Notes), but the use of pepoitha en kyriō later in this epistle and elsewhere in Paul barely tips the scales in favor of the second interpretation (see Rom. 14:14; Gal. 5:10; Phil. 2:24; 3:3, 4; 2 Thess. 3:14).

An interesting question raised in our day by v. 14 is whether the preaching of the gospel is the responsibility of Christians generally or of ordained church officers only. Verses 15–17 (see comments below) suggest that Paul has in view recognized church leaders rather than believers generally. On the other hand, "most of the brothers" in v. 14 cannot reasonably be restricted to ministers. This verse was of course not written for the purpose of answering the question we are posing, and surely it would be a grave mistake to downplay the necessity for and distinctiveness of church offices (such expressions as "Every believer an evangelist!" can be dangerous and misleading). Nevertheless, Phil. 1:14 leaves little doubt that Paul encouraged believers in general "to speak the word of God without fear."

Additional Notes

1:12 γινώσκειν δὲ ὑμᾶς βούλομαι, ἀδελφοί: This formula occurs with some variation in a large number of Pauline passages, particularly for the purpose of introducing a new section (with either δέ or γάρ): θέλω ὑμᾶς εἰδέναι; γνωρίζω(-ομεν) ὑμῖν, ἀδελφοί; and οὐ θέλω(-ομεν) ὑμᾶς ἀγνοεῖν, ἀδελφοί (Rom. 1:13; 11:25; 1 Cor. 10:1; 12:1; 11:3; 2 Cor. 1:8; Col. 2:1; 1 Thess. 4:13). Although Hwth. states that the particular formula used here does not occur elsewhere in Paul "at this particular point of transition," in at least two passages (2 Cor. 1:8 and Gal. 1:11; perhaps also Rom. 1:13) the expression does serve to introduce the body of the letter; 2 Cor. 1:8 is a particularly close parallel.

τὰ κατ' ἐμέ ("my circumstances"): This expression is used by Paul in two other places (Eph. 6:21; Col. 4:7), both of them also against the background of his imprisonment; notice similarly Acts 24:22 and 25:14 with reference to judicial proceedings.

ἐλήλυθεν: For the meaning "turn out," BAGD refer to Wis. 15:5: the sight of idols ἄφροσιν εἰς ὄρεξιν ἔρχεται, "for fools results in lust."[2]

1:13 ὥστε: It would be pedantic to understand this conjunction as introducing an *additional* result (that is, the imprisonment resulted in the progress of the gospel and *this in turn* resulted in the events described in v. 13); rather, the conjunction should be regarded as

---

2. See A. T. S. Goodrich, *The Book of Wisdom with Introduction and Notes.* The Oxford Church Bible Commentary. (New York: Macmillan, 1913), pp. viii n. and 310.

epexegetical, explaining the previous clause. This conjunction then rules two infinitival clauses, one in v. 13 and the other in v. 14, each of which explains in what way the gospel has advanced.

ἐν ὅλῳ τῷ πραιτωρίῳ: Though in some respects dated, Ltf.'s excursus on this point (pp. 99–104) is still valuable. Assuming a Roman imprisonment, he argues that the most suitable meaning of *praetorium* in this passage is "a body of men" rather than a place. A brief, but also very clear and up-to-date, discussion may be found in Bruce (pp. xxii–xxiii). He points out that there is no evidence that the term was used "for the headquarters of a proconsul in a senatorial province such as Asia was at this time" (thus an Ephesian imprisonment as the setting for Philippians seems unlikely). The headquarters of the governor of Judea could indeed be called a *praetorium* (Mark 15:16; Acts 23:35), but Bruce considers that Caesarea, a political backwater, "offers too restricted a setting" for Paul's comments here. Ltf. and Bruce are probably correct that Paul is referring to the emperor's bodyguard in Rome. For a different view see Hwth. and the bibliography he provides.

1:14 τοὺς πλείονας τῶν ἀδελφῶν ἐν κυρίῳ πεποιθότας ("most of the brothers, trusting in the Lord"): In favor of this translation is the fact that to construe τῶν ἀδελφῶν with ἐν κυρίῳ ("the brothers in the Lord") results in an expression that occurs nowhere else and that some commentators regard as redundant (cf. Vincent, Hwth., and esp. Schenk); this objection is not decisive, however, because one could also speak of ἅγιοι ἐν Χριστῷ (v. 1) as redundant. Those who prefer to translate "the brothers in the Lord" point out that πεποιθώς normally occurs first in its clause; however, Ltf. argues plausibly that in 1:14 ἐν κυρίῳ stands first for emphasis (but see Lohmeyer). It appears then that these various arguments and objections cancel out each other. As pointed out in the comments above, Paul's apparent preference for using the verb πέποιθα with the preposition ἐν argues for construing ἐν κυρίῳ with πεποιθότας here, as the *NASB* translates.

τοῖς δεσμοῖς μου: Whether we take this dative as causal (cf. *NIV* and *NASB*) or as instrumental ("by, through"; cf. Vincent) makes no substantive difference.

τὸν λόγον: MSS. F and G add τοῦ κυρίου, whereas the Alexandrian MSS., followed by *NIV* and *NASB*, add τοῦ θεοῦ. The *UBSGNT* committee has chosen the reading of P[46] (also the Majority Text, but with weak early support), which is simply τὸν λόγον, on the principle that the shorter reading is preferable. (Metzger: the other readings "have the appearance of scribal expansions.") However, P[46] is characterized by many careless omissions (see Introduction: Textual History), so the question must remain open, as I have tried to indicate with brackets in my translation.

2. BLESSING MIXED WITH ADVERSITY (1:15–17)

Translation

It is true [as you have heard] that some are preaching Christ motivated by envy and strife, but there are also those who do it motivated by goodwill. *The latter do it out of love, knowing that I am divinely appointed to defend the gospel, while the others preach Christ out of partisanship, with impure motives, supposing that they will *add pressure to my chains.

Exegesis and Exposition

The connection between these verses and those that precede is expressed by the conjunction *kai* (usually "and") at the beginning of v. 15. But what is its force? Some commentators interpret the conjunction as an adversative and draw a sharp distinction between the "brothers" of v. 14 and the group mentioned in 15*a*. There is some force to Vincent's argument that "the motives of envy and strife [in vv. 15–17] . . . cannot be reconciled with" Paul's description in v. 14, "trusting the Lord because of my imprisonment" (the latter phrase indicates good motives). The answer to this problem is not a sharp artificial separation between vv. 14 and 15*a* but the simple recognition that Paul's syntax is not always subject to precise logical analysis (see Introduction: Language and Style). The flourishing evangelism referred to in v. 14 surely includes the preaching/proclamation of Christ mentioned in vv. 15*a* and 17; moreover, the term ἀδελφοί (*adelphoi*, "brothers") is applicable to Paul's opponents. But it is also true that the particular terms of description in v. 14 reflect Paul's estimate only of those who preach from goodwill—clearly they are not terms the apostle would have chosen as an adequate description of his opponents.

We may therefore view *kai* as having a transitional but emphatic force. This idea is captured well by both the *NIV* ("It is true that") and the *NASB* ("to be sure"), and one is tempted to supply, "as you have heard." The reference in v. 14 to renewed evangelistic activity among believers led Paul naturally to acknowledge a painful situation that had very likely come to the Philippians' attention: not all who were taking part in this activity did so impelled by pure motives.

Of course, Paul did not ignore those whose work arose from goodwill and love. Those believers had been emboldened to speak the word because of their recognition that Paul was divinely commissioned. The last word in v. 16, κεῖμαι (keimai, lit. "lie, recline"), is often used in the sense "appointed" and can be translated "destined" (see esp. Luke 2:34 and 1 Thess. 3:3). The predestinarian motif in Paul's description of his own call is particularly vivid in Gal. 1:15–16, where the divine activity is emphasized repeatedly: "He who set me apart [aphorizō] from my mother's womb and called me [kaleō] by His grace [charis] was pleased [eudokeō] to reveal [apokalyptō] His Son in me, in order that I might preach Him among the Gentiles" (it is generally recognized that Jeremiah's call provides the pattern for this description; see Jer. 1:5).

But Paul's description of the sincere Christian workers takes secondary importance. In chiastic fashion (see Additional Notes) Paul begins and ends this paragraph with what was uppermost in his mind: the brothers whose preaching arose from a heart of strife. These individuals were actuated by impure motives (οὐχ ἁγνῶς, ouch hagnōs): they merely pretended (πρόφασις, prophasis, v. 18) to be concerned for the gospel when their real desire was to aggravate Paul's sufferings. The last clause of v. 17, οἰόμενοι θλῖψιν ἐγείρειν τοῖς δεσμοῖς μου (oiomenoi thlipsin egeirein tois desmois mou), is best translated literally, "supposing that they will add pressure to my chains," a rendering that preserves Paul's play on words (see Additional Notes).

The apostle's meaning is clear enough; what is not at all plain is why his opponents would think that their preaching created grief for him. In other words, if their real motivation was to mortify Paul, why would they go about it in such a way—proclaiming Christ? How one answers this question depends on one's prior identification of these opponents (see Introduction: Paul's Opponents). For Ltf., who identified them as Judaizers, these individuals "sought to annoy and wound" the apostle by forming "a compact party in the Church bound to the observance of the law." Most expositors, however, prefer to see no doctrinal question involved at all and attribute the opponents' behavior to "personal animosity and rivalry."[3] This latter

---

3. So Hwth., who provides a brief but useful survey of the various interpretations that have been set forth. Chrysostom, incidentally, believed that Paul was referring to unbelievers who evangelized "in order that the Emperor's wrath might be increased at the spread of the Gospel, and all his anger might fall on the head of Paul" (perhaps this is also Calvin's point). This explanation is simply unsatisfying, however. Walter Schmithals, *Paul and the Gnostics* (Nashville: Abingdon, 1972), pp. 74–75 n. 45, sees vv. 15–17 as parenthetical and referring to the situation in Philippi. Perhaps there is a small (but suggestive) measure of truth in this proposal.

alternative fails to provide an adequate answer to our question. Indeed, would it really occur to anyone that one way of hurting the apostle was to preach precisely what Paul himself had been preaching, especially when such an activity would brand them as "Pauline" and thus bring danger to them?

Although Ltf. was almost surely wrong in his description of the opponents, he perceived correctly that some issues of doctrinal significance must have been at stake. Without necessarily preaching heresy such as we read about in Galatians, these individuals opposed the more distinctive features of Paul's gospel and sought to undermine his ministry to the Gentiles. Yes, men and women were being brought to a saving knowledge of Christ, and for that Paul rejoiced. But this evangelistic success was being used by some to subvert the apostle's authority and to establish a form of Gentile Christianity that was friendlier to Judaizing influences. It is no wonder they believed their efforts would add misery to Paul's sufferings.

Additional Notes

1:15 διὰ φθόνον καὶ ἔριν ("from envy and strife"): In v. 17 Paul uses a different preposition and a different noun (ἐξ ἐριθείας) but it would be a mistake to stress these differences. It may be that the preposition ἐκ more clearly than διά calls attention to attitudes as sources of behavior, but it is just as possible that the variation is purely stylistic and that the semantic distinction between the two prepositions is neutralized in this context. Similarly, it seems best not to look for subtle distinctions between the nouns, even though different English equivalents may indeed be necessary in different contexts. One should also note that, in spite of their phonetic similarity, ἔρις and ἐριθεία are not etymologically related;[4] yet it seems clear that popular etymologizing tended to link them (cf. Ltf.). Therefore, ἐριθεία may be translated "strife" or "partisanship" rather than "selfish ambition" (the latter is preferred by *NIV* and *NASB*).

δι' εὐδοκίαν (lit. "on account of goodwill"): In v. 16 we have "out of love" (ἐξ ἀγάπης). Perhaps εὐδοκία was used first because it provides a clear contrast to the selfish motivation expressed by φθόνος and ἔρις; then, for stylistic reasons, Paul avoided the repetition of εὐδοκία and made use of a word that had become indicative of distinctly Christian ideals. Schenk considers the words contextual synonyms.

---

4. See Pierre Chantraine, *Dictionnaire étymologique de la langue grecque. Histoire des mots* (Paris: Klincksieck, 1968–), pp. 371–72.

1:16–17 The Majority Text, represented in English by *KJV*, transposes these two verses, so that the structure of the clauses becomes parallel (AB-AB) rather than chiastic (AB-BA). This textual variant, though found in a majority of (late) MSS., is not attested earlier than the sixth century; indeed, its attestation is so poor that it is not even mentioned in *UBSGNT*. The variant is a convincing example of the tendency (common in the Byzantine or Majority Text) to smooth what may have appeared stylistically awkward to some scribes.

1:17 ἐγείρειν ("to raise, cause"): The Majority reading is the synonym ἐπιφέρειν ("to bring, inflict on"), which has very poor attestation.

οἰόμενοι θλῖψιν ἐγείρειν τοῖς δεσμοῖς μου ("supposing that they will add pressure to my chains"): If we take δεσμοῖς as an instrumental dative, we could translate, "meaning to make use of my imprisonment to stir up fresh trouble" (so *NEB* mg.), but this construction, which seems to import an alien meaning into the text, is rightly ignored by commentators. A satisfactory translation must, first of all, do justice to the contrast between εἰδότες ("knowing," v. 16) and οἰόμενοι ("imagining"; Collange's "imagining rightly" in effect does away with the contrast). Second, we should note (with Ltf.) that Paul here revives the dead metaphor θλῖψις ("friction, pressure" → "oppression, affliction") by combining it with δεσμός ("chain" → "imprisonment" by metonymy), a stylistic element missed altogether by most versions. Third, ἐγείρειν, too, is being used figuratively.[5] Though not all of these features can be reproduced, the English reader can easily understand the basic figure of the Greek with a literal translation, as above.

B. PAUL'S ATTITUDE (1:18–26)

Paul's description of the circumstances in which he found himself (vv. 12–17) already carried with it an indication of his emotional response to them. But something more explicit was needed, and so we are treated to a remarkable passage in which the apostle lays his heart bare and reveals the deepest motives of his life. We may see a threefold progression in this paragraph. In vv. 18–20 Paul expresses unbounded joy on account of his assurance of salvation. In vv. 21–24

---

5. As in Lucian's *De dea Syria* 18, "Do not, then, out of spite bring grief [πένθος ἐγεῖραι] to the whole kingdom." See Harold W. Attridge and Robert A. Oden, *The Syrian Goddess* (SBLTT 9; Missoula, Mont.: Scholars Press, 1976), p. 27.

he makes clear how that salvation is not in any way threatened by the possibility of death. Finally, he reassures the Philippians (vv. 25–26) by expressing his confident hope that he will be released from prison.

1. JOY IN SALVATION (1:18–20)

Translation

What then [shall I say about my troubles]? Quite simply that Christ is being preached—however this may happen, whether by pretense or in truth—and for this result I rejoice. Indeed [try as they may to discourage me] I will continue to rejoice, because I am confident that these adversities will result in my salvation through Jesus Christ's provision of His Spirit in answer to your prayers. Such is in fact my hopeful expectation: that I may suffer disgrace in no way, but that with all boldness, now as always, through my life or my death, Christ may be magnified in my body.

Exegesis and Exposition

NA marks the beginning of a new paragraph with the last three words of v. 18, ἀλλὰ καὶ χαρήσομαι (*alla kai charēsomai*, "and indeed I will rejoice"). This understanding is supported by Hwth., who comments on the "progressive" character of the combination *alla kai*, which he paraphrases, "*And in addition* I will be glad for another reason." One can just as easily argue that the initial question "What then?"[6] begins the new paragraph by resuming the thought of v. 12: "whatever my circumstances, the gospel is advancing and thus there is reason for rejoicing." At any rate, v. 18 is clearly a transitional unit, bringing the previous paragraph to an end and opening a new, but closely related, thought.

A more substantive question is raised by Hwth.'s comments, namely, the precise relationship between *alla kai charēsomai* and the earlier phrase ἐν τούτῳ χαίρω (*en toutō chairō*, "in this I rejoice"). This is certainly an intriguing repetition, and its emphatic and abrupt character is not satisfactorily explained by Paul's desire to give an additional reason. Ltf. shows more sensitivity to the emotion of the passage when he remarks that the expression "reflects the conflict in the Apostle's mind: he crushes the feeling of personal annoyance, which rises up at the thought of this unscrupulous antagonism." We would go too far if we imagined Paul gritting his teeth as

---

6. τί γάρ: the causal use of γάρ gives way to the transitional, so that this phrase is roughly equivalent to τί οὖν ("what therefore?").

he speaks of rejoicing, but we may be sure that his joyful response was not natural and easy; it would have been unexpected in view of his trials, and therefore it required explanation. (Cf. also Schenk's comments on the significance of the future tense.)

The explanation is Paul's assurance that the adversities he has experienced will result in his salvation: οἶδα γὰϱ ὅτι τοῦτο μοι ἀποβήσεται εἰς σωτηϱίαν (*oida gar hoti touto moi apobēsetai eis sōtērian,* "for I know that this shall turn out for my salvation," v. 19). A common interpretation of this statement is that Paul is certain he will be released from prison (see esp. Martin and Hwth.). No doubt the word *sōtēria* can sometimes be translated "deliverance," as *NIV* and *NASB* do here; and it is certainly plausible to see in this verse a reference to what Paul describes clearly and explicitly in vv. 25–26, his expected release from prison and subsequent visit to Philippi.

This plausibility, however, is only superficial, for the interpretation runs against insurmountable difficulties. In the first place, Paul specifically ties in his adversity with his deliverance. It is not merely that he will be delivered, but that his adversity *will result* in his deliverance. It makes little sense to say that what Paul has suffered (whether the imprisonment itself or the work of his opponents) will lead to his release. One must note the conceptual parallelism between this statement and the basic thesis of v. 12:

v. 12	v. 19
ta kat' eme	*touto* [see Vincent]
eis prokopēn tou euangeliou	*eis sōtērian*
elēlythen	*apobēsetai*

The basis for Paul's encouragement is not merely that things will turn out all right in spite of the problems, but that the problems themselves assist us in our Christian experience. For greater detail on Paul's conception, compare Rom. 5:3–5; in that passage, which provides an interesting parallel, the apostle describes the process that leads from tribulation (*thlipsis*) to a hope that does not make us ashamed.

Second, the deliverance that Paul speaks about is one that he will experience *irrespective* of what happens to him in prison: εἴτε διὰ ζωῆς εἴτε διὰ θανάτου (*eite dia zōēs eite dia thanatou,* "whether through life or through death," v. 20). Hwth.'s minimizing of this phrase—by calling it a stock expression that means "totally"—has the ring of special pleading, particularly in view of the significance that the death/life antithesis takes on in the subsequent verses. As Calvin comments: "For it is evident from what follows, that he is not speaking of the safety of the body" (cf. also Greijdanus).

Third, most commentators recognize that Paul is here alluding to Job 13:13–18 in the LXX, but they rarely point out that this passage clearly deals with matters affecting Job's eternal destiny: "Be silent so that I may speak and relieve my anger.... Though the Mighty One should lay hand on me,...I will speak, and plead before him. And this will turn out for my salvation [*touto moi apobēsetai eis sōtērian*], since deceit will not come before him.... Behold I am near judgment: I know that I will appear just." It is Job's own standing *before God* that is at issue here. The soteriological import is moreover present in the other occurrences of *sōtēria* in Philippians (see comments on 1:28 and 2:12).

Fourth, we cannot minimize the pathos in Paul's striking comment, κατὰ τὴν ἀποκαραδοκίαν καὶ ἐλπίδα μου (*kata tēn apokaradokian kai elpida mou*, "according to my eager expectation and hope"); such language ill suits a mere reference to his desire for physical freedom. The word *apokaradokia* is particularly emphatic; its only other occurrence is in reference to the eager desire of creation for the final redemption, a desire also described as a groaning (Rom. 8:19, 22). With regard to *elpis*, this is Paul's standard term for the distinctive and certain hope of the believer (also in the Romans passage, 8:24–25), a hope that will not make us ashamed (Rom. 5:4 and see below). Why Paul would use such (soteriologically) charged terms in describing his desire to be released from prison defies explanation.[7]

Fifth, Paul expresses his hope (or goal or motivation) in terms that turn our attention to matters of eternal import: "I will have nothing to be ashamed of [αἰσχυνθήσομαι, *aischynthēsomai*], but with all boldness [παρρησία, *parrēsia*]...Christ will be glorified [μεγαλυνθήσεται, *megalynthēsetai*] in my body" (v. 20).[8] The association of *aischynomai* with *elpis* in this verse reminds us of Rom. 5:4, where the compound *kataischynomai* is used in the context of Christian faith and perseverance. Of course, this idea derives from such key passages as Isa. 28:16, quoted in Rom. 9:33 and 10:11, "He who believes in Him will not be ashamed [LXX, *ou kataischynthēsetai*]." The shame of which this verse and many other OT parallels speak is less a subjective feeling of guilt (such as we seem to have in Rom. 1:16) than the

---

7. Hwth. attempts an explanation (p. 41), but I do not find it persuasive.
8. Hwth. points to Rom. 1:16 and 2 Cor. 3:12 and argues that here in Philippians Paul was expressing his commitment not to be ashamed of the gospel; even a Roman tribunal would not embarrass him but rather provide a platform for bold testimony. This is Hwth.'s strongest argument for his reading of vv. 18–20, but the alternate interpretation offered here is both possible and attractive.

objective disgrace experienced by those on whom the judgment of God falls. Schenk properly calls attention to the contextual synonymy between *kataischynō* and *katargeō* ("to nullify") in 1 Cor. 1:27–28. Within the context of the believing community, "being put to shame" is in effect the fate of the apostate, a conception reflected in 1 John 2:28: "And now, little children, abide in Him so that when He appears we may have boldness [*parrēsian*] and not be ashamed to face Him [*kai mē aischynthōmen ap' autou*] at His coming."

The main difficulty with this understanding of v. 20 is that *parrēsia* is characteristically used by Paul with reference to the bold proclamation of the gospel (see esp. 2 Cor. 3:12; Eph. 6:19). In response, we should note that a less specific use of the term is clearly attested in Paul (2 Cor. 7:4, "we have confidence in you"). What is more, we need to avoid a false dichotomy between (1) our confidence in God's salvation and (2) the boldness for witness that flows from that confidence. In other words, my emphasis on a soteriological interpretation of Phil. 1:19–20 does not necessarily exclude some of the concerns expressed by the view that Paul desired and expected to be released from prison to continue the work of evangelization.[9]

All of those considerations point unmistakably to the position that, even if *sōtēria* in v. 19 alludes in some way to deliverance from prison (could we have a deliberate ambiguity in Paul's use of this term?), the primary reference is to Paul's perseverance in faith: the magnification of Christ—not his own freedom or even his life—is Paul's salvation. The great significance of this point is brought out dramatically by Paul's forms of expression in his last epistle. In 2 Timothy 4, where Paul shows no expectation of physical deliverance (4:6), he utters a cry for salvation: "The Lord will rescue [*rhysetai*] me from every evil work and will bring me safely [*sōsei*] to His heavenly kingdom" (4:18). Or to phrase it in terms of his perseverance: "I have kept the faith" (4:7).

An additional and remarkable point is Paul's recognition, in v. 19, that his perseverance does not take place automatically but rather through (1) the prayers of the Philippians and (2) the support provided by Jesus' Spirit. Commentators have debated a few points of syntax in this verse (for which see Additional Notes). The point to note here, however, is that even Paul's *personal* growth—his sanctification—does not take place *in isolation* from the support of the

---

9. Cf. Funk, "The Apostolic *Parousia*," p. 262 n. 1. Schenk, who suggests that Rom. 8:35–38 provides a close parallel to Phil. 1:19, argues against a false dichotomy between present acquittal and eschatological fulfillment.

church. It is indeed a sobering thought that our spiritual relationship with God is not a purely individualistic concern; we are dependent on the Spirit's power in answer to the intercessory prayers of God's people. And we may add that the Spirit's help itself is normally manifested through the *koinōnia* of fellow-believers. The godly Ignatius, early bishop of Antioch, learned this lesson well, as we can tell from his comment to the church in Philadelphia as he was on his way to martyrdom: "your prayer will perfect me."[10]

Additional Notes

1:19 διὰ τῆς ὑμῶν δεήσεως καὶ ἐπιχορηγίας τοῦ πνεύματος (lit. "through your prayers and the provision of the Spirit"): The fact that Paul does not repeat the article (τῆς) before the second clause has led some commentators to relate the two clauses very closely, even to the point of making ὑμῶν qualify both δεήσεως and ἐπιχορηγίας. But pressing the syntactical principle[11] yields an awkward sense here: "the prayer and Spirit's help that you supply." Vincent argues persuasively against this construction, but not so as to exclude the idea that the Spirit's help comes in answer to prayer.

On the force of the genitives in these clauses see especially Vincent and Hwth. The most important one is ἐπιχορηγίας τοῦ πνεύματος, interpreted by most commentators as a subjective genitive, "the help given by the Spirit" (so *NIV;* Schenk sees here a chiasm that rules out an objective genitive). On the other hand, Gal. 3:5 (ὁ ἐπιχορηγῶν ὑμῖν τὸ πνεῦμα) offers striking support for the view that the Spirit Himself is here regarded as the divine provision. Either an objective or (with Chrysostom) an appositional genitive yields this meaning.

1:20 κατὰ τὴν ἀποκαραδοκίαν καὶ ἐλπίδα μου (lit. "according to my expectation and hope"): This combination should probably be regarded as an instance of hendiadys, as my translation above suggests. Schenk agrees, though he goes too far in saying that the use of a single article precludes a semantic differentiation between the two nouns.

ὅτι ἐν οὐδένι αἰσχυνθήσομαι (lit. "that in nothing shall I be put to shame"): In support of his general interpretation of this passage, Hwth. argues that ὅτι here is ruled by οἶδα (v. 19; Schenk agrees, though with very different conclusions) and thus introduces a second and distinct reason for Paul's assurance. The only substantive argu-

10. *Phld.* 5:1, ἡ προσευχὴ ὑμῶν με ἀπαρτίσει.
11. Cf. BDF § 276; Rob., pp. 785–89.

ment he offers (p. 42) is that the object of ἐλπίς is normally expressed, not by a clause introduced with ὅτι, but by a genitive. Such a genitival construction, however, is only possible when that object consists of one or two words. Surely, if Paul needed a sentence to describe the object of his hope, a genitive would not do. (Besides, it is possible that the ὅτι here is a causal conjunction.)

ἐν τῷ σώματί μου: Hwth. translates "because of me," following the interpretation of σῶμα as "person" rather than "body," but R. H. Gundry argues persuasively, on the basis of the whole context, that the presence of which Paul speaks "is specifically physical."[12]

2. DEATH NO THREAT (1:21–24)

Translation

[I speak with such boldness] because my life is wholly devoted to Christ and so death would result to my advantage. If nevertheless living in the flesh means fruitful labor, then I cannot decide what to do. You see, I am in straits between the two choices, because on the one hand I do wish to depart so I can be with Christ, since this is much better. On the other hand, remaining *in the flesh is necessary because of you.

Exegesis and Exposition

The very last phrase of v. 20 alerts us to the startling thought, now to be developed, that Paul's deliverance does not depend on whether he lives or dies. As we noted in the previous section, Paul can speak of his being delivered from all evil even when he expects to lose his life (2 Tim. 4:18). Such a perspective is jarring not merely to someone unacquainted with the Scriptures but even to a believer who may have noticed the repeated OT references depicting divine blessing in terms of physical safety from enemies and deliverance from death. Indeed, one can argue that the OT phrase "being put to shame" is often equivalent to "dying."[13] Therefore, for Paul to say that even through death he will be ashamed in nothing demands an explanation. Even more surprisingly, Paul's explanation does not express hope *in spite* of death but focuses on death as the more advantageous alternative.

---

12. R. H. Gundry, *Sōma in Biblical Theology: With Emphasis on Pauline Anthropology* (SNTSMS 29; Cambridge: Cambridge U., 1976), p. 37.
13. In Ps. 22:5, for example, the phrase "they were not ashamed (or disappointed)" becomes equivalent to "they were saved"; in Ps. 31:17 "being put to shame" is equated with "lying silent in the grave."

Before considering the substance of Paul's teaching here it is necessary to discuss a difficult syntactical question, the ambiguity of v. 22: εἰ δὲ τὸ ζῆν ἐν σαρκί τοῦτό μοι καρπὸς ἔργου καὶ τί αἱρήσομαι οὐ γνωρίζω (*ei de to zēn en sarki touto moi karpos ergou kai ti airēsomai ou gnōrizō*). The traditional understanding of this statement is to mark the main pause after *karpos ergou* (lit. "fruit of work"), so that the protasis (or "if" clause) extends from *ei* ("if") to *ergou* and the last five words constitute the apodosis (or "then" clause). The resulting translation is: "But if living in the flesh means fruitful work for me, then I do not know what I would choose." This interpretation makes good sense and fits nicely in the context, but other possibilities must be kept in mind (see Additional Notes).

As it turns out, all of the syntactical possibilities yield basically the same sense. Yet it is useful to appreciate the nature of the ambiguities in this verse because the style tells us something of exegetical value regarding the emotional context of Paul's words. The spontaneity of Paul's writing (that bubbling forth out of the heart that Wilamowitz spoke of[14]) sometimes finds expression in anacoloutha and disjointed clauses. The point is that the apostle here is not making an objective, detached theological statement, nor does he treat us to a sustained contrast between life and death for its mere stylistic impact.

Rather, Paul is laying bare his soul and frankly admitting to having some "embarrassing" feelings; he acknowledges a tension—a trying, and perhaps almost unbearable, tension—between personal desire (τὴν ἐπιθυμίαν ἔχων, *tēn epithymian echōn*, v. 23) and Christian duty (ἀναγκαιότερον, *anankaioteron*, v. 24). "I am in straits [συνέχομαι, *synechomai*]," says Paul (v. 23). The verb *synechomai*, when used of personal feelings, indicates at the very least the idea of constraint (cf. 2 Cor. 5:14), and at worst that of torment: in Luke 4:38 of suffering from a fever; in Luke 8:37 of being overcome by fear or terror; in Luke 12:50 of Jesus' distress as He anticipates His baptism of suffering. Although we cannot simply import the meaning of these references into Philippians, we surely miss the real import of this passage if we fail to see in it an echo of Paul's psychological ordeal.

The nature of Paul's tension is described most briefly and powerfully in v. 21, words that have rung from the lips of the faithful during all the Christian centuries: "For to me, to live is Christ, and to die is

14. Ulrich von Wilamowitz-Moellendorf in *Die griechische und lateinische Literatur und Sprache*, 2d ed. (Die Kultur der Gegenwart 1.8; Berlin: Teubner, 1907), p. 159.

gain." Formally, there is a certain logical imbalance in the statement: surely, not only in life but also in death Paul is bound with
Christ. Accordingly, Calvin interprets the force of these words as follows: "to me Christ is gain in life and in death." But this move is
quite unnecessary and dilutes the apostle's emphasis on the advantageous character of death for him (v. 23). The lack of symmetry in v.
21 is itself what lends special force to the statement; precisely because his life finds its total meaning in Christ, his dying—which
entails being with Christ (v. 24)—must be viewed as an advantage.
Those commentators are surely correct who see a genuine correspondence between "to live is Christ" here and "Christ lives in me" = "I
live by faith in the Son of God" in Gal. 2:20 (cf. Schenk).

One further matter requires consideration, namely, the bearing
of this passage on the debate regarding soul-sleep.[15] Verse 23 has
traditionally been used as a proof-text for the doctrine that, upon
death, the believer finds himself immediately in the presence of
Christ, even prior to the resurrection. Proponents of soul-sleep argue
that death in fact does away with time as far as the consciousness of
the believer is concerned; when he awakens at the resurrection, no
time has passed for him, and so Paul's words are consonant with the
doctrine of soul-sleep.

Others simply refuse to use this verse to settle a question that
most likely was not in the apostle's mind at all. Indeed, it would be
unwise to build a whole locus of theology on the basis of this one
statement. Nevertheless, the debate on the doctrine of soul-sleep has
a clear and direct relevance to our exegesis of this passage. For truly,
if Paul had any notion at all that death meant a prolonged sleep for
him, then the tension that is so prominent in the passage would be
dissolved immediately. It is hardly credible that Paul would have
viewed the choice as difficult as he describes it if leaving the work of
the gospel did not in fact entail his being in the presence of Christ.
Surely in the consciousness of those for whom it is necessary that
Paul remain, time is not done away with.

Additional Notes

1:21 τὸ ἀποθανεῖν κέρδος: The aorist ἀποθανεῖν has inexplicably
led commentators astray. Hwth. says it "accentuates the act of

---

15. We are not concerned here with the controversy about whether or not this
passage contradicts, or marks theological development from, Paul's
views on death as contained in 1 Corinthians 15. To my mind, the supposed discrepancy is a pseudo-difficulty that deserves little attention (cf.
Vincent).

dying" (the aorist tense accentuates nothing).[16] Martin takes things to quite an extreme by suggesting that this aorist infinitive has the fate of martyrdom in view. Even Ltf. shows confusion: "The tense denotes not the act of dying but the consequence of dying, the state after death." This information comes from v. 23, not from the tense. Most surprising of all is Schenk's emphasis on the specificity of the aorist ("Momentanbegriff"; his reference to the Kühner-Gerth grammar does not really support the claim). There is probably no semantic significance in the tense (ζῆν is a present tense because the aorist ζῆσαι is normally used of "to come to life"); the most one can say is that the aorist is the natural tense to use when referring to an event that in the very nature of the case is neither progressive nor repetitive.

1:22 εἰ δὲ τὸ ζῆν ἐν σαρκί, τοῦτό μοι καρπὸς ἔργου, καὶ τί αἱρήσομαι οὐ γνωρίζω: Several translations are possible. The *NASB* rendering, "But if I am to live on in the flesh, this will mean fruitful labor for me; and I do not know which to choose," is perhaps the least likely, for it assumes an ellipsis (which Vincent regards as "inadmissible") of the predicate in the protasis. The view that limits the apodosis to three words (καὶ τί αἱρήσομαι, "...then what shall I choose? I cannot tell") finds support in 2 Cor. 2:2, where καί also introduces the apodosis as a direct question.[17]

Still another interpretation is that of Ltf., who thinks that the true apodosis ("what then?") is not at all expressed, in which case εἰ introduces a question: "But what if living in the flesh means fruitful work for me? In that case [καί = "in fact, surely"] I cannot tell what I would choose." This is a harsh construction and few have followed Ltf. (see esp. Vincent's objections). The traditional understanding (adopted in the exposition above) takes the second half of the verse as the apodosis and presents two minor problems: one is the superfluous τοῦτο, but such an emphatic restatement of the subject is quite possible and even elegant; the other difficulty is taking καί as introducing the apodosis (some other conjunction, e.g., τότε, or no conjunction at all is more common), but this use is attested elsewhere (cf. Vincent).

γνωρίζω: The meaning found in all other occurrences, "to make known," is inappropriate here, for the resulting translation, "I do not

---

16. Cf. D. A. Carson, *Exegetical Fallacies* (Grand Rapids: Baker, 1984), pp. 69–75.

17. See BDF § 442.7–8. Schenk stresses the possible Semitic background of this syntax and proceeds, with no substantive grounds, to explain subsequent instances of καί in this passage in the same way.

reveal," implies that Paul does know but refuses to let the Philippians in on the secret (Hwth. defends this rendering). BAGD, sensing this difficulty, give "to know" as the meaning for both this passage and *Diogn*. 8.5. It should be pointed out, however, that the references given in support of it have an incipient force, "to obtain knowledge of, discover, recognize, become acquainted with."[18] Ltf.'s "I do not perceive" is a good attempt, but in fact none of the usual English equivalents for γνωρίζω seems appropriate here, and so the rendering "I do not know" (*NASB, NIV*, etc.) wins by default. The paraphrase "I cannot tell" is satisfactory, but only so long as it is taken in the colloquial sense of "I do not know" (that is, this rendering should not be chosen on the grounds that it preserves the Greek nuance of "to make known").

1:24 [ἐν] τῇ σαρκί: Though the term "flesh" does not have its strongly pejorative sense here, Calvin is probably right when he says that it reflects contempt "from comparing it to a better life."

The preposition ἐν is omitted by Sinaiticus and Alexandrinus, a few other uncials, and some important minuscules (e.g., 33, 1739). It could have been omitted accidentally; it could also have been a deliberate change if the scribe felt an incongruity with ἐπί (in ἐπιμένειν). On the other hand, it might have been added on the basis of v. 22, τὸ ζῆν ἐν σαρκί. Since Vaticanus in Paul is suspect when accompanied by "Western" witnesses (D F G), one could argue that the omission has greater external support (in spite of P[46]). The decision is very difficult, however, and it would be a mistake to attribute the difference to semantic reasons. Pauline usage of ἐπιμένω (Rom. 6:1; 11:22, 23; Col. 1:23) supports omission of ἐν; however, 1 Cor. 16:8 is a close parallel (note the local use of the preposition).

ἀναγκαιότερον ("more necessary"): This word is a comparative adjective that Vincent regards as "slightly illogical," presumably because nothing in the preceding context has been described as necessary. Following Ltf., he thinks the form may have been used on the analogy of κρεῖσσον ("better," v. 23), but could we not see it as an emphatic word reflecting Paul's desire to reassure the Philippians?

3. A WORD OF REASSURANCE (1:25–26)

Translation

So [being well aware of this need] I am confident that I will stay and remain with all of you so that you may make progress and re-

---

18. Even for *Diogn*. 8.5 cf. Edgar J. Goodspeed, *The Apostolic Fathers: An American Translation* (New York: Harper & Brothers, 1950), p. 280: "No

joice in the faith. In this way your glorying in Christ will abound through my ministry when I come back to you.

Exegesis and Exposition

Paul's positive remarks about departing to be with Christ might carry with them the suggestion that he expects death to be imminent. Possibly to forestall such a conclusion, he had already in v. 24 spoken of remaining alive as "more necessary" (see Additional Note on that verse). At any rate, vv. 25–26 most certainly expand on this concern. Paul emphatically assures the Philippians that he will be released and resume his ministry among them.

The emphasis is achieved, first, by the construction τοῦτο πεποιθ- ὼς οἶδα (*touto pepoithōs oida*, "being convinced of this [i.e., of the necessity that he remain for the Philippians' sake], I know"). The verb *oida* does not stress certainty in contrast to *ginōskō*,[19] but either verb (in opposition, for example, to *oiomai*, cf. v. 17) would indicate Paul's strong conviction on this matter. Second, note the combination μενῶ καὶ παραμενῶ (*menō kai paramenō*, "I will stay and remain"). Attempts have been made to distinguish between the two verbs by attributing a distinctive semantic component to *paramenō*. Some appeal to the verb's etymology and stress the force of the preposition (with the resulting meaning "stand fast alongside"); others say it means "to continue for a long time" (so Calvin, for whom *menō* = "stay a little while"); still others suspect a reference to Christ's coming. The evidence for those distinctions is not forthcoming, however. Besides, such an approach misses the significance of stylistic reinforcement (see Introduction: Language and Style): Paul may at times add a word not to introduce a new meaning but to make a greater impact on his readers.

Apart from questions of style, the apostle comforts the Philippians by a moving description of the purpose that will be served by his release: (1) their progress in the faith, (2) their joy in that faith, (3) their abounding glory in Christ through Paul. Paul had already spoken about the progress of the gospel in v. 12; now he focuses on the

---

man has ever seen him or *discovered* him, but he has revealed himself" (italics added).

19. I have argued this point in my article, "The Pauline Style as Lexical Choice: γινώσκειν and Related Verbs," *Pauline Studies: Essays Presented to F. F. Bruce*, ed. D. A. Hagner and M. J. Harris (Grand Rapids: Eerdmans, 1980), pp. 184–207. If, with Ltf., we construe τοῦτο with οἶδα, then the construction becomes even more emphatic, for πεποιθώς would have to be understood adverbially ("I know with confidence") and as referring to the content of v. 25 rather than v. 24.

Philippians' participation in that progress. Just as in prison he had become an instrument for the advance of God's Word, so upon his release he will be used to bring greater spiritual health to the believers in Philippi. The effect of his future ministry among the Philippians will be a confirmation that it was indeed necessary for Paul to be released.

One cannot avoid detecting an allusion to the serious difficulties that were manifesting themselves among the Philippian believers. Yet Paul's ministry of spiritual correction was intended to bring, not fear and sorrow, but joy. In different circumstances the news of the apostle's παρουσία (*parousia*, "coming, presence") could raise expectations of judgment (cf. 2 Cor. 13:1–3, 10), so Paul uses this opportunity once again to underscore the joy of Christian experience, one of the great themes of Philippians. In v. 25 we find the common term for joy, χαρά (*chara*), but in the next verse he shifts to the stronger word καύχημα (*kauchēma*, "pride, grounds for glorying") and assures them that their confident joy can only increase.

An important problem arises in v. 26. The phrase ἐν ἐμοί (*en emoi*, "in me") could be construed directly with *kauchēma*, yielding such a translation as that of the *NASB*, "so that your proud confidence in me may abound in Christ Jesus." One need not object to this rendering on theological grounds, because it expresses an unquestionably Pauline concept, as we can gather from 2 Cor. 1:14, "we are your grounds for boasting [*kauchēma hymōn esmen*], as you also are ours, in the day of our Lord Jesus." If this interpretation of v. 26 is correct—it is supported by Ltf., Vincent, and others—we may relate the thought to that in Phil. 2:16, where Paul counts the Philippians' sanctification as his reason for confidence (see also the additional note on 1:11).

On the other hand, it must be pointed out that when Paul uses the verb καυχάομαι (*kauchaomai*, "boast") with the preposition *en*, he consistently admonishes believers to boast in God, not man, as in 1 Cor. 1:31 and 2 Cor. 10:17, "Let him who boasts boast in the Lord" (a reference to Jer. 9:23–24). In 1 Cor. 3:21 Paul writes, "Let no one boast in men," and in Philippians itself he characterizes believers as those who "glory in Christ Jesus" (3:3). The cognate noun *kauchēsis* too is used with *en* in reference to Christ (Rom. 15:17; 1 Cor. 15:31). When the ground of boasting is properly a human being, Paul seems to prefer the preposition *hyper*, as in 2 Cor. 5:12; 7:4; 8:24; 9:3. We have good reason then to take the *en emoi* of Phil. 1:26 as instrumental: "so that your boasting may abound in Christ Jesus *through my ministry* when I return to you."

Additional Notes

1:25 οἶδα ὅτι μενῶ: Toward the end of his third missionary journey, Paul told the Ephesian elders, "I know [οἶδα] that you all will no longer see my face" (Acts 20:25). On the basis of this verse J. van Bruggen[20] has argued that Paul indeed never returned to Asia Minor and that the traditional chronology must be wrong. The apparent discrepancy between these two verses is satisfactorily dealt with by Ltf., who points out that we do not have here "a prophetic inspiration, but a personal conviction" (cf. also Calvin).

1:26 τῆς ἐμῆς παρουσίας: Beare's inference that Paul may expect a "king's welcome" puts too much weight on the associations of the word παρουσία. There is certainly no thought of pageantry in other comparable uses of the term (1 Cor. 16:17; 2 Cor. 7:6–7; 10:10; Phil. 2:12).

---

20. *Die geschichtliche Einordnung der Pastoralbriefe* (Wuppertal: R. Brockhaus, 1981), pp. 29–30.

3
A Call to Sanctification (1:27–2:30)

The relationship between 1:12–26 and this new section of the epistle is marked by the transitional word μόνον (*monon,* "only"). Though Schenk, following Gnilka, views the word not as restrictive but as emphatic ("above all"), the exceptive or adversative nuance should not be ignored. This use of *monon* is found most clearly in Gal. 2:10 and 5:13 (cf. also 2 Thess. 2:7). The first of these passages is particularly instructive. According to Gal. 2:7–9, the Jerusalem leaders assured Paul that everything was in order. There was *only* one thing, however, that they must ask of him, and that was to remember the poor in Jerusalem.

Similarly, here in Philippians Paul had given his readers a word of assurance: everything will work out well (vv. 24–26). *Nevertheless,* there was one matter that concerned him (Barth sees here "a warning finger"). The Philippians were in danger of overlooking their Christian duty to maintain spiritual unity; intimidated by their opponents, they may slacken their zeal in conflict. The apostle's injunction must therefore be taken as a serious and fundamental concern in the letter.

Indeed, with 1:27 we reach what must be considered the central section of Philippians (see Introduction: Literary Structure). In spite of the disproportionate and isolated attention that scholars have paid to 2:5–11, one must insist on the coherence of 1:27–2:18 as an injunction to holy conduct—an element reflected in the outlines of Lohmeyer, Schenk, and others. The conduct in view is set against the background of the Philippians' own opponents (1:28), a subject that Paul will return to in chapter 3. But the primary focus is that of the united front that Christian humility creates. We may divide this passage into three subsections: (1) the duties of Christian citizenship (1:27–2:4); (2) a description of Christ's conduct as the model of Christian humility (2:5–11); and (3) a more general, concluding exhortation to Christian obedience (2:12–18).

A. CHRISTIAN CITIZENSHIP (1:27–2:4)

The heading I have chosen for this passage arises from the view that the main verb in 1:27, πολιτεύεσθε (*politeuesthe*), probably preserves its semantic overtones of the conduct expected of citizens in a state (*polis*). The early meaning "to be (live as) a (free) citizen" is widely attested (see Additional Notes). The term could often be used also in the general sense of "to deal with, conduct oneself, live," and this is certainly the verb's meaning in its only other occurrence in the NT, Acts 23:1 (but see Ltf.). However, Paul's use of the term πολίτευμα (*politeuma*, "citizenship") in Phil. 3:20 suggests that already here in 1:27 he may be appealing to the Philippians' sense of civic duty: "You know the pride and responsibility attached to living in a Roman colony: remember that you have a higher allegiance calling you to faithful conduct."[1] This citizenship requires a tenacious spirit (1:27–28) in the face of suffering (1:29–30), something possible only through the strength of Christian unity (2:1–4).

---

1. Similarly, Hendriksen argues against the extreme alternatives of Raymond R. Brewer, who sees here a command to discharge civic obligations ("The Meaning of *Politeuesthe* in Phil. 1:27," *JBL* 73 [1954]: 76–83), and of Lenski, who sees no reference to citizenship at all. Schenk believes that the use of this verb, as opposed to περιπατέω, is motivated by Paul's concern with the social aspect of the conduct he enjoins here. Ernest C. Miller, Jr., "Πολιτεύεσθε in Philippians 1.27: Some Philological and Thematic Observations," *JSNT* 15 (1982): 86–96, claims that the verb had a special nuance in Judaism (to live according to the Torah), that Paul uses it here as part of his ecclesiology (the church as the true Israel), and that this use supports the integrity of the letter (1:27 anticipates chap. 3). While some of Miller's references are suggestive, he assumes that the verb must take on the sense conveyed by its modifiers. At any rate, his thesis greatly overloads the verb.

1. TENACITY (1:27–28)

Translation

[Regardless of my circumstances,] what really matters is that you behave as citizens of heaven, in a manner worthy of the gospel of Christ, so that whether I am able to come and actually see you or remain absent *the news about you will be the same; namely, that you are standing steadfast in unanimity of spirit by struggling jointly with unanimity of soul for the faith proclaimed in the gospel. Moreover, do not be intimidated by your opponents; your behavior will be a sign to them that they will be destroyed but that you will receive salvation—and a salvation that comes from God.

Exegesis and Exposition

The term *politeuesthe* itself reminds us that Christian responsibility is not a transient affair but a permanent obligation that requires the fundamental virtue of perseverance. "Nothing is so incongruous in a Christian, and foreign to his character, as to seek ease and rest" (Chrysostom on 3:18). Hendriksen chooses the apt term *tenacity* to describe this virtue, and the importance that it has for Paul may be gathered by the force of his expressions.

First, the apostle tells the believers in Philippi that their proper Christian behavior must continue "whether I come and see you or remain absent." There is no respite from Christian obligation. Just as Timothy must be ready for faithful ministry "in season and out of season" (2 Tim. 4:2), so the Philippians must maintain a consistent witness regardless of their circumstances. It is worth noting, however, that Paul focuses on his own presence/absence to underscore their need for consistency. No doubt this concern is to be explained by the immediately preceding context, where the apostle has assured the Philippians that his absence from them will not be permanent.

Still, one can only wonder why his presence/absence surfaces again in 2:12, also in a context where the readers are enjoined to lead obedient lives. Is it possible that Paul's absence had discouraged some in the Philippian community? Not even Timothy would be able to visit Philippi immediately (2:19–24), and Paul possibly feared that the troubles being experienced by the church could worsen because of his inability to deal with them in person. At any rate, Paul makes clear that his absence did not justify a relaxing of their Christian obligations. Perseverance does not admit of interruptions.

Second, Paul uses two verbs that stress the importance of spiritual tenacity: στήκετε (*stēkete*, "you are standing firm") and

91

συναθλοῦντες (*synathlountes*, "contending together"). The verb *stēkō* is used by Paul in several of his epistles;[2] it is simply a late form derived from the perfect tense of ἵστημι (*histēmi*, "to stand") and not to be sharply distinguished in meaning from it.[3] In addition to the firmness and steadfastness suggested by this verb, Christian citizenship requires conscious effort, for it consists in a struggle, as the second verb, *synathleō*, indicates. The simple form *athleō* occurs in 2 Tim. 2:5; the only other occurrence of the compound form is also in Philippians and, interestingly, in close proximity to *stēkō* (4:1, 3; see comments on these verses for the possibility of a literary *inclusio*).

Third, Paul stresses the tenacity required of Christian believers by pointing out the need for unanimity. This thought is already intimated by *synathleō* (the prefixed *syn-*, "with," speaks of a joint struggle), but we also find an express command made even more forceful by a chiastic pattern:

A	*stēkete*	you are standing firm
B	*en heni pneumati*	in one spirit
B'	*mią psychę*	[with] one soul
A'	*synathlountes*	contending together

Paul will develop this concern in 2:1–4 (see comments on that passage) and return to it several times throughout the letter. At the very outset he alerts us to the fundamental thesis that Christian sanctification cannot be reduced to an individualistic exercise. The struggles of the Christian citizen must be faced within the fellowship of the believing community.

Fourth, in v. 28 Paul makes explicit reference to spiritual opposition (already implied by the verb *synathleō*): καὶ μὴ πτυρόμενοι ἐν μηδενὶ ὑπὸ τῶν ἀντικειμένων (*kai mē ptyromenoi en mēdeni hypo tōn antikeimenōn*, lit. "and not being frightened in any way by the opponents"). Whether the Philippian church was experiencing opposition from the pagan environment (so Martin; cf. Acts 16:19–24) is difficult to prove. Because Paul appears to be greatly concerned about Judaizers (see comments on 3:2), it is reasonable to assume that the same group is primarily in view here as well. In any case, the struggle is real and likely to intimidate any believer.

---

2. Rom. 14:4; 1 Cor. 16:3; Gal. 5:1; Phil. 4:1; 1 Thess. 3:8; 2 Thess. 2:15; elsewhere in Mark 3:31; 11:25; John 8:44 (v.1); Rev. 12:4. See Grundmann's useful summary in *TDNT* 7:636–38.
3. See esp. Rom. 5:2; 11:20; 14:4 (both forms); 1 Cor. 10:12; 15:1; 2 Cor. 1:24; Eph. 6:11, 13, 14; Col. 4:12. For the possible metaphor of soldiers who persist in guarding their posts, cf. Lohmeyer.

But the Philippians must not be intimidated so as to give up their struggle. Indeed, the very struggle they were experiencing was "a sign to them of [their] destruction but of your salvation." The grammar of v. 28 is difficult (see Additional Notes), but Paul seems to be saying that the conflict of the Philippians should be understood as a reminder that they were but a part in the greater conflict between God and the prince of darkness—if God was with them, who could be against them (Rom. 8:31)? The last clause, "and this from God," probably does not refer exclusively to the word σωτηρία (sōtēria, "salvation," a feminine noun, is not the grammatical antecedent of the neuter pronoun τοῦτο, touto, "this") but rather to the whole complex of ideas: conflict, destruction, perseverance, and salvation. The true grounds for the Philippians' encouragement was the profound conviction that nothing in their experience took place outside God's superintendence.

Additional Notes

1:27 πολιτεύεσθε: In support of the view that the verb preserves the nuance of citizenship, cf. Philo, De confusione linguarum 77–78: "all whom Moses calls wise are represented as sojourners.... To them the heavenly region, where their citizenship lies [ἐν ᾧ πολιτεύονται], is their native land; the earthly region in which they became sojourners is a foreign country." The Epistle to Diognetus 5.9 (a Christian writing of the second or third century) describes Christians as those who "pass their time upon the earth, but...have their citizenship in heaven [ἐν οὐρανῷ πολιτεύονται]." 1 Clement uses the verb on several occasions with the more general sense "live," but the idea of citizenship becomes explicit in 54.4, "those who live without regrets as citizens in the city of God [οἱ πολιτευόμενοι τὴν ἀμεταμέλητον πολιτείαν τοῦ θεοῦ]."[4]

ἵνα εἴτε ἐλθὼν καὶ ἰδὼν ὑμᾶς εἴτε ἀπὼν ἀκούω τὰ περὶ ὑμῶν (lit. "so that, whether coming and seeing you or being absent, I may hear about you"): As Ltf. helpfully points out, the expected syntactical symmetry is lost when Paul uses the finite verb ἀκούω instead of the participial phrase καὶ ἀκούων. He may be wrong, however, in his view that ἀκούω refers to the second clause only; Meyer argues that

---

4. Translations from LCL: Philo 4:51–53 and Apostolic Fathers 2:361; 1:101. The reference in 1 Clement is emphasized by Sigfred Pedersen, "Mit Furcht und Zittern," ST 32 (1978): 1–31, esp. p. 6. By linking that passage with chap. 51, Pedersen sees an allusion to Moses' example (cf. Deut. 9:12–14). See also, below, comments on 2:14–16.

93

Paul's construction is a valid use of zeugma. At any rate, this is a good example of Paul's relative indifference to tight grammatical constructions (Calvin: "We need not...worry over the words, when the meaning is plain"). As for the εἴτε, Meyer is probably correct that it does not cast doubt about Paul's deliverance from prison but rather assumes such a deliverance. My paraphrase ("the news about you will be the same") attempts not only to smooth the syntax but also to bring out the nuance attached to the idiomatic τὰ περὶ ὑμῶν (cf. on τὰ κατ᾽ ἐμέ, 1:12).

The present subjunctive ἀκούω is the Alexandrian reading (with additional support from D). The Majority Text gives the aorist form ἀκούσω, with some significant early support, such as the second corrector of Sinaiticus (see Introduction: Textual History). If the present is indeed original, the accompanying aorist participles may have influenced the change. No semantic distinction is likely to have affected scribal changes here.

ἐν ἑνὶ πνεύματι, μιᾷ ψυχῇ (lit. "in one spirit, [with] one soul"): The view of Martin et al. that πνεῦμα here refers to the Holy Spirit seems very unlikely in light of its parallelism with ψυχή (see esp. Hwth.). Assuming then that both terms are anthropological, the question arises whether they are to be distinguished. Calvin, for example, believes that the spirit is the faculty of the understanding, whereas the soul is that of the will; Ltf. sees here the more general distinction between spirit as the principle of the higher life and soul as the seat of the affections. In the present context, however, the rhetorical effect of using two terms appears to overrule sharp semantic distinctions (see Introduction: Language and Style). One should certainly not be misled to think that steadfastness is the particular function of the spirit while the soul specializes in struggling. In any case, the apostle here is not concerned with ontology or human psychology, but with mental harmony, singleness of purpose, harmonious attitudes.

συναθλοῦντες τῇ πίστει τοῦ εὐαγγελίου: How we render this clause depends on whether we take τῇ πίστει as a dative of advantage ("for the faith"; perhaps instrumental, as Calvin suggests) or as ruled by συν- ("with the faith"). Ltf. finds the former construction "harsh and improbable" and prefers to translate, "striving in concert with the faith"; but Paul's emphasis on the Philippians' unanimity is the simplest explanation for the preposition ("contending jointly").

A further question is whether or not πίστει should be taken in the objective sense of "message"; if so, then εὐαγγελίου is functioning as a subjective genitive (cf. Hwth.: "to preserve the faith brought about by the gospel") or as epexegetical ("the faith, namely the gospel").

Others, less convincingly, prefer to view πίστει as subjective and εὐαγγελίου as an objective genitive: "with trust in the gospel" (or, following Schenk, "for the greater reception of the gospel"). Still a third possibility is to see here the passive sense of "faithfulness" (*NBE:* "por la fidelidad a la buena noticia"), which agrees well with the emphasis of the context on steadfastness. Perhaps the best solution is Vincent's attempt to find a middle way: "the rule of life which distinctively characterises" the gospel.

1:28 ἥτις ἐστὶν αὐτοῖς ἔνδειξις ἀπωλείας, ὑμῶν δὲ σωτηρίας (lit. "which is to them a sign of destruction, but of your salvation"): The syntax of these words is difficult, partly because the grammatical antecedent of "which" (ἥτις) is ambiguous, partly because the dative pronoun αὐτοῖς leads one to expect the dative ὑμῖν (rather than the genitive ὑμῶν; indeed the Majority Text smooths the sentence in this way). Most commentators, beginning with Chrysostom, identify the antecedent of ἥτις as the immediately preceding clause, i.e., the Philippians' fearlessness in the face of opposition, though it was suggested above that the more general thought of the conflict itself is the sign of which Paul speaks (see also comments on vv. 29–30). The feminine gender of ἥτις is plausibly explained by most writers as attraction to ἔνδειξις. As for the apparent incongruity of ὑμῶν, one need look no further than v. 27 to be reminded of Paul's relative lack of concern for strict syntax. In any case, writers such as Gnilka and Schenk are correct in pointing out that Paul did not have in mind one sign for the enemies and another one for the believers; both signs were directed at the Philippians' opponents.

Hwth. probably exaggerates the problems here when he describes the clause as "extraordinarily difficult to interpret." He then proposes that ὑμῶν applies to both ἀπωλείας and σωτηρίας, with this resulting idea: "For although they see your loyalty to truth [ἥτις referring to πίστει] as inevitably leading to your persecution and death . . . you see it as leading through persecution to the salvation of your souls." The sense thus achieved is attractive but the syntax is barely defensible. Moreover, the close conceptual parallel in 2 Thess. 1:4–8 argues strongly against this new interpretation: "The fact that [the Thessalonians] are enduring persecution and affliction for Christ's sake is a sure token of God's righteous judgment, which will be vindicated in them and in their persecutors at the Advent of Christ."[5] This parallel, incidentally, makes plain that "destruction"

5. F. F. Bruce, *1 and 2 Thessalonians* (WBC 45; Waco, Tex.: Word, 1982), p. 149.

and "salvation" in Phil. 1:28 should be understood in their strongest soteriological sense.

2. SUFFERING (1:29–30)

Translation

[Indeed, you have no reason to fear,] since your suffering no less than your faith is God's gracious gift to you on behalf of Christ. Evidence of this truth is the fact that the conflict you are experiencing is the same conflict you saw me go through—and in fact you have heard *that I am still experiencing it.

Exegesis and Exposition

Verse 29 begins with the causal conjunction ὅτι (*hoti*, "for, because"), and it would be a mistake to ignore its significance. The conjunction γάρ (*gar*, "for") is used very frequently as a transitional particle and thus one cannot always assume a causal function. Paul's use of *hoti* rather than *gar* makes clear that v. 29 is intended as the reason or explanation for the surprising statement in v. 28, particularly the emphatic clause at the end, "and this from God."

The relationship between the two verses may be brought out by a paraphrase: "The conflicts that you are experiencing may appear frightening and thus threaten to discourage you, but you cannot allow that to happen. Perhaps you are tempted to interpret these conflicts as a bad omen, as though God is displeased with you and intends to destroy you. But that is exactly wrong. You must interpret what is happening as evidence of God's design to save you! Why? *Because* suffering is the way to glory, God's gift of salvation for His children."

Paul's description of suffering as a gift, ὑμῖν ἐχαρίσθη (*hymin echaristhē*, "to you it has been granted"), is lexically unique in the NT. It is also startling. Believers find it difficult enough to accept the inevitability of suffering; we feel we are making spiritual progress if we resign ourselves to the fact that grief cannot be avoided. But here the apostle challenges the Philippians' theology and asks them to understand their afflictions not merely as inevitable but as a manifestation of God's gracious dealings with them.

In fact, however, this statement is only the explicit expression of a thought that appears consistently in Scripture, particularly in the Pauline material. According to Luke, Paul told the believers in Asia Minor that tribulations are necessary (*dei*) if we would enter the kingdom of God (Acts 14:22); and this "divine necessity" of suffering would become a major theme for the Macedonian believers during Paul's second journey (*keimetha*, "we were destined," 1 Thess. 3:3–4; cf. 2:14 and 2 Thess. 1:4–7). To the Romans he presents suffering as a condition of glorification and therefore as part of that which God works out for their good (Rom. 8:17, 28–30; cf. 2 Cor. 4:10; 2 Tim. 2:12; 1 Pet. 4:13). Moreover, if our requests to God, which so often arise from our afflictions, are to be brought with thanksgiving (Phil. 4:6; cf. Eph. 5:20; Col. 3:15; 1 Thess. 5:18), then clearly the believer is being taught to view sufferings in a positive light. Therefore, when Paul in Phil. 1:29 sets up affliction as a correlative of faith—a necessity and a gift[6]—he is giving vivid expression to an underlying biblical theme, a fundamental truth of Christian citizenship.

Two more factors must be noted. First, Paul qualifies the suffering of which he speaks as a suffering that takes place for the sake of Christ. Whether the words ὑπὲρ Χριστοῦ (*hyper Christou*) may be translated "in Christ's stead" (so Hwth., appealing to Col. 1:24–25) is doubtful, for the simplest and contextually most natural idea is that of suffering out of devotion for, on account of our identification with, Christ (cf. *hyper tou onomatos*, "for the name," Acts 5:41). Yet it must be acknowledged that the relationship in view is one of union with Christ, so that in this very letter Paul can speak about sharing in Christ's sufferings (3:10; see the comments there for a discussion of this difficult concept).

(Though not strictly an exegetical issue, the important question arises whether or not physical persecutions, or afflictions suffered as a *direct* result of the believer's Christian identity, are the only experiences that qualify as suffering for Christ. Neither this passage nor the NT more generally gives an explicit and unequivocal answer to the question. We may consider, however, that for the person whose life is committed in its totality to the service of Christ, every affliction and

---

6. That faith is both a necessity and a gift is suggested by the whole thrust of Eph. 2:8–9, even though πίστεως is not the grammatical antecedent of τοῦτο (cf. the discussion in Ridderbos, *Paul*, p. 234n.). Notice also the striking parallelism between the language there (καὶ τοῦτο οὐκ ἐξ ὑμῶν, θεοῦ τὸ δῶρον) and in Phil. 1:28 (καὶ τοῦτο ἀπὸ θεοῦ). One ought to be careful, incidentally, not to draw the wrong conclusions from what Paul says about suffering as a divine gift. Suffering is not in itself a good thing but an evil characteristic of this sinful world (and certainly we must not think of evil, in the sense of sin, as proceeding from God). Believers certainly are not admonished to thank God for experiencing personal tragedy. But we may, indeed we must, thank Him that he does not isolate us from evil experiences; we are to praise Him that in His wisdom He uses them to strengthen us and thus to accomplish His saving purposes in us.

every frustration becomes an obstacle to fulfilling the goal of serving Christ. It surely would be impossible to think that believers who enjoy freedom of religion and so suffer no physical persecution or religious discrimination are thereby deprived of an essential element in their sanctification.)[7]

Second, Paul reinforces these words on Christian suffering by calling attention to the correspondence between the Philippians' experience and his own conflicts (v. 30). Already in v. 7 Paul had described his readers as co-participants with him in ministry and suffering, though the reference there is primarily to their support of Paul's ministry. Here, on the other hand, he is quite explicit about what that participation entails: the disciple is no greater than his master. Just as Paul had comforted and encouraged the Thessalonians by appealing to the example of the churches in Judea and even of their Lord (1 Thess. 2:14–16), so here he reminds his readers of his own experiences, both while he was in Philippi (cf. Acts 16:19–40) and at the present time: "you are going through the same conflict I endure; you have seen it with your own eyes and now you hear that it still persists." Clearly, Paul's injunction to his churches to become imitators of him (see on 3:17) entailed a great deal more than may appear on the surface.

Additional Notes

1:29 ἐχαρίσθη: Schenk's comment that the aorist refers to the "Anfangszeit" (temporal beginning) is a surprising overloading of the tense.

ὑπὲρ Χριστοῦ: This phrase is not to be construed with what precedes, as is suggested by some English translations (e.g., *NASB*, "to you it has been granted for Christ's sake"), but rather with πάσχειν, so "to suffer for Christ's sake." As Ltf. points out, "The sentence is suspended by the insertion of the after-thought" (namely, the clause οὐ μόνον τὸ εἰς αὐτὸν πιστεύειν), then it is resumed with ἀλλὰ καί. This syntax, however, can hardly be reproduced in a translation.[8]

1:30 ἔχοντες: This participle is in the nominative case. One expects the dative ἔχουσιν in agreement with the pronoun ὑμῖν, to which the participle refers—still another example of syntactical looseness.

---

7. For a fine biblico-theological discussion, see R. B. Gaffin, Jr., "The Usefulness of the Cross," *WTJ* 41 (1978–79): 228–46, esp. pp. 235–40.
8. On the anaphoric use of the article with the infinitive see BDF § 399.

ἀγῶνα ("contest"): Paul's use of this word in Col. 2:1 and 1 Thess. 2:2 does not clearly suggest the athletic imagery, but 1 Tim. 6:12 and 2 Tim. 4:7 do so (cf. Heb. 12:1). Here in Philippians the presence of συναθλέω in 1:27 and the more explicit imagery in 2:16 and 3:13–14 justify seeing an athletic allusion in 1:30.

ἐν ἐμοί: The second occurrence of this phrase is omitted in P⁴⁶, possibly one more example of the scribe's carelessness (see Introduction: Textual History). Since the omission is supported by minuscule 81, however, a desire to avoid repetition could account for the variant.

3. UNITY (2:1–4)

Translation

Therefore, if you have experienced at all the exhortation that comes from union with Christ, the encouragement that love provides, the fellowship produced by the Spirit, and the compassion that flows from the heart, make my joy complete: adopt the same frame of mind, sharing the same love—[yes,] you must adopt the *only frame of mind [that is proper for those who are] united in their soul. *Your disposition must not be characterized by selfishness or vain conceit; you must rather in humility regard one another as more excellent than yourselves, and *each of you must look out not for your own interests [only] but also for those of others.

Exegesis and Exposition

The very close connection between this passage and the preceding verses is apparent, not only from the particle οὖν (*oun*, "therefore," 2:1—resumptive rather than causal, as Schenk points out), but more substantively from the fact that Paul had made spiritual unanimity a central concern at the very opening of the section (1:27). What had been briefly expressed there with the phrases "in one spirit, with one soul," becomes here a whole paragraph brimming with emotional force.

The structure of the paragraph may be delineated with a literal translation thus:⁹

A.   if any exhortation in Christ (1*a*)
      if any encouragement of love (1*b*)

---

9. For a very similar yet independent arrangement, see David Alan Black, "Paul and Christian Unity: A Formal Analysis of Philippians 2:1–4," *JETS* 28 (1985): 299–308.

         if any fellowship of the Spirit (1c)
         if any affection and compassion (1d)
   B.   make my joy complete (2a)
   C.   that you may think the same thing (2b)
         having the same love (2c)
         joined in soul (2d)
         thinking the one thing (2e)
   D.   nothing according to selfishness or empty conceit (3a)
         but with humility regarding one another as more
            important than yourselves (3b)
         not looking out for your own things (4a)
         but also for those of others (4b)

Without arguing for a clear poetic structure, one must recognize
the rhythmic consistency of the short clauses, the repeated parallelism, and the strophic quality of sections A, C, and D. For reasons
that will become apparent as we proceed, it will be helpful to begin
with a discussion of the second section.

Section B: The note of joy. Grammatically, vv. 1–4 constitute but
one sentence with one main clause, the imperative of v. 2a, "make my
joy complete" (πληρώσατέ μου τὴν χαράν, *plērōsate mou tēn charan*).
To be sure, the main verb of a sentence does not necessarily convey
the writer's main concern. It is plain here that the Philippians' unanimity of mind, enjoined in the *subordinate* clauses that follow, and
not Paul's yearnings for joy, is the primary thought of the whole
passage (cf. Hwth.).

Nonetheless, it would be a mistake to minimize the nature of
Paul's appeal. The Philippians' afflictions have brought discouragement to the community. Because they have lost, or at least are in
danger of losing, the fundamental Christian perspective of joy, the
apostle in this letter exhorts them repeatedly to rejoice (2:18; 3:1; 4:4;
see Introduction: Distinctive Teaching). Moreover, Paul reinforces his
exhortation by emphasizing the joy that the Philippians have
brought to him in spite of his afflictions (1:4). Perhaps Paul recognizes that the key to joy consists in shifting our attention away from
ourselves and onto the needs of others. In any case, Paul once again
addresses the issue of the Philippians' unity as the one matter that
concerns him (see above on *monon*, 1:27), as the one problem that is
preventing *him* from experiencing full joy with regard to his Philippian brethren.

Section C: Spiritual oneness. The central thought of this passage is
conveyed by the four brief clauses that constitute section C. The first
and last of these (2b, ἵνα τὸ αὐτὸ φρονῆτε, *hina to auto phronēte:* 2e, τὸ

ἕν φρονοῦντες, *to hen phronountes*) are virtually identical, though the use of *hen* perhaps makes 2e more emphatic than 2b (so Ltf.). Unity of mind is therefore Paul's pervasive concern in this exhortation (on the significance of *phroneō* see Introduction: Distinctive Teaching).

The two intervening units (2c-d, τὴν αὐτὴν ἀγάπην ἔχοντες, σύμψυ-χοι, *tēn autēn agapēn echontes, sympsychoi*) are not intended to bring up additional factors, but to reinforce that main concern. In other words, to have the same love and to be "soul-joined" are in effect explanatory of *to auto/hen phronein*. The latter expression certainly does not focus on intellectual uniformity but on a whole frame of mind that we can perhaps best describe as spiritual oneness (cf. the corresponding expression in 1 Cor. 1:10, *to auto legēte*, lit. "that you speak the same thing," explained by the following clause, "so that there may be no divisions among you"). Paul's fourfold repetition of this concern cannot be viewed as carelessness of style; rather, it is a deliberate "tautology of earnestness" (Ltf., p. 67) intended to move the hearts of his readers and awaken them to the importance of the injunction.

Section D: Humility as the key to unity. Verses 3–4, which expand the central exhortation of section C, consist of two units, each of which contains a negative clause; in turn, each of these is followed by a positive clause introduced with ἀλλά (*alla*, "but"). The overarching concern of this section is sounded out by ταπεινοφροσύνη (*tapein-ophrosynē*, "humility"), which alludes to the verb *phroneō*, as Chrysostom suggests: "This virtue is called humble-mindedness, because it is the humbling of the mind [*phronēma*]." More precisely, the term is in effect contextually defined by its opposition to such ex-pressions as "selfishness" and "looking out for oneself." The term "selfishness" (ἐριθεία, *eritheia*) must have struck a sensitive nerve among the Philippians because Paul had used it earlier to describe his opponents who preach the gospel with impure motives (1:17; note also the presence of *phthonon*, "envy," in 1:15).

The true obstacle to unity is not the presence of legitimate dif-ferences of opinion but self-centeredness. Shifting attention away from ourselves becomes the challenge: "regard one another as better than yourselves, look out for the interests of others" (the verbs *hēgeomai* and *skopeō* continue to emphasize the mental disposition; Schenk views *skopeō* as a contextual synonym for *phroneō*). Not sur-prisingly, Paul expresses similar concerns when writing to the most blatantly schismatic of his churches, Corinth. As a capstone to his discussion of Christian liberty Paul says, "Let no one seek his own good, but that of others" (1 Cor. 10:24). And the love referred to in Phil. 2:2 is described in 1 Cor. 13:5 as one that "does not seek its own."

Section A: The grounds of Paul's exhortation. The fourfold exhortation of v. 2 is grounded in the fourfold appeal of v. 1. One advantage of postponing consideration of section A until this point is that now we are in a better position to appreciate the rhetorical qualities of the passage and can therefore be less concerned about identifying in precise detail all the references in this verse. Does ἀγάπης (*agapēs*) refer to God's love, or Paul's, or the Philippians'? Are παράκλησις (*paraklēsis*) and παραμύθιον (*paramythion*) to be distinguished or not—and do they have an objective or subjective reference here? (Cf. Hwth.'s substantive treatment of these issues and see the Additional Notes.) These and other questions cannot be answered with any certainty. Nor should they. The clauses are deliberately compressed and vague, since the appeal is primarily emotional. That is, v. 1 is not intended to function as a set of four rational, theological arguments but rather as impassioned pleading.

The Greek text has no verb expressed in these four clauses, and the *NASB* supplies "there is." This translation is of course grammatically correct but it may leave the impression that the apostle is appealing to the (general) existence of these qualities, whereas he surely has in mind the Philippians' specific experience of them (cf. *NIV*, "if you have..."). Of various attempts to clarify the force of these clauses, Ltf.'s paraphrase continues to commend itself: "If then your experiences in Christ appeal to you with any force, if love exerts any persuasive power upon you, if your fellowship in the Spirit is a living reality, if you have any affectionate yearnings of heart, any tender feelings of compassion, listen and obey." (In contrast, Chrysostom views Paul as the object of the implied verbs: "if ye wish to give me any comfort in my temptations." Cf. also Heriban, pp. 174–76, for alternate views.)

The impact of these words should make it clear that Paul's exhortation to unity arose out of very real and particular shortcomings in the Philippian community. These Christians, no doubt, constituted a healthy church, but the seeds of dissension had been sown and they were not to be allowed to sprout, lest Paul's work among them should prove to have been in vain (2:16).

Additional Notes

2:1 εἴ τις: The conjunction does not suggest doubt any more than comparable English expressions such as "if you love me" (= show

102

your love for me), but one should resist the tendency to translate with "since" (cf. Schenk), for this rendering weakens the rhetorical force of the passage. The repetition of the indefinite pronoun has led to some changes in the textual tradition. None of them is strongly attested, nor do they have an effect on the sense.

παράκλησις...παραμύθιον: After pointing out, rightly, that these two nouns "cannot be sharply distinguished," Hwth. goes on to suggest, without any clear evidence, that "the idea of 'consolation' comes to the fore in παραμύθιον" (similarly Schenk). The coupling of the cognates in 1 Thess. 2:12 and 1 Cor. 14:3, to which he refers, would seem to support contextual synonymy (cf. also 1 Thess. 5:14). Interestingly, Calvin suggests, on the basis of the context, that παράκλησις too should be rendered "consolation." My exposition above basically follows Ltf.

κοινωνία πνεύματος: On the term κοινωνία see comments on 1:5. The genitive, like ἀγάπης, is best understood in the sense, "brought about by."

σπλάγχνα καὶ οἰκτιρμοί: These two nouns are joined grammatically in Col. 3:12, σπλάγχνα οἰκτιρμοῦ ("heart of compassion" = compassionate heart or heartfelt compassion; cf. also σπλάγχνα ἐλέους, "heart of mercy," Luke 1:78). Possibly we have here a hendiadys with the same meaning. On the other hand, σπλάγχνα was used in 1:8 of the affection itself rather than of the seat of the affections (the heart), and so it would be defensible to render, "tenderness and compassion" (so *NIV*).

2:2 ἵνα τὸ αὐτὸ φρονῆτε: (lit. "so that you may think the same thing"): The ἵνα here does not indicate purpose but probably introduces the content of an implied exhortation (supply παρακαλῶ, "I beseech"). The rendering "by being like-minded" (*NASB*, similarly *NIV*) is as good a translation as one can come up with.

σύμψυχοι, τὸ ἓν φρονοῦντες (*NASB*, "united in spirit, intent on one purpose"): Meyer, followed by Alford, Vincent, et al., makes of these words one clause: "with harmony of soul cherishing the one sentiment." There is much to be said for this construction, which is perhaps reflected in the *NIV* ("being one in spirit and purpose"), but it has not been picked up by recent scholars. The change from ἕν to αὐτό in some MSS. (including the first hand of Sinaiticus), whether accidental or intentional, reflects a proper contextual identification of the two words (contrast Heriban, p. 191, who stresses the function of the article).

2:3 μηδὲ κατὰ κενοδοξίαν: A few minuscules have ἢ κατὰ, whereas others omit either the μηδέ (P⁴⁶ and an important corrector of Sinaiticus) or the κατά ("Western" witnesses followed by the Majority Text). These variations, possibly to be viewed as stylistic improvements, do not affect at all the sense of the passage.

The term κενοδοξία, which is attested as early as Polybius (in 3.8.9 with τῦφος, "delusion"), occurs nowhere else in the NT but Paul uses the cognate κενόδοξος in Gal. 5:26, where it appears to be understood as involving a spirit of envy and provocation. Perhaps that is the nuance here in Philippians. Heriban (pp. 198–200) provides a critique of various speculative interpretations of v. 3.

2:4 For the textual variations of ἕκαστος and ἕκαστοι see Ltf.'s fine discussion. My translation of this verse with the added words "not only" reflects the implications of the καί in the second part of the verse. The omission of that conjunction in "Western" witnesses is best interpreted as accidental, and so the brackets in NA are not really necessary. (It is however possible that the conjunction was added by scribes who may have thought that, without it, Paul's injunction was too strong—as though it were wrong to look out for one's own interests at all.)

B. CHRISTIAN HUMILITY (2:5–11)

The meaning of this well-known passage will only be ascertained if we can determine how the passage functions in the context of the whole letter. In what way do these verses contribute to achieving the apostle's purposes? The question is hotly debated, as the subsequent exposition will show. Yet careful attention to the earnest concerns of the previous section (1:27–2:4) suggests a simple answer.

If the opposition being experienced by the Philippians calls for steadfastness, if steadfastness is impossible without spiritual unity, and if unity can come about only from an attitude of humility, then surely Paul must reinforce the critical importance of humility in the heart of believers. And what better way to reinforce this thought than by reminding the Philippians of the attitude and conduct of Him to whom they are united in faith? When admonishing the Corinthians to contribute generously for the sake of the poor in Jerusalem, Paul sets before them the example of Christ: "though He was rich, He became poor on account of you, so that through His poverty you might become rich" (2 Cor. 8:9). Similarly here he appeals to the spirit of servanthood that brought Jesus to His death—a death which, incidentally, has overflowed in life for the Philippians.

Modern scholarship has been greatly preoccupied with the question of whether vv. 6–11 come originally from Paul or whether he has simply made use of an already existing poem that puts us in touch with the worship and doctrine of the early church. The question is of considerable importance, because the historical reconstruction of the earliest Christian period provides one of the contexts against which the NT must be interpreted. Although it would therefore be a mistake to minimize the significance of these issues as having "merely historical interest," Strimple is certainly correct in insisting that the proper exegesis of Phil. 2:5–11 must be based on its literary setting.[10] Whether or not Paul composed these words originally, he certainly used them to support the argument of vv. 1–4, and it is primarily in that light that the words must be exegeted. Much of the present exegetical confusion, in fact, may be blamed on the tendency to overemphasize the pre-Pauline setting of our passage, and thus to wrest it from the only context in which it has come down to us.

Closely related to the issue of authorship is that of structure, but this matter has greater relevance to the exegetical task. Although one can hardly prove that vv. 6–11 in whole or in part constitute a formal poem or hymn, it would be foolhardy to deny the strong poetic qualities of the passage. Even the label "elevated prose" does not do justice to the rhythm, parallelisms, lexical links, and other features that characterize these verses. Unfortunately, a baffling diversity of opinion exists regarding the proper way of arranging these lines; indeed, at least half a dozen arrangements can be easily defended.[11]

---

10. Robert B. Strimple, "Philippians 2:5–11 in Recent Studies: Some Exegetical Conclusions," *WTJ* 41 (1978–79): 247–68, esp. pp. 250–51. Caird had already made this point forcefully in his commentary: "The meaning of this passage *in Philippians* is the meaning Paul intends it to have, the meaning he has imposed on the ambiguities of its language. . . . There may be some justification for [isolating this passage from its context] when we are speculating about early Christian origins, but not when we are expounding a letter of Paul" (p. 104). It is refreshing to note the growing number of recent publications that recognize this principle. Note also the recent piece by David Alan Black, "The Authorship of Philippians 2:6–11: Some Literary-Critical Observations,: *Criswell Theological Review* 2(1988): 269–89.

11. Cf. Paul D. Feinberg, "The Kenosis and Christology: An Exegetical-Theological Analysis of Philippians 2:6–11," *TrinJ* 1 N.S. (1980): 21–46, esp. pp. 24–27. The character of this problem is most clearly reflected in Morna D. Hooker's oft-quoted remark, "I myself have produced six or seven different analyses—and found each of them convincing at the time!" See her article, "Philippians 2:6–11," in *Jesus und Paulus. Festschrift für Werner Georg Kümmel zum 70. Geburtstag*, ed. E. E. Ellis and E. Grasser (Göttingen: Vandenhoeck & Ruprecht, 1975), pp. 151–64, esp. p. 157.

This factor alone should be sufficient to shatter one's hopes of rediscovering "the original hymn," if there was such a thing.

Without claiming to be able to determine the correct (original?) structure of vv. 6–11, I nevertheless find Lohmeyer's identification of six three-line stanzas attractive in its simplicity and exegetically useful.[12] The first three stanzas speak of Jesus' humiliation, the last three of His exaltation. The accents provided on the following transliteration suggest *one* possible way of reading the lines with a fairly consistent (but certainly not perfect) rhythm. The literal translation is deliberately artificial in order to convey something of the rhythm of the original.

hos en morphḗ theoú hypárchōn	who in the form of God existing
oúch harpagmón hēgḗsato	not an advantage considered
to eínai ísa theǭ	His being equal with God
allá heautón ekénōsen	but nothing He made Himself
morphḗn doúlou labṓn	the form of a servant adopting
en homoiṓmati anthrṓpōn	in likeness of men
genómenos	becoming
kai schḗmati heuretheís hōs	and in appearance being found as
ánthrōpos	man
etapeínōsen heautón	He humbled Himself
genómenos hypḗkoos mechri	becoming obedient to death
thanátou	
—thanátou de stauroú	—and death of a cross
dio kai ho theós autón hyperýpsōsen	therefore also exalted Him God
kai echarísato autǭ to ónoma	and granted Him the name
to hypér pan ónoma	that's above ev'ry name
hína en tǭ onómati Iēsoú	so that in the name of Jesus
pan góny kámpsǭ epouraníōn	ev'ry knee may bow of those in heav'n
kai epigeíōn kai katachthoníōn	and on earth and under the earth
kai pása glṓssa exomologḗsētai	and every tongue may confess
hoti kýrios Iēsoús Christós	that Jesus Christ is Lord
eis dóxan theoú patrós	to God the Father's glory

The word *epouraníōn* (middle line of fifth stanza) may well belong in the following line, as Lohmeyer's own arrangement suggests. Indeed, most scholars see *epouraníōn kai epigeíōn kai katachthoníōn* as constituting one line. The words *thanatou de staurou* at the end of the third stanza create a problem for any attempt to bring out a strophic arrangement (see the comments on that phrase). Other difficulties with this arrangement will be considered below.

12. E. Lohmeyer, *Kyrios Jesus. Eine Untersuchung zu Phil. 2,5–11* (Heidelberg: Carl Winters, 1928), pp. 5–6.

1. PAUL'S EXHORTATION (2:5)

Translation

*Adopt *[then] this frame of mind in your community—which indeed [is proper for those who are] in Christ Jesus.

Exegesis and Exposition

The traditional rendering of v. 5 is sometimes referred to as the ethical interpretation because it understands Paul to say that Christ is our pattern of behavior: "Have this mind in you which was also in Christ Jesus" (so *KJV;* similarly *NASB* and *NIV,* both of which use the word "attitude"). This approach takes ἐν ὑμῖν (*en hymin*) in the sense of "within you" and supplies the verb ἦν (*ēn,* "was") in the second part of the verse.

Since Käsemann's 1950 contribution,[13] however, disenchantment with the ethical interpretation has led many scholars to reject this handling of the syntax and to adopt the view, lucidly defended by Deissmann,[14] that the verb to be supplied in the second part of the verse is φρονεῖτε (*phroneite,* "you think"). The resulting translation is, to be literal, "Think among you that which you also think in Christ Jesus." Various nuances are then possible, such as: "Think among yourselves as it is necessary to think in view of your corporate union with Christ."[15]

This paraphrase, which yields a very good sense, brings out clearly the main point of the debate. According to Deissmann and those who follow him, the clause "which also in Christ Jesus" is not a reference to the inner thoughts of Jesus but is rather to be taken in the usual sense of the Pauline formula ἐν Χριστῷ (*en Christō*). If, in fact, the verse appeals to the Philippians' union with Christ and not to His attitude, interpreters then feel justified in abandoning the ethical understanding of vv. 6–11. Particularly influential has been the interpretation of Käsemann, according to whom v. 5 corresponds to

---

13. Ernst Käsemann, "A Critical Analysis of Philippians 2:5–11," in *God and Christ: Existence and Province,* ed. Robert W. Funk, Journal for Theology and Church 5 (New York: Harper & Row/Tübingen: J. C. B. Mohr, 1968; German orig. 1950), pp. 45–88.
14. G. A. Deissmann, *Die neutestamentliche Formel "in Christo Jesu"* (Marburg: N. G. Elwert'sche Verlagsbuchhandlung, 1892), pp. 113–17.
15. Supplying φρονεῖν δεῖ (cf. also Gnilka, φρονεῖν τρέπει). Other possibilities are: "Let your bearing towards one another arise out of your life in Christ Jesus" (so *NEB*); "Have the same thoughts among yourselves as you have in your communion with Jesus Christ" (BAGD, following C. H. Dodd).

passages like Rom. 6:1–11, where Paul deduces "Christian conduct from the act of salvation." If so,

> Paul did not understand the hymn as though Christ were held up to the community as an ethical example. The technical formula "in Christ," whatever else might be said about it, unquestionably points to the salvation-event.... The salvation-event is indivisible and serves as the basis for the Christian's condition either altogether or not at all.[16]

Now it must be stated at the outset that the traditional understanding of the syntax, adopted by most conservative writers, is very difficult to defend. In the first place, τοῦτο φρονεῖτε ἐν ὑμῖν (*touto phroneite en hymin*) almost certainly means, "think this [have this disposition] *among* you." The idea of individuals thinking *to* or *within* themselves would normally be expressed with *heautois* rather than *hymin* (cf. *legein en heautois*, Matt. 3:9); moreover, this idea is not expressed with *phronein en* elsewhere. The translation "among" is accepted by some recent defenders of the traditional view, such as Strimple,[17] but that concession gives up one of the strongest arguments for the traditional view, namely, the insistence that the preposition *en* should have the same force in both parts of the clause.[18] If the first *en* does not express the notion of something (thought, attitude) being in or within someone, then the reader would hardly expect such a reference in the second occurrence of the preposition.

In the second place, the possibility of supplying the verb *ēn* ("was") in the second half of the verse is not likely to have occurred to a Greek speaker. If we begin with the English, "Have this mind in you," then it may seem natural to interpret the second clause as has been done traditionally, but the Greek simply says, "think." In short, there is nothing in the first clause to suggest that a verb other than *phroneō* should be supplied in the second clause. Ltf., aware of this difficulty, suggests that we supply the imperfect passive form *ephroneito* (yielding the translation, "which was also thought in

---

16. Käsemann, "Critical Analysis," p. 84.
17. Strimple, "Philippians 2:1–5," p. 253.
18. Cf. esp. Vincent. Hwth. in fact places so much weight on "the clear parallel nature of the two halves of this sentence" (p. 81) that he is led to accept the reading of the Majority Text and then to supply a passive verb in the second half: τοῦτο φρονείσθω ἐν ὑμῖν ὃ καὶ [ἐφρονεῖτο] ἐν Χριστῷ Ἰησοῦ, "let this be thought by you that was also thought by Christ Jesus." Surely this is a counsel of despair, since Hwth. himself acknowledges that the variant φρονείσθω appears to be "an effort to explain more easily" the two clauses as parallel (p. 76).

Christ Jesus") but he recognizes the irregular character of the resulting construction.[19]

A third objection to the traditional view is Deissmann's appeal to two important parallels, namely, the only other occurrences of the combination *phronein en* in the NT.[20] One of these is in this very epistle: "I urge Euodia and I urge Syntyche to think the same thing in the Lord" (*to auto phronein en kyriǭ*, 4:2). The context is the same: an appeal to unity and humility, qualities that must come to expression by virtue of our bond in Christ. The other passage, Rom. 15:5, provides an even fuller parallel: Paul prays that God will grant the Romans "to think the same thing among each other according to Christ Jesus" (*to auto phronein en allēlois kata Christon Iēsoun*). This verse throws light on both clauses of Phil. 2:5: just as *en hymin* corresponds to *en allēlois* (which can hardly mean "within yourselves"), so *en Christǭ Iēsou* corresponds to *kata Christon Iēsoun*, "according to Christ Jesus," a deliberately general expression that calls attention to our relationship with Christ (although it may well *include* a reference to Jesus' example; see below).[21]

We conclude, therefore, that *en Christǭ Iēsou* in Phil. 2:5 is a reference to the Philippians' relationship to Christ and that the verse is best understood thus: "Be so disposed toward one another as is proper for those who are united in Christ Jesus." Does this conclusion lead us to abandon the ethical interpretation of vv. 6–11? By no

---

19. If one were to follow the traditional interpretation of v. 5 it would be least objectionable to supply the verb βλέπετε, "which you also *see* in Christ Jesus," a suggestion made by Lohmeyer on the basis of Phil. 1:30; 4:9; *Test. Simeon* 4:5. Heriban (pp. 89–90) appeals to the Greek fathers in support of the individual sense of ἐν ὑμῖν, but they did not address this issue directly. The fact that they adopted the ethical interpretation does not really tell us how they understood the grammar (besides, they worked under the assumption that the text read φρονείσθω).
20. Deissmann, *Formel*, p. 116.
21. C. F. D. Moule, "Further Reflexions on Philippians 2:5–11," in *Apostolic History and the Gospel: Biblical and Historical Essays Presented to F. F. Bruce on His 60th Birthday*, eds. W. W. Gasque and R. P. Martin (Grand Rapids: Eerdmans, 1970), pp. 264–76, esp. pp. 265–66, appeals to Phil. 4:2 and Rom. 15:5 in support of the traditional translation, but the logic of his argument is not at all clear. Heriban (pp. 108–10) has a very full and instructive discussion of the parallels between Phil. 2:1–11 and Rom. 15:1–6, yet he ignores the relevance of ἐν ἀλλήλοις for our understanding of ἐν ὑμῖν. Remarkably, Martin dismisses Rom. 15:7 and 2 Cor. 8:9 because they "are short statements, not comparable with an extended passage such as verses 6–11 in our letter."

means. Much of the current discussion is plagued by false dichotomies. Strimple rightly argues against "drawing a superficial antithesis between Heilsgeschichte and ethics" and quotes some apt comments by Morna Hooker: "It is only the dogma that the Jesus of History and the Christ of faith belong in separate compartments that leads to the belief that the appeal to a Christian character appropriate to those who are in Christ is not linked to the pattern as seen in Jesus himself."[22]

We should note in this regard Paul's desire to share in the sufferings of Christ (Phil. 3:10). Even though these words clearly speak of union with Christ, they hardly preclude the idea that believers suffer as Jesus suffered (1 Thess. 2:14–15). Those who are united with Christ live as He did (cf. 1 John 2:6), and so the notion of Jesus as an ethical example is implicit in Phil. 2:5 by the very nature of the subject matter. It should be pointed out, moreover, that Rom. 15:5 (which I cited earlier against the traditional view of 2:5) is set precisely in the context of an appeal to Christ as the model of one who "did not please Himself" (Rom. 15:3).

Finally, we should consider the objection that the ethical understanding of the Christ-hymn renders vv. 9–11 irrelevant. According to Martin, "On any other interpretation than Käsemann's, verses 9–11 are left 'in the air' and must be treated as an excursus, because Christ's elevation to world rulership cannot be the theme of the Christian's imitation."[23] This is a puzzling criticism that can only be made on the assumption, already disputed, that redemptive-historical events and ethical example are antithetical ideas. Moreover, the

---

22. Strimple, "Philippians 2:5–11," p. 255; Hooker, "Philippians 2:6–11," p. 154. See also Heriban, p. 104, and L. W. Hurtado, "Jesus as Lordly Example in Philippians 2:5–11," in *From Jesus to Paul: Studies in Honour of Francis Wright Beare*, ed. Peter Richardson and John C. Hurd (Waterloo, Ont.: Wilfrid Laurier U., 1984), pp. 113–26, esp. p. 121: "However we translate the somewhat elliptical *ho kai en Christō Iēsou*, the following verses determine more fully the interpretation to be given to the passage as a whole."

23. Martin, p. 93. In *Carmen Christi: Philippians 2:5–11 in Recent Interpretation and in the Setting of Early Christian Worship*, rev. ed. (Grand Rapids: Eerdmans, 1983), p. xiii, Martin mentions that Strimple's article ("Philippians 2:5–11") does not deal in detail with vv. 9–11 and adds: "In my judgment, this is a fatal deficiency." This comment, plus his further statements on pp. xiv–xv, indicate how much weight Martin gives to this objection. Contrast Calvin's words on v. 9: "By adding consolation, he shows that abasement . . . is in the highest degree desirable. . . . Who will now refuse submission, by which he will ascend into the glory of the heavenly Kingdom?"

objection flies in the face of substantive evidence that the promise of vindication is a central biblical theme, used as the basis for encouragement to those undergoing suffering and humiliation. Without pausing to consider the numerous relevant passages in the OT prophets, we may recall such sayings of Jesus as Mark 8:34–35 and 10:28–30, and well-known paraenetic sections like Heb. 12:1–2; James 5:7–11; 1 Pet. 3:17–22; 4:12–13; and virtually the whole book of Revelation.

Paul is even more explicit in linking Jesus' humiliation/exaltation with that of believers: "...if we suffer with Him, so that we may also be glorified with Him" (Rom. 8:17; cf. 2 Tim. 2:11). More to the point, Philippians itself makes repeated references to the promise of vindication in the Last Day as a source of encouragement for proper Christian conduct (1:6, 9–11, 27–28; 2:14–16; 3:10–14, 17–21; 4:5). One is therefore baffled to read that, because the Philippians were plagued by disunity and selfishness, "the last thing Paul needed to do...was to appeal to some hedonistic ethic that promised a future glory if only the Philippians would take the road of humility."[24] No church had greater problems with disunity and selfishness than the Corinthian community, yet to them Paul says: "Do you not know that those who run in a race all run, but one receives the prize? Run in such a way that you may get it" (1 Cor. 9:24).

Additional Notes

2:5 τοῦτο φρονεῖτε (lit. "think this"): Two interesting textual variants should be noted. The Majority Text reads τοῦτο γάρ, whereas the omission of γάρ is the clear Alexandrian reading. One does not expect a causal particle introducing an exhortation. Indeed, a GRAMCORD search revealed only three instances of γάρ with an imperative: Eph. 5:5 (better understood as an indicative); James 1:7 (not a real parallel); 1 Pet. 4:15 (the role of the conjunction unclear). Metzger (supported by Heriban, p. 86 n.) therefore misleads when he comments that "no good reason can be found for its deletion." If anything, an *inferential* conjunction would be natural; not surprisingly, the improved reading οὖν, "therefore," is found in a few

---

24. Martin, *Carmen Christi*, p. xxxvii; on the next page he speculates that the sectarian teachers in Philippi had used the Christ-hymn to introduce a *theologia gloriae* that is in fact far removed from "true Christian living." Hurtado ("Jesus as Lordly Example") is one of many recent scholars critical of Käsemann's attack on the ethical interpretation; he perceptively suggests that this attack may have been an overreaction to nineteenth-century liberalism.

medieval MSS. Inasmuch as the Majority Text is characterized by grammatically smooth readings, how then does one explain this γάρ here? It must be original, because it receives support from the weighty combination of P⁴⁶ and the "Western" text. The omission can then be explained as either accidental (see Introduction: Textual History) or as an early Alexandrian attempt to improve the style.

The second variation is the third person passive imperative φρονείσθω, also found in the Majority Text. In this case, however, there is no support from the other textual traditions and the variation can be easily explained as an attempt to smooth out what was probably perceived as a syntactical irregularity (cf. Ltf.). UBSGNT does not even list this variant, which is rejected by virtually all authorities. Hwth.'s attempt to resurrect it is surprising and unsuccessful (see exposition above and n. 18).

2. CHRIST'S HUMILIATION (2:6–8)

Translation

Though He existed in the form of God, Christ took no advantage of His equality with God. Instead, He made Himself nothing by assuming the form of a servant, that is, *by becoming incarnate. And having appeared as a mere man, He further humbled Himself by becoming obedient to the point of death—and no less than the death of the cross.

Exegesis and Exposition

Perhaps the strongest argument that can be advanced against the six-strophe arrangement/structure suggested above is the striking parallelism that appears when vv. 6–8 are arranged as two stanzas of four lines each:[25]

---

25. Cf. Joachim Jeremias, "Zu Phil ii 7: ἑαυτὸν ἐκένωσεν," NovT 6 (1963): 182–88, esp. p. 186. (Cf. also Ulrich B. Müller, "Der Christushymnus Phil 2 6–11," ZNW 79[1988]: 17–44, esp. p. 19.) To make vv. 9–11 fit the pattern, Jeremias needs to get rid of the last five words in v. 10 and the last four in v. 11. If Paul was so insensitive as to disrupt the poetic structure of the hymn by adding so much material, it would seem that Jeremias's structuring tells us very little about how the apostle himself understood the poem. Comparable to Jeremias's proposal is that of Pierre Grelot, "Deux notes critiques sur Philippiens 2,6–11," Bib 54 (1973): 169–86, an article that includes a retroversion into Aramaic. For a better retroversion (which seems to support Lohmeyer's arrangement), see Joseph A. Fitzmyer, "The Aramaic Background of Philippians 2:6–11," CBQ 50(1988): 470–83.

hos en morphę theou hyparchōn *en homoiōmati anthrōpōn genomenos*
ouch harpagmon hēgēsato *kai schēmati heuretheis*
 to einai isa theǫ   *hōs anthrōpos*
alla heauton ekenōsen   *etapeinōsen heauton*
morphēn doulou labōn   *genomenos hypēkoos mechri*
           thanatou

who in the form of God existing in likeness of men becoming
not an advantage considered   and in appearance being found
 His being equal with God   as man
but nothing He made Himself He humbled Himself
the form of a servant adopting becoming obedient to death

In this arrangement, the first stanza begins and ends with the noun μορφή (*morphē*, "form"), whereas the second stanza begins and ends with the participle γενόμενος (*genomenos*, "having become"). This feature can easily be interpreted as *inclusio* (see Introduction: Literary Structure) and may suggest that indeed these lines begin and end discrete units. Moreover, each line of the first stanza finds some parallelism in the corresponding line of the second stanza. In both stanzas the first line contains a participle, and the participle rules a prepositional phrase. The contrast between God and man in that line is repeated in the second line. The third line of each stanza describes Christ's voluntary act ("He emptied/humbled Himself"). Finally, both stanzas conclude with a participial clause. Whether or not such an arrangement puts us in touch with the original structure of the hymn, it is certainly suggestive and may have a bearing on exegesis.

In any case, the apparent meaning of these striking lines is that the divine and preexistent Christ did not regard the advantage of His deity as grounds to avoid the incarnation; on the contrary, He was willing to regard Himself as nothing by taking on human form. Then He further lowered Himself in servanthood by obeying God to the point of ignominious death. A great deal of modern scholarship, to be sure, has been directed to show that this apparent meaning is not the real meaning, but the effort has been completely unsuccessful. We shall look at these verses under the following headings: the initial clause (v. 6a); Christ's voluntary act negatively stated (v. 6b-c); Christ's voluntary act positively stated (vv. 7–8).

a. *The initial statement* (v. 6a). Much of the debate centers on the first line, "although He existed in the form of God," particularly the force of the word "form" (*morphē*). If we stress the classical usage of this term, the technical sense of Aristotelian philosophy suggests itself: *morphē*, although not equivalent to *ousia* ("being, essence"), speaks of essential or characteristic attributes and thus is to be dis-

113

tinguished from *schēma* (the changeable, external "fashion"). In a valuable essay on *morphē* and *schēma*, Ltf. argued along these lines and remarked that even in popular usage these respective meanings could be ascertained.[26] The many references where *morphē* is used of physical appearance (see Additional Notes) make it difficult to maintain Ltf.'s precise distinction, though there is an important element of truth in his treatment, as we shall soon see.

Käsemann emphatically rejects the classical background on the basis of parallels in the literature of the Hellenistic religions, since "the conceptual language of the hellenistic period moves within an ideological framework quite different from that...of the classical Greek era." According to this new language, *morphē* "no longer means the individual entity as a formed whole, but a mode of being [*Daseinsweise*] in a specific direction, such as, for example, being in divine substance and power." In his discussion, Käsemann overstresses the significance of the prepositional construction.[27] Moreover, Käsemann's dependence on the gnostic "heavenly man" myth fails to take seriously the substantial differences between it and the Philippians passage.[28] Although this solution therefore cannot be regarded as acceptable, it would nevertheless be a grave mistake to ignore Käsemann's point that in the literature of the Hellenistic religions *morphē theou* and *isotheos physis* "are parallel and even become synonymous."[29]

Dissatisfaction with approaches that rely heavily on either the classical philosophical usage (Ltf.) or the usage in Hellenistic religions (Käsemann) has led many scholars to reconsider the Jewish

---

26. See Ltf., pp. 127–33, and cf. Trench, *Synonyms*, pp. 261–67.
27. "One may possess a form, type, or attitude; but one is not spatially 'in it,' as it were. [For Paul, ἐν] designates the realm in which one stands and by which one is determined, as in a field of force" (Käsemann, "Critical Analysis," p. 61; the two previous quotations are from pp. 59, 60).
28. See especially D. Georgi, "Der Christushymnus im Philipperbrief in liturgiegeschichtlicher Sicht," in *Zeit und Geschichte. Dankesgabe an R. Bultmann zum 80. Geburtstag*, ed. E. Dinkler (Tübingen: J. C. B. Mohr, 1964), pp. 263–93, esp. p. 264: "Es lässt sich sogar noch deutlicher zeigen, dass diese Form des gnostischen Mythos bei der Entstehung unseres Textes überhaupt nicht Pate gestanden haben kann."
29. Käsemann, "Critical Analysis," p. 62. He adds: "Here we also come upon the main argument for my contention that, whether or not one chooses to differentiate between 'divine form' and 'equality with God,' both terms are at least co-ordinated with one another. . . . Whoever overlooks this fact and separates these two terms in order to consider them in isolation, can hardly be credited with a methodologically sound procedure."

background, especially the LXX material, as the most promising source for arriving at a solution. Unfortunately, the LXX evidence is meager and ambiguous, so that interpreters have come up with a wide range of ideas: from the rather vague notion of "visible appearance,"[30] to the very specific equation of *morphē* with *doxa*, "glory" (so Meyer and many after him), and on to the elaboration of an Adam-Christology based on the relation between *morphē theou* and *eikōn tou theou*, "image of God" (Col. 1:15).[31] The discussion of LXX backgrounds is often complicated by fuzzy linguistic arguments and by the implication that the various theses proposed are mutually exclusive.

In view of the great variety of contexts in which *morphē* may be used, Hwth. makes a significant point in admitting that the word's "precise meaning is elusive" (unfortunately, he then proceeds to adopt the precise definition in MM). To put it differently, *morphē* is characterized by semantic extension;[32] it covers a broad range of meanings and therefore we are heavily dependent on the immediate context to discover its specific nuance. Here in Phil. 2:6 we are greatly helped by two factors. In the first place, we have the correspondence of *morphē theou* with *isa theǭ*. Käsemann, as we have noticed, was absolutely right in emphasizing that being "in the form of God" is equivalent to being "equal with God." To go beyond this equivalence and inquire whether *morphē* tells us precisely in what respects Jesus is equal with God (in essence? attributes? attitude? appearance?) is asking too much from one word.

In the second place, and most importantly, *morphē theou* is set in antithetical parallelism with μορφὴν δούλου (*morphēn doulou*, "form of a servant"), an expression further defined by the phrase ἐν ὁμοιώματι ἀνθρώπων (*en homoiōmati anthrōpōn*, "in the likeness of men"). It is possible to cite parallels (already noted by Bauer) in

---

30. So Strimple, "Philippians 2:5–11," p. 260; cf. Kennedy, Heriban (p. 245), and others.
31. See Martin's survey of the arguments in *Carmen Christi*, pp. 106–19, and note the important study by Seyoon Kim, *The Origin of Paul's Gospel* (Grand Rapids: Eerdmans, 1982), chap. 6, esp. pp. 193–205.
32. Cf. Silva, *Biblical Words*, p. 77. Heriban (pp. 213–14, n. 17, following Dibelius) shows the difficulties of taking the terms in a rigorous technical sense. Cf. also Vern S. Poythress, *Symphonic Theology: The Validity of Multiple Perspectives in Theology* (Academie Books; Grand Rapids: Zondervan, 1987), esp. pp. 74–79 on the differences between biblical language and technical theological terms; and John M. Frame, *The Doctrine of the Knowledge of God* (Phillipsburg, N.J.: Presbyterian and Reformed, 1987), pp. 222–26.

which *morphē* is used to designate what is distinctively divine in contrast to what is distinctively human.[33] It appears then that Ltf., although misguided in seeing here a more or less philosophical meaning of "essence," was *not* off the track in detecting a contrast between "the true divine nature of our Lord" and "true human nature" (p. 133). And it moreover follows that the Philippians passage, although not written for the purpose of presenting an ontological description of Christ, is very much consonant with the trinitarian formulas of the fourth-century church.

These conclusions, however, do not preclude several other ideas that have been put forward over the years. I would not want to argue strongly for them, but it seems misleading to present them as mutually exclusive of each other. For example, the meaning "condition" or "status" is not clearly attested for *morphē*, but the combination *morphēn doulou* in v. 7 plus the parallel in 2 Cor. 8:9 strongly suggest that connotation. Again, it is an overstatement to equate *morphē* with *doxa*, but who can deny that the *morphē theou* manifests itself in glory? Finally, the parallel with Adam has been illegitimately pressed by some writers, but there is an undeniable network of associations between Philippians 2 and Genesis 1–3 (mediated by such passages as Rom. 5:19; 8:29; 1 Cor. 15:41; 2 Cor. 3:18; 4:4; Phil. 3:21; Col. 1:15; 3:10), and Herman Ridderbos in particular has shown the theological coherence of these associations.[34]

b. *Christ's voluntary act negatively stated* (v. 6b-c). The ambiguous phrase in v. 6, οὐχ ἁρπαγμὸν ἡγήσατο (*ouch harpagmon hēgēsato*), has created a literature far more extensive than it probably deserves. In particular, one is impressed by the futility of trying to reach a deci-

---

33. Philo, for example, ridicules Gaius's claims to divinity by stating that the θεοῦ μορφή "cannot be counterfeited as a coin can be" (*The Embassy to Gaius* 110; LCL 10:55); and Josephus, in speaking of God's uniqueness, links μορφή and μέγεθος ("greatness") as qualities that cannot be described or visually represented (*Against Apion* 2.190–91; LCL 1:369). In a recent study ("Erwägungen zu Phil 2₆₋₇b," *ZNW* 78 [1987]:230–43), Hermann Binder seeks to understand δοῦλος in the light of Mark 10:45.

34. Ridderbos, *Paul*, pp. 68–78. C. A. Wanamaker, "Philippians 2.6–11: Son of God or Adamic Christology?" *NTS* 33 (1987): 179–93, argues that those who deny the theme of preexistence by means of the Adamic interpretation cannot account for the contrast between being in the form of God and taking the form of a slave. Unfortunately, a very weak treatment of v. 6b-c leads him to deny that the passage teaches the absolute divinity of Christ. Preexistence plus divinity is strongly argued by L. D. Hurst, "Re-Enter the Pre-Existence of Christ in Philippians 2.5–11?" *NTS* 32 (1986): 449–57, and by T. Yai-Chow Wong, "The Problem of Pre-Existence in Philippians 2,6–11," *ETL* 62 (1986): 267–82.

sion regarding Jesus' preexistence and deity on the basis of whether *harpagmon* here has an active or a passive meaning.[35] The subsequent choices then become rather confusing: if one opts for the passive idea, is the nuance positive ("windfall, advantage") or negative ("booty, prize")? Further, if it carries a negative nuance, we must decide whether it speaks of a thing already possessed, which one is tempted to hold on to (*res rapta*), or a thing *not* possessed, which one may be tempted to snatch (*res rapienda*). In the last instance, the inference is drawn that the Christ-hymn speaks of the human (not preexistent) Christ, who was tempted to snatch the status of lordship but instead chose the path of obedience (vv. 9–11). We may outline these options thus:

> *active* (or abstract: the act of snatching, robbery, usurpation):
> "precisely *because* he was in the form of God he reckoned equality with God not as a matter of getting but of giving"
> *passive* (or concrete: the thing possessed or to be snatched):
> (1) *positive* (windfall, piece of good luck): "Jesus did not regard equality with God as a gain to be utilized"
> (2) *negative* (booty, prize)
>   (a) *res rapta*: "He, though existing before the worlds in the form of God, did not treat His equality with God as a prize, a treasure to be greedily clutched and ostentatiously displayed"
>   (b) *res rapienda*: "He did not regard the being on an equality with God as a thing to be seized, violently snatched"[36]

This very diversity of interpretations should warn us not to move from the ambiguous word to the meaning of the passage as a whole, but vice versa. Now the context provides two important clues. First, the phrase in question is contrasted with ἑαυτὸν ἐκένωσεν (*heauton ekenōsen*, "He emptied Himself," v. 7) and ἐταπείνωσεν ἑαυτόν (*etapeinōsen heauton*, "He humbled Himself," v. 8). One could argue, on that ground alone, that v. 6 is simply concerned to state negatively what the main verbs in vv. 7–8 state positively: Jesus refused to make a selfish choice with respect to His divinity. If so, any other questions

---

35. An active meaning ("the act of snatching, robbery") is the usage found in the few attested occurrences of the word outside the NT and Christian writers; a passive meaning ("the thing possessed or to be snatched") is only attested for the form ἅρπαγμα.
36. The paraphrases above come, respectively, from Hwth. (quoting Moule), Foerster (*TDNT* 1:474), Ltf., and Kennedy. Note that each of these interpretations is given a variety of twists by different writers; cf. Martin, *Carmen Christi*, pp. 134–64.

117

regarding the phrase should probably remain quite subordinate. In the second place, it is certainly no accident that the verb *hēgeomai* is also used in v. 3, and this fact alerts us to the parallel expressions, "each of you must regard one another as more important than himself" and "looking out . . . for the interests of others." These clauses in turn are contrasted with *eritheia*, "selfishness." Third, a more distant—but as we have already noted very important—parallel is Rom. 15:1–7; in v. 3 of that passage we are told that "Christ did not please Himself." These three pieces of contextual data leave no doubt about the force of v. 6b-c: *Christ refused to act selfishly.*

Whether Christ's unselfishness expressed itself in a decision not to aspire for something greater than He already had (*res rapienda*) or in a decision not to use selfishly what He already had (*res rapta*) can be decided on the basis of three factors. First, the presence of the article in *to einai isa theǭ* suggests strongly the definiteness that in English is more commonly expressed with the possessive pronoun,[37] "his equality with God"; at the very least it points back to *en morphē theou hyparchōn* (so Hwth.).

Second, an extensive and persuasive discussion by Roy W. Hoover has demonstrated the mistake of focusing on the word *harpagmos* itself rather than on the combination of that word (and comparable nouns) with *hēgeomai* (and comparable verbs). Building on the researches of W. W. Jaeger (who however stressed the idea of "windfall") Hoover states that in all instances examined, the "idiomatic expression refers to something already present and at one's disposal." His translation of the Phil. 2:6 passage is: Christ "did not regard being equal with God as . . . something to use for his own advantage."[38] Hoover's essay, which reflects thoroughness and a clear-headed method, must be regarded as having settled this particular question.

Third, the notion of Christ's aspiring (or being tempted to aspire) for equality with God is completely foreign to the NT; conversely, the notion that Christ set aside His "advantageous" position for the sake of others is at the very heart of the NT message (cf. again 2 Cor. 8:9).

---

37. Cf. Herbert Weir Smyth, *Greek Grammar*, rev. Gordon M. Messing (Cambridge, Mass.; Harvard U., 1956), sect. 1121.
38. Roy W. Hoover, "The Harpagmos Enigma: A Philological Solution," *HTR* 64 (1971): 95–119, esp. p. 118. The basic soundness of Hoover's research is accepted by, among others, Heriban (pp. 262–65) and N. T. Wright, "ἁρπαγμός and the Meaning of Philippians 2:5–11," *JTS* 37 (1986): 321–52. Wong ("The Problem of Pre-Existence," pp. 277–78) rejects Hoover's conclusions, but on very weak grounds.

c. *Christ's voluntary act positively stated* (vv. 7–8). The central thought of the whole Christ-hymn is embodied in the two main verbs, *ekenōsen* and *etapeinōsen*, which illumine each other. It is specious to drive a sharp wedge between these verbs; only a wooden approach to this poetic passage would insist that the verbs refer to two different and separate stages. It may well be, of course, that the first verb speaks of the incarnation generally whereas the second focuses more specifically on Jesus' death, but one would be greatly mistaken to suggest that the self-emptying is not part of the humiliation or— what is more to the point—that Jesus' humiliation unto death is not included in the statement, "He emptied Himself."

These preliminary comments alone should make us suspicious of the extensive debates seeking to answer the question, "Of what did Christ empty Himself?" Once again, sensitivity to the contextual demands of the passage should discourage us from focusing excessively on the meaning of one word. As Vincent aptly puts it, *heauton ekenōsen* is used as a "graphic expression of the completeness of his self-renunciation. It includes all the details of humiliation which follow, *and is defined by these.* Further definition belongs to speculative theology."[39]

Moreover, the well-established figurative meaning of the verb, "to nullify, make of no effect," is elsewhere used by Paul and suits the present passage well. For example, in Rom. 4:14 Paul states that "if those who are of the Law are heirs, faith has been emptied" (*kekenōtai hē pistis*), but no one thinks of asking, "Of what is faith made empty?" Clearly, the idea is that faith would come to nought, as the following clause confirms: "and the promise has been nullified" (*kai katērgētai hē epangelia*). Similar examples are found in 1 Cor. 1:17; 9:15; 2 Cor. 9:3.[40]

In short, we are fully justified in translating our phrase with a comparable English idiom: "He made Himself nothing" (cf. *NIV*). Whether or not the phrase focuses on the initial act of humiliation ("He became flesh," John 1:14), it surely points forward to His death.

---

39. Italics added (the word *speculative* need not have a negative nuance, however); cf. also Heriban, p. 286.
40. Apparently, this is the way the author of *The Shepherd of Hermas* understood the Christ-hymn, for in describing believers who please themselves (ἑαυτοῖς ἀρέσκοντες, cf. Rom. 15:3 again) he says: "for this high-mindedness [ὑψηλοφροσύνην; contrast ταπεινοφροσύνην] therefore many have been made worthless [ἐκενώθησαν] by exalting themselves [ὑψοῦντες ἑαυτούς; cf. Phil. 2:9, ὑπερύψωσεν]" (*Similitudes* 9.22.3; LCL 2:275).

119

In other words, the phrase is intended to encapsulate for the readers the whole descent of Christ from highest glory to lowest depths.[41]

In addition to the two main verbs *ekenōsen* and *etapeinōsen,* vv. 7–8 contain four participial clauses that modify either or both of the verbs. How should these four participles be related to the main thought? All four are aorists (*labōn, genomenos, heuretheis, genomenos*), and aorist participles usually refer to actions that have taken place prior to the action of the verbs they modify. If we were to press this rule, we would need to translate each clause somewhat woodenly: for example, "having taken (or, after He had taken) the form of a servant." This grammatical "rule," however, admits of many exceptions, and most writers recognize that some flexibility is needed here, particularly in view of the poetic quality of the passage.

The smoothest option, followed by *NASB* and *NIV,* is to translate the first three participles as referring to simultaneous action. The *NASB* then interprets the fourth explicitly as a participle of means: "by becoming obedient." Implicitly, however, the first two clauses also indicate means: "by taking the form of a servant, by being made in the likeness of men." Hwth. takes even the third participial clause in this way ("by being recognized as a man"), but the resulting syntax is awkward, because it requires that the first three participles modify the first verb. In both of the strophic arrangements that have won most acceptance, the third participial clause is connected with the second main verb, *etapeinōsen,* and that seems the most natural reading of the clause, that is, as providing the background for the statement of v. 8.

Much more difficult is the decision whether the second participial clause—"being made in the likeness of men"—should be construed with what precedes, as in Lohmeyer's arrangement, or with what follows, as in Jeremias's proposal. Since both strophic arrangements are plausible and at the same time speculative, we must make a judgment on other grounds. Jeremias argues forcefully that *en homoiōmati anthrōpōn genomenos* must not be separated from *kai schēmati heuretheis hōs anthrōpos* because both clauses have substantives that end in *-ma,* each of which attests to Christ's humanity.[42] This

---

41. Such a formulation is reminiscent of the Johannine perspective. Note esp. C. H. Dodd, *The Interpretation of the Fourth Gospel* (Cambridge: Cambridge U., 1953), pp. 247–48 and passim. Not suprisingly, some scholars appeal to John 13 in their interpretation of Phil. 2:6–11 (e.g., Hwth., Heriban). For a connection with the synoptic gospels, cf. E. Schweizer, "Die Christologie von Phil 2, 6–11 und Q," *TZ* 41 (1985): 258–63.
42. Jeremias, "Zu Phil ii 7," p. 85 (following Dibelius).

argument is hardly decisive, however. Besides, the resulting idea does not yield a particularly good sense: if the stanza begins with "being made in the likeness of men," what significance do we attribute to the additional clause, "and being found in appearance as a man"?

On the other hand, if we construe the second participial clause with what precedes, a clear progression of thought results. According to this approach, the clause "taking the form of a servant" is expanded and explained by "being made in the likeness of men." Once that point has been clearly established, a transition is marked by the conjunction *kai* ("and") so that the clause "being found in appearance as a man," by *summarizing* the previous thought, introduces or sets the stage for the next main verb, *etapeinōsen*.

The exegetical significance of these considerations is, first, that we need not see a sharp difference between the first two clauses. The words *morphē* and *homoiōma*, whatever distinctions one may detect in some contexts, are interchanged here for stylistic rather than semantic reasons. Moreover, we need not look for substantive theological differences between *doulos* and *anthrōpos;* the first term of course stresses Christ's attitude of servanthood, but the latter simply reminds us that He gave expression to that attitude by becoming man (cf. Rom. 8:3). In the second place, it becomes clear that the use of *schēma* is not intended primarily to be contrasted with *morphē* (as Ltf. tried to prove). Rather, the whole clause recapitulates the thrust of the two previous clauses by making a succinct statement of the incarnation. As the *NBE* puts it, "Así, presentándose como simple hombre. . ." ("Thus, presenting Himself as no more than man . . .").

Special attention needs to be given, finally, to the last participial clause, "becoming obedient to death."[43] The description of Christ as "obedient" (*hypēkoos*) will serve as a key word in relating Christ's humiliation to the Philippians' conduct (*hypēkousate*, v. 12). The terminology of obedience is common enough in Paul, but only on one other occasion, Rom. 5:19, does he use it to describe Jesus' conduct: "For as through one man's disobedience [*parakoēs*, parallel to *paraptōmatos* "transgression" in v. 18] the many were constituted sinners, so also through one man's obedience [*hypakoēs*, parallel to *di-*

---

43. The participle itself, γενόμενος, is also in the aorist tense, but it cannot possibly refer to antecedent action (the translation would yield no reasonable sense: "He humbled Himself after He had become obedient to death"). This fact confirms the usual handling of the other participles as referring to simultaneous action.

kaiōmatos "act of righteousness" in v. 18] the many will be constituted righteous" (Jesus is also described as learning obedience in
Heb. 5:8). While we need to be careful not to import into Philippians,
on the basis of one word, all of the theological ideas presented in
Romans, the parallel is real and throws light in two directions.

First, it adds weight to the suspicions that the Adam-Christ analogy, although not dominant in the Christ-hymn, has played a role in
it (see the exposition of v. 6a). Second, it reminds us that Paul can
hardly speak of Christ's death without thinking of its redemptive
effect. In other words, although the Christ-hymn speaks of Jesus'
death primarily in reference to Christ's humiliation, so that its main
purpose is not to make a statement about its sacrificial character, yet
the latter cannot be wrenched from the total meaning of the text.[44]
Surely, both for Paul and for his readers, Christ's death was not only
an example of utter obedience and humiliation, but also the very
basis on which the believer's sanctification (sōtēria, v. 12) could become a reality.

But why is one more clause added, thanatou de staurou ("and
death of the cross")? No doubt to emphasize the extent and depth of
Christ's humiliation, because death by crucifixion was considered by
the Romans the most degrading penalty. (Philippian criminals, if
sentenced to death, would have been treated more honorably as Roman citizens, for whom decapitation was the capital punishment.)
There is more, however. The way Paul speaks of the cross (e.g., 1 Cor.
1:17–18; Gal. 3:1, 13; 6:12–14) has led many scholars to conclude
that the manner of Christ's death may have been the major stum-
blingblock for Paul prior to his conversion.[45]

The offensive character of that death repelled many pious Jews
and may have been a source of embarrassment for Jewish Christians.
Paul viewed his Jewish opponents as wanting to avoid the offense of
the cross (Gal. 6:12); indeed, in Phil. 3:18 he describes them as "enemies of the cross." We may have in the Christ-hymn a subtle anticipation of the polemic of chapter 3. It is certainly intriguing that the
clause thanatou de staurou in 2:8 breaks the poetic pattern of all
major strophic arrangements of the passage. We may speculate that
in fact Paul was making use of a well-known hymn but then inserted

---

44. Cf. the parallel use of ὁμοίωμα in Rom. 8:3, a passage where the thought
of sacrifice is predominant. In contrast to my exposition, Martin in his
commentary argues that "no soteriology . . . is implied" (p. 100).
45. Cf. among others F. F. Bruce, *Paul: Apostle of the Heart Set Free* (Grand
Rapids: Eerdmans, 1977), pp. 70–71.

this clause to impart his own distinctiveness to it and to reinforce one of his major concerns in writing this letter. (If there is any merit to this suggestion, which in one form or another has been adopted by not a few writers, we have an additional reason for affirming the integrity of the epistle. See Introduction: Literary Integrity.)

Additional Notes

2:6 ὅς: On the analogy of 1 Tim. 3:16, this relative pronoun is often thought to be an introductory formula for early Christological hymns.

ὑπάρχων ("existing"): The *NASB* is justified in bringing out the concessive force of the participle (contra Meyer, Hwth.), and that in turn sheds light on the second part of v. 6. It seems unnecessary to see any special significance in the use of ὑπάρχω (as opposed to εἰμί).

ἐν μορφῇ θεοῦ: Ltf.'s claim that μορφή (opposite σχῆμα) refers to unchangeable essence can be sustained by some references, but too many passages speak against it. Plato asks if God can manifest Himself in different aspects (ἄλλαις ἰδέαις) and alter "his shape in many transformations" (τὸ αὐτοῦ εἶδος εἰς πολλὰς μορφάς). Xenophon reports Socrates as advising not to wait "for the gods to appear to you in bodily presence" (τὰς μορφὰς τῶν θεῶν ἴδῃς). Philo describes Gaius's attempts to prove himself divine "by remodelling and recasting what was nothing but a single body into manifold forms" (ἑνὸς σώματος οὐσίαν μετασχηματίζων καὶ μεταχαράττων εἰς πολυτρόπους μορφάς). Lucian relates the Egyptian story of a certain occasion when one god "in his terror entered into a goat, another into a ram, and others into other beasts or birds; so of course the gods still keep the forms they took then" (διὸ δὴ εἰσέτι καὶ νῦν φυλάττεσθαι τὰς τότε μορφὰς τοῖς θεοῖς). Elsewhere Lucian describes the ugly physical appearance of the god Heracles (τὸ εἶδος τοῦ θεοῦ) according to the Celts, who thereby committed an offense against his form (παρανομεῖν τοὺς Κελτοὺς ἐς τὴν μορφὴν τὴν Ἡρακλέους). A still later writer, Libanius (fourth century), states that "any man who really approximates to the divine, does so not by any physical likeness" (οὐχ ὁ τοῖς θεοῖς τὴν μορφὴν ἐοικώς).[46]

---

46. The references are, respectively, to Plato, *Republic* 2.19 = 380D (LCL 1:189); Xenophon, *Memorabilia* 4.3.13 (LCL 305); Philo, *The Embassy to Gaius* 80 (LCL 10:41); Lucian, *On Sacrifices* 14 (LCL 3:171) and *Heracles* 1–2 (LCL 1:63); Libanius, *Fifteenth Julian Oration* 34 (LCL 1:169). I owe the last three references to my former student Roy Kotanski; the first two are listed by Bauer. For more linguistic references, see Ceslas Spicq, *Notes de lexicographie néo-testamentaire* (OBO 22; Fribourg: Editions Universitaires, 1978), 2:568–73.

οὐχ ἁρπαγμὸν ἡγήσατο (lit. "did not regard as robbery"): It may
be that too much emphasis has been placed on this negative statement, with the implication that Christ was tempted but refused to
yield. Glen Ker, a former student of mine, has suggested that the οὐχ
. . . ἀλλά contrast is used here for rhetorical effect: the particle οὐχ
could be viewed as negating the whole clause (not the verb alone),
with the resulting idea, "We should not think that He regarded. . . ."
Still another possibility is that οὐχ governs not the verb but the noun,
as Carmignac has argued with erudition but unpersuasively.[47]

τὸ εἶναι ἴσα θεῷ (lit. "the being equal to God"): The fact that ἴσα
can be described grammatically as a "weakened" adverbial form of
the adjective ἴσος has misled some scholars (e.g., Gnilka and Schenk)
into thinking that this phrase cannot refer to complete equality with
God. The most thorough attempt to establish this view is by Grelot.[48]
The confusion shows up especially when a scholar states: "The fact
that ἴσον . . . is not employed suggests that 'being equal with god'
does not denote an equality of persons."[49] No doubt if the text did use
the adjectival form, someone would point to Matt. 20:12 (and probably other texts) as proof that even ἴσος need not refer to complete
equality of nature. Theological inferences drawn from grammatical
nuances (and in a quasi-poetic passage to boot) seldom are worth
considering seriously.

---

47. Jean Carmignac, "L'importance de la place d'une négation: οὐχ ἁρπαγμὸν ἡγήσατο (Philippiens II.6)," *NTS* 18 (971–72): 131–66. On p. 140 he
points out that in 204 instances (against four, namely, 2 Cor. 2:11; 5:12;
Rom. 7:15, 19) the particle negates what immediately follows, but note
the criticisms of P. Grelot, "La valeur de οὐχ . . . ἀλλά . . . dans Philippiens 2,6–7," *Bib* 54 (1973): 25–42, who rightly explains the position of
οὐχ as emphatic negation (p. 35). Carmignac also appeals to Chrysostom
in support of his view (p. 142), but the evidence is not as clear as he makes
it out to be; indeed, his treatment of the relevant passage is misleading.
In any case, his resulting translation, "Il a estimé que ce n'était pas une
usurpation d'être égal à Dieu," has not proved attractive to most scholars, with the notable exception of Hooker ("Philippians 2:6–11").
48. P. Grelot, "Deux expressions difficiles de Philippiens 2,6–7," *Bib* 53
(1972): 495–507. Interestingly, he believes that equality of nature is in
fact expressed in this passage, but by the previous clause, v. 6a, not v. 6c.
Rather disappointing is his method of establishing an equivalence between ἴσα and Hebrew k- on the basis of Isa. 51:23, LXX, (a paraphrastic
rendering that really means "equal in level with the ground") and several
references in LXX Job (with further appeal to the Qumran *Targum of
Job!*); see p. 500. For some reason neither he nor other writers have referred to passages where the sense of equality seems strong, e.g., Wis. 7:3.
49. Wanamaker, "Philippians 2.6–11," p. 187.

2:7 ἑαυτὸν ἐκένωσεν (lit. "emptied Himself"): The view taken here—namely, that this phrase should be understood figuratively—is objected to by Oepke on the basis that a metaphorical meaning "is ruled out by the resultant weak tautology of" ἐταπείνωσεν ἑαυτόν.[50] Even if we allowed that the latter clause is equivalent to the former, Oepke's objection is strange when one considers the "tautology of earnestness" that characterizes 2:1–11 (see Introduction: Language and Style).

But if our interpretation is correct, what are we to say then about the large number of attempts to explain the phrase? Martin catalogs seven distinct interpretations, most of which can be plausibly defended.[51] As in my final comments regarding μορφὴ θεοῦ, we can and should recognize that the phrase ἑαυτόν ἐκένωσεν may well have evoked a larger network of associations, and those would be part of the "total" meaning. Particularly intriguing is the possible connection with Isa. 53:12, where the Servant of the Lord (cf. δοῦλος in Phil. 2:7) is said to have "poured (out) Himself [lit. His soul] unto death." The fact that Phil 2:11 quotes Isa. 45:23 increases the probability that we may have an allusion to Isa. 53:12. But an allusion is not a direct reference.[52] To say that the Christ-hymn is primarily an attribution to Jesus of the Servant of the Lord description seems to me to be an overstatement; much less is it acceptable to argue that "He emptied Himself" actually means "He suffered the death of the Servant of the Lord."

In similar fashion, we may want to deny that the passage speaks primarily to ontological issues regarding the nature of the Trinity, but it would appear futile to deny that Phil. 2:5–7 has some strong implications for these issues. These verses cannot serve as the total basis for a formula regarding the two natures of Christ, but the description of Christ in this passage reflects certain ontological commitments that lead rather naturally to the later orthodox formulations.

ἐν ὁμοιώματι ἀνθρώπων γενόμενος (lit. "having become in the likeness of men," which I have paraphrased above with "by becoming

---

50. Oepke, *TDNT* 3:661. Contrast above, Introduction: Language and Style.
51. Martin, *Carmen Christi*, pp. 169–94.
52. For the literature on this subject, and a formulation similar to mine, see Heriban, pp. 160–62. In his view, the Isaianic passage provides the thematic background of humiliation and exaltation, and as such it is significant. Cf. most recently G. Wagner, "Le scandale de la croix expliqué par le chant du Serviteur d'Isaïe 53. Réflexion sur Philippiens 2/6–11," *ETR* 61 (1986): 177–87.

incarnate" to stress the connection of this clause with what precedes): The variant ἄνθρωπον (P⁴⁶ supported by some versional and patristic evidence) instead of the plural form is surely not to be explained on the basis of theological motivation, but as a simple assimilation to the singular δοῦλον, reinforced by ὡς ἄνθρωπος. This kind of scribal error is common in P⁴⁶ (see Introduction: Textual History; in the course of writing this section of the commentary, I have made the same mistake several times).

μορφὴν . . . ὁμοιώματι . . . σχήματι: The literature dealing with these words (and such related terms as δόξα, εἶδος, εἰκών, etc.) is very extensive and covers a wide range of problems.⁵³ Whatever distinctions may be posited are subject to contextual adjustments, including semantic neutralization, which is most likely what we have here. It would be difficult to prove that if these three terms were interchanged, a substantive semantic difference would result. No doubt μορφή was chosen first to provide an explicit contrast with μορφὴ θεοῦ in v. 6; ὁμοίωμα (a close synonym to ἴσος, cf. ἴσα in v. 6) serves to delimit more precisely the range of μορφή (that is, although μορφή covers a very wide semantic range, only that area that overlaps with ὁμοίωμα is in view); finally σχῆμα, which has an even greater range than μορφή, is perhaps the most useful term available to provide a general summary of what the two previous clauses have stated.

3. CHRIST'S EXALTATION 2:9–11

Translation

For this very reason God has exalted Him above all things by granting to Him as a gift the name that is above every name, so that the whole universe may bow in adoration before the name of Jesus— indeed, so that every tongue *may confess that Jesus Christ is the divine Lord, for the glory of God the Father.

Exegesis and Exposition

The second part of the Christ-hymn contrasts with the first not only conceptually (exaltation opposed to humiliation), but in other respects as well. To begin with, in this second part we are not faced with numerous lexical and exegetical problems such as we encountered in vv. 6–8. Indeed, most commentators are able to deal with vv.

---

53. A helpful summary, including well-selected bibliographies, may be found in *NIDNTT* 1:703–14; 2:44–52, 284–93, 496–508.

9–11 in about half the space they required for the first section. (Yet, as we shall see, these verses raise two or three questions that have major doctrinal implications.) Moreover, the structure of vv. 9–11 is not characterized by the large number of parallel and contrasting items that have been recognized in vv. 6–8.

Verses 9–11 constitute one sentence, composed of (1) two closely related main verbs, ὑπερύψωσεν, ἐχαρίσατο (hyperypsōsen, "exalted"; echarisato, "granted"), of which God, not Jesus, is the subject; and (2) a purpose clause (introduced with ἵνα, hina, "in order that") also consisting of two verbs, the subjunctives κάμψῃ and ἐξομολογήσηται (kampsē, "bow"; exomologēsētai, "confess"). This sentence is introduced in v. 9 with the inferential conjunction διό (dio, "therefore," reinforced with καί, kai, "also"—see Additional Notes), and commentators have debated the precise relationship between the two parts of the hymn.

On the surface, it would appear that God is spoken of as rewarding Jesus with "the Name which is above every name" because of His faithful obedience (so Meyer, Eadie, et al.). Partly because of certain abuses of this idea, Calvin reacted strongly against it. In recent times it has been opposed by Barth and others; Collange, for example, appeals to the verb echarisato as indicating "pure grace" or "the gracious sovereign act of God," in contrast to the idea of recompense. Hwth. speaks of a "natural or logical outcome," "an inflexible law of God's kingdom," namely, "that in the divine order of things self-humbling leads inevitably to exaltation."[54]

One must question, however, whether it is useful to oppose these various aspects to one another. The "inflexible law" of which Hwth. speaks is hardly an impersonal rule; when Jesus taught that "whoever humbles himself shall be exalted" (Matt. 23:12), He was not speaking of an automatic sequence of events but of a deliberate act on God's part, as we also have here in Philippians. God's act does not entail submission to some higher, arbitrary law. In other words, to speak of a logical consequence does not exclude the question of whether or not a personal reward is in view.

Moreover, is it necessary to deny the notion of reward if we wish to do justice to the gracious element of God's act? The question, though quickly dismissed in some Protestant circles as reflecting a medieval aberration, is a highly complicated one that does not admit

---

54. Hwth., p. 90, no doubt building on Lohmeyer's work (see esp. *Kyrios Jesus*, pp. 47–48).

of brief and definitive answers. On the one hand, if we emphasize the reward/merit element in a passage that presents Christ as our example, we may appear to undermine the doctrine of salvation by grace (as though people *achieve* their final salvation as Christ achieved His Messianic exaltation). On the other hand, if we emphasize the element of grace in a passage where Christ's vicarious obedience is in view, we appear to undermine a correlative soteriological principle, namely, that Christ's meritorious work as the last Adam fully satisfied the claims of divine law and justice (Rom. 5:18–19).[55]

It may help us to see our way out of this dilemma if we consider, first, that the Christ-hymn, though it certainly describes Christ's sacrificial work, does not have as its primary object setting forth the vicarious character of His obedience. In other words, we need not fear that an emphasis on the gracious character of God's act in exalting Jesus subverts the principle of Christ's meritorious obedience on behalf of His people. Second, the Christ-hymn implies a correspondence between Christ's experience and the believer's sanctification leading to glorification, not between Christ's exaltation and the sinner's justification. Surely, believers are exhorted to persevere in their Christian race so that they may receive the prize (Phil. 3:13–14), but we need not for that reason fear that the notion of reward conflicts with Paul's doctrine of justification (Rom. 4:5, "to the one who does not work . . .").

Gnilka then is quite correct in pointing out both that we cannot exclude the notion of reward from this passage and at the same time that we must restrict its application in view of Jesus' uniqueness (though Gnilka's own qualifications are debatable). Similarly, Martin clarifies the issue by accepting in this context the concept of reward while rejecting that of merit:

> It is not so much the thought that because He rendered this obedience He was glorified as that, having accomplished the mission He came into the world to fulfil, God interposed and reversed the seeming finality of death in raising Him to the place of dignity. The obedience of Christ did not force the hand of God, as a doctrine of merit implies. The action of God is but the other side of that obedience, and a vindication of all that the obedience involved.[56]

We must move on and inquire what is the nature of Christ's exaltation. It is not farfetched to view the second *kai* of v. 9 as epex-

---

55. Cf. Meredith G. Kline, "Of Works and Grace," *Presbyterion* 9 (1983): 85–92, esp. p. 87.
56. Martin, *Carmen Christi*, p. 232.

egetic; certainly Christ's exaltation is here defined as receiving "the name which is above every name." But what is that name? Most contemporary writers assume that this name (ὄνομα, *onoma*) is in fact the title κύριος (*kyrios*, "Lord"). This interpretation makes sense in view of v. 11 and may well be correct, but it requires some critical comments.

(1) The equation of *onoma* with *kyrios* is an inference, not an explicit statement in the text. (2) Although the phrase *epi* [or *en*] *tǭ onomati tinos* may indicate a title or category,[57] we may question whether "title" is an adequate equivalent for the absolute use of *onoma*, as in v. 9.[58] (3) To take the genitive *Iēsou* in v. 10 as indicating possession (the name that belongs to Jesus = Lord) is at variance with usage.[59] (4) The Greek *onoma*, like its Hebrew counterpart שֵׁם (*šēm*), often calls attention to the honor and dignity of the bearer (cf. Ltf.), but one must question the approach that focuses exclusively on this aspect and suggests that *onoma* here does not mean "name" but rather "office and power."[60]

All of these are substantive objections that lead us to doubt the standard interpretation. It would be an overreaction, however, to argue that *onoma* in v. 9 is a reference to Jesus and not to Lord, for the connection between these two names is too close and basic. Very helpful in this regard is noticing the combination *onoma kyriou Iēsou* in Acts 8:16; 19:5, 13, 17; 21:13; Col. 3:17 (cf. also 1 Cor. 5:4; 2 Thess. 1:12; 3:6). Moule gives us a satisfactory statement:

> God, in the incarnation, bestowed upon the one who is on an equality with him an earthly name which, because it accompanied that most God-like self-emptying, and has come to be, in fact, the highest of names, because service and self-giving are themselves the highest of divine attributes. Because of the incarnation, the human name, "Jesus," is acclaimed as the highest name; and the Man Jesus thus comes to be acclaimed as Lord, to the glory of God the Father.[61]

---

57. See Wilhelm Heitmüller, *"Im Namen Jesu." Eine sprach- und religionsgeschichtliche Untersuchung zum Neuen Testament, speziell zur altchristlichen Taufe* (Göttingen: Vandenhoeck & Ruprecht, 1903), p. 50.
58. Certainly LSJ do not give such an equivalent; Bauer's treatment (p. 573) is confusing.
59. The phrases ὄνομα θεοῦ (Rom. 2:24; 10:13; 1 Tim. 6:1; Rev. 3:12; 16:9), ὄνομα κυρίου (Matt. 21:9 and parallels; Acts 2:21; 15:26; 1 Cor. 1:2, 10; 5:4; 6:11; Eph. 5:20; 2 Thess. 1:12; James 5:10, 14), ὄνομα Ἰησοῦ (Acts 4:18, 30; 5:40; 9:27, 28; 26:9), ὄνομα Χριστοῦ (1 Pet. 4:14), and ὄνομα Ἰησοῦ Χριστοῦ (Acts 2:38; 3:6; 4:10; 8:12; 10:48; 16:18) never indicate the possession of a name other than the one given in the genitive case.
60. So Martin, *Carmen Christi*, p. 236.
61. Moule, "Further Reflexions," p. 270.

Moule rightly appeals to Eph. 1:20–23, where Christ's exaltation is described as His being seated above all powers and above "every name that is named" (*hyperanō . . . pantos onomatos onomazomenou*), with all things brought under His authority (cf. also Matt. 28:18). It should be noted, finally, that the idea of a new significance given to Christ's name in connection with His exaltation may be present also in Rom. 1:3–4 and Heb. 1:3–4 (with reference to *huios*, "son").[62]

One additional problem needs to be considered in connection with the twofold purpose clause in vv. 10–11, namely, is the homage spoken of voluntary or involuntary? Calvin rightly comments that the devils, for example, "are not, and never will be, subject of their own accord and by cheerful submission; but Paul is not speaking here of voluntary obedience." Hwth. finds this view objectionable, claiming that (1) the subjunctive *exomologēsētai* does not allow this interpretation, which would require the inferior reading in the indicative mood, (2) not even God's purposes are always fulfilled, and (3) the passage only expresses God's hope that intelligent beings will voluntarily choose submission.

We may respond to these points in order. (1) The weight that Hwth. places on *hina* plus subjunctive is unbearable. John 3:16, for example, uses this construction (*hina pas ho pisteuōn eis auton mē apolētai all' echę̄ zōēn aiōnion*), but who will argue that God only hopes that those who believe will not perish? The certainty that God will give eternal life to all who believe is not undermined by the subjunctive verbs *apolētai* and *echē*. In any case, the grammatical category that we call the subjunctive mood cannot of itself convey assurance or lack thereof (certainly not any more than the English construction "in order that" can settle those kinds of questions).

(2) Hwth. equivocates on the term "purpose," which sometimes can refer to God's commands, as in Luke 7:30, a passage to which he appeals (the Pharisees "rejected God's purpose [*boulē*]"). Contrast such a passage as Isa. 46:10, "My purpose will stand, and I will do all that I please" (*NIV*; note also 14:24–27). The question is then whether Phil. 2:11 speaks of what God hopes people will do or of what He, by divine decree, has granted to the Son, namely, the placing of all things under His feet (Eph. 1:22).

(3) Statements that point to the eschatological purposes of God

---

62. See M. Silva, "Perfection and Eschatology in Hebrews," *WTJ* 39 (1976–77): 60–71.

are always characterized by firmness and certainty.[63] Of particular importance here is Paul's affirmation that, when the end comes, all powers will be abolished and all things will be subjected to Christ (1 Cor. 15:24–28). Moreover, Phil. 2:10–11 is virtually a quotation of Isa. 45:23, LXX (which Paul cites verbatim in Rom. 14:11), a passage that rings with triumphal certainty concerning the sovereign Lordship of God over all. It is only natural, however, that the manner in which this submission is expressed here focuses on the thankful praise of God's people.

In conclusion, we must pause to appreciate the stunning implications of applying Isa. 45:23 to Jesus. Isa. 45:18–25 (excerpts below from the literal *NASB*) constitutes one of the most powerful OT affirmations of the uniqueness of the God of Israel in the context of His redeeming work:

> I am the Lord [Yahweh], and there is none else. . . .
> They have no knowledge,
> Who carry about their wooden idol,
> And pray to a god who cannot save. . . .
> . . . there is no other God besides Me,
> A righteous God and a Savior;
> There is none except Me.
> Turn to Me, and be saved, all the ends of the earth;
> For I am God, and there is no other.
> I have sworn by Myself, . . .
> That to Me every knee will bow,
> every tongue will swear allegiance.

Whether or not Paul composed the Christ-hymn, it patently expresses His own conviction that the worship of Jesus Christ does not compromise Israel's monotheistic faith. On the contrary, Jesus Christ the righteous Savior bears the name of the one Lord, Yahweh, "to the glory of God the Father."[64]

Additional Notes

2:9 διὸ καί: The precise nuance of this combination of particles is debatable. Ltf. simply states the the καί "implies reciprocation"; the

---

63. Hwth. without good reason denies the eschatological element here. With regard to George Howard's view that the passage has in view Jesus' resurrection rather than His enthronement, see Heriban, pp. 329–31.
64. It is not my position that ὄνομα in Phil. 2:9–10 is a direct reference to Yahweh, as a few scholars have argued with some persuasiveness. I would prefer to speak about that reference as a necessary implication of Paul's teaching that the granting of the name serves as the basis on which worship takes place.

resultant idea, presumably, would be, "As for God, this is what He did in response." Vincent claims that the καί expresses "the consequence corresponding to the humiliation." BAGD describes the force of this combination in its various occurrences by saying that it denotes "that the inference is self-evident" (p. 198), but the passages do not bear this out. Is such an inference self-evident in Rom. 4:22, which has διὸ καί, but not in Rom 1:24, which has διό alone? In any case, this construction is not an adequate basis for Hwth.'s view of a "natural or logical outcome." The inherent difficulties in trying to identify a precise meaning for this expression, combined with the consideration that in a (semi-)poetic passage other factors (such as rhythm) may have influenced the writer, lead us to see the καί simply as strengthening or enhancing the διό (so Lohmeyer). The force of the expression is surely equivalent to that of διὰ τοῦτο in Isa. 53:12, LXX; the contrast between suffering and vindication in that passage may well have had some influence in the composition of the hymn, as pointed out earlier.

ὑπερύψωσεν: This compound form, if its etymology is pressed, conveys a comparative meaning: "God exalted Him more." This has led some writers to speculate concerning what is the basis of the comparison, and a common answer is that God has now exalted Christ to a higher dignity than He enjoyed in His preincarnate existence (v. 6).[65] Whether or not the conception is valid, it seems rather foreign to the text. At best, the verb may anticipate ὑπὲρ πᾶν ὄνομα, "above every name."[66] At any rate, BAGD lists more than forty ὑπερ-compounds, the vast majority of which are translated as elatives (e.g., ὑπεραυξάνω, "increase abundantly," 2 Thess. 1:3) or as superlatives (e.g., ὑπερεκπερυσσῶς, "most highly," 1 Thess. 5:13). The BAGD translation of Phil. 2:9 is quite defensible: "raise . . . to the loftiest height."

2:10 ἐν τῷ ὀνόματι Ἰησοῦ: The *NASB* and *NIV* rendering, "at the name of Jesus," could be interpreted to mean that (the name of) Jesus is the object of worship (so Hwth.) or that worship should take place when His name is uttered.[67] Some commentators argue, however, that we have here the language of prayer and that a literal translation, "in the name of Jesus," properly calls attention to Jesus' mediating role (so Beare). This last option, however, would not necessarily

---

65. Cf. Martin's survey in *Carmen Christi*, pp. 239f., esp. n. 2 on p. 240.
66. Cf. Gerhard Delling, "Zum steigernden Gebrauch von Komposita mit ὑπέρ bei Paulus," *NovT* 11 (1969): 127–53, esp. p. 147, but Delling would not object to my comments.
67. Moule, "Further Reflexions," p. 270.

exclude the idea that Jesus is also the object of worship, as the context clearly indicates. Vincent's more general interpretation is perhaps the most satisfactory: "He who believes on the name of the Lord believes on the Lord himself. Hence, to bow the knee in the name of Jesus is to pay adoration in that sphere of authority, grace and glory for which the name stands; as being consciously within the kingdom of which he is Lord, as recognising the rightfulness of the title 'Jesus,' 'Savior,' 'Lord,' and as loyally accepting the obligations which those titles imply." Cf. also Kennedy: "This *name*, which declares the true character and dignity of Jesus Christ, is both the basis and the object of worship."

ἐπουρανίων καὶ ἐπιγείων καὶ καταχθονίων ("of those who are in heaven, and on earth, and under the earth"): We would be misguided to attempt an identification of three specific groups.[68] The interest is clearly to stress the universality of Christ's lordship. Ltf. is therefore right in denying that the reference is limited to intelligent beings. A lack of literal knees and tongues does not prevent the heavens from proclaiming God's glory (Ps. 19:1–6; cf. Ps. 148), and Paul himself was capable of a bold personification of inanimate nature (Rom. 8:19–22).

2:11 ἐξομολογήσηται: An impressive combination of Alexandrian (A C), "Western" (D F G), and Byzantine witnesses have the indicative ἐξομολογήσεται, which if pressed would indicate a grammatical break from the ἵνα clause, with the resulting translation: "and every tongue will confess." Grammatically, therefore, the indicative is the more difficult reading, and it is quite possible that an original indicative, perceived by scribes as an irregularity, led to the smoothing of the style through the very minor (semi-conscious?) change from an ε to an η.[69] If the indicative is indeed original, however, it would not in my opinion convey greater certainty than the purpose clause (see Exposition).

εἰς δόξαν θεοῦ πατρός: Clearly, the worship of Jesus as Lord does not imply competition with the Father, who receives even greater glory through the glorification of the Son.

---

68. The least objectionable classification is spirits in heaven, men on earth, and the dead in Sheol (cf. Heriban, pp. 350–51).
69. If so, this may be an instructive example of a change that cannot be neatly categorized as either deliberate or accidental but as occupying a psychological area where the two overlap. Cf. M. Silva, "Internal Evidence in the Text-Critical Use of the LXX," in *La Septuaginta en la investigación comtemporánea*, ed. N. Fernández Marcos (Madrid: C.S.I.C., 1985), pp. 151–67, esp. pp. 161–62.

C. CHRISTIAN OBEDIENCE (2:12–18)

The connection that obtains between the Christ-hymn and its surrounding context is made clear by v. 8. The first part of that verse emphasizes Christ's *humility* (ἐταπείνωσεν, *etapeinōsen*), a concept that links the Christ-hymn very closely with the immediately preceding section (ταπεινοφροσύνη, *tapeinophrosynē*, v. 3). But this self-humbling is further described in v. 8 as an act of *obedience* (ὑπήκοος, *hypēkoos*), and this concept, now picked up in v. 12 (ὑπηκούσατε, *hypēkousate*, "you have obeyed"), becomes the central thrust of vv. 12–18.

When one further considers the strong link provided by ὥστε (*hōste*, "therefore") in v. 12, one must wonder how anyone could deny that in vv. 6–11 Jesus is indeed viewed as our ethical example. In addition, as several commentators have noted, the theme of Paul's presence/absence links v. 12 with 1:27. Quite possibly, then, the *hōste* not only serves as a transition from what immediately precedes but also resumes the call to Christian citizenship, that is, unity in the struggle for the faith.

The structure of vv. 12–18 is clear. We have first a general but powerful exhortation and encouragement to lead obedient lives (vv. 12–13). There follows a more specific instruction to avoid dissension in the community (vv. 14–16). Paul then concludes with an appeal to his own ministry (vv. 17–18).

1. THE BELIEVER'S WORK (2:12–13)

Translation

Therefore, my loved ones, [in view of Christ's obedience, I call upon you once again to live as Christian citizens:] In the same way that you have always shown an obedient attitude, I urge you to bring about with all godly fear your own salvation—something to be done not only *when I am present, but much more so now during my absence. [You may approach this awesome task with confidence] because God Himself is the one [who makes it possible] by producing in your lives both the will to work and the working itself, and all for the sake of His gracious will.

Exegesis and Exposition

This remarkable passage has occasioned considerable controversy, partly because of several distinct exegetical problems. It is no exaggeration, however, to say that our understanding of these two verses hinges on the force of the imperatival phrase, τὴν ἑαυτῶν σωτηρίαν κατεργάζεσθε (tēn heautōn sōtērian katergazesthe, "bring about your own salvation"), which constitutes the main thought of the passage. Verse 12 could be construed as a chiasm (but see Additional Notes):

hypēkousate	obeyed
en tǭ parousia mou	in my presence
en tǭ apousia mou	in my absence
katergazesthe	work

Whether or not we wish to press this structure, we may reasonably deduce that to work one's salvation is a more specific—or at least a more suggestive—way of expressing the idea of obedience.

But what could Paul possibly mean by such an expression? Any careful reader of the Pauline letters is brought up short by it, since hardly anything is more fundamental to the apostle's theology than the doctrine that God saves "the one who does not work" (tǭ mē ergazomenǭ, Rom. 4:5).[70] Moreover, by going on to explain that it is God who works, Paul may appear to render the command meaningless. The conceptual tension between v. 12 and v. 13 seems unbearable—apparently, an extreme formulation of the paradox of divine sovereignty and human responsibility.

Under the influence of J. H. Michael's work, some commentators (including such prominent writers as Bonnard, Gnilka, Collange, Martin, and Hwth.) have sought to put us at ease by arguing that these verses address a sociological rather than a strictly theological issue. In other words, Paul is here concerned with the well-being of the community, not with the question of individual salvation. A number of plausible arguments have been advanced in support of this relatively new interpretation.

In the first place, we are told that ἐν ὑμῖν (en hymin, v. 13) should be translated "among you" rather than "in you." This rendering is of course quite possible, and we saw how it seemed preferable in v. 5. One must ask, however, how it is that God works in the midst of people if not through personal transformation. To state that the passage refers *not* to individual salvation but to the church's well-being

---

70. It would be sheer linguistic perversion to attempt a solution to this problem by driving a wedge between the compounded form κατεργάζομαι and the simple ἐργάζομαι, as though the former referred to what we may legitimately do and the latter to what God alone does. See the Additional Notes for further comments on these verbs.

already assumes a conceptual dichotomy that is both false and lethal. As we noted in connection with 1:19 and 27, personal sanctification takes place precisely in the context of the Christian community.

As a matter of fact, it is not at all certain or even probable that in this particular passage *en hymin* means "among you." The proper translation depends on the particular syntactical combination being considered. In v. 5 we noted that the combination of this phrase with the verb *phroneite* most likely means, "think among you," but a different thrust is apparent when the verb is *energeomai*. A particularly clear example is 2 Cor. 4:12, "death works [*energeitai*] in us [*en hēmin* = Paul], but life in you [*en hymin*]"; here *en hymin* must have the same force as *en hēmin*, and the latter cannot reasonably be translated "among us" (similarly, the verb is used with *en* + sg. noun/pronoun in Eph. 1:20; Col. 1:29). The translation "works in" for *energeō* + *en* + pl. noun is always possible and in at least two passages most probable (Rom. 7:5 and 1 Cor. 12:6).[71]

In the second place, it is argued that *sōtēria* need not have its technical theological force, because the meaning of "health" is well-attested. It must be objected, however, that out of nearly twenty occurrences of this noun in the Pauline corpus, not one instance requires the translation "well-being"; the vast majority require—and all of them admit—the theological sense. (The nontheological sense "deliverance" is possible in 1:19, but even there "well-being" is not possible; see the comments on that verse and on 1:28.) That the context of 2:12 does not require the sense "well-being"—indeed, that its usual theological sense is preferable—should become clear in the course of our discussion.

Proponents of the new view appeal, thirdly, to the context as not being consonant with the traditional understanding. Martin, for example, states that "after the passage in 2:5–11 it would be inappropriate to stress personal salvation," but he does not spell out the

---

71. Eph. 2:2 and 1 Thess. 2:13 are ambiguous; the rendering "among" is preferable in Gal. 3:5. In his very fine article "Mit Furcht," Pedersen prefers the collective interpretation of the phrase but wisely remarks that, because Paul does not separate the collective from the individual, the question is irrelevant. Even less relevant is the force of ἑαυτῶν in v. 12, a reflexive pronoun which, claims Schenk, always emphasizes cooperation. In fact, the parallel to which he appeals for support (v. 3) undermines his point because there τὰ ἑαυτῶν refers to one's own interests *as opposed* to those of others. The translation "your own salvation" for v. 12 is quite proper, though I would not argue against such a rendering as "your common salvation," since there is no denying that Paul has the community, not isolated individuals, in mind.

argument and it is difficult to see its force. Martin also argues that v. 12 "cannot mean that each church member is to concentrate on his own soul's salvation, since Paul has bidden them to do the opposite in 2:4." The difficulty with this argument is its suggestion that concern for one's soul is tantamount to selfishness (what is forbidden in 2:4). On the contrary, Gal. 6:1–5 shows us how easily Paul can move from the need for spiritual self-concern ("looking to yourselves," v. 1) to concern for others ("bear one another's burdens," v. 2) and back again ("let each one examine his own work," v. 4). More satisfactory is Martin's appeal to the emphasis of Phil. 2:1–4 and 14 on Christian relationships. But as we shall see, the traditional understanding of v. 12 is hardly inconsistent with such an emphasis.

These arguments, therefore, whether viewed separately or in concert, utterly fail to dislodge the view that v. 12 speaks of personal salvation (though one must underscore that the personal salvation in view manifests itself primarily in healthy community relationships). Perhaps the strongest objection to the new interpretation is that it lends itself so easily (though not necessarily, cf. Michael's handling of v. 13) to a remarkably weakened reading of a remarkably potent text. Martin, for instance, sees in this passage little more than an apostolic reminder that God's help is available to the Philippians even if Paul himself cannot be with them. Hwth., for his part, believes that a good summary of Paul's teaching is a saying by Aeschylus roughly equivalent to "God helps those who help themselves" (see p. 106).

A better understanding of our passage begins with the recognition that the phrase ὁ ἐνεργῶν ἐν ὑμῖν (ho energōn en hymin, "He who works in you") finds a close parallel in 1:6, ὁ ἐναρξάμενος ἐν ὑμῖν ἔργον ἀγαθόν (ho enarxamenos en hymin ergon agathon, "He who began a good work in you"). In the exegesis of that passage we noticed how easily the apostle moves from a commendation of the Philippians' own conduct (v. 5) to an acknowledgment that God is the one who both began that good work and will surely complete it (then, just as easily, he shifts back in v. 7 to commend them for their constancy). The striking verbal correspondence between 1:6 and 2:13 suggests strongly that the two verses reflect a common, and profound, conceptual link. But the only concept that fits both passages is the paradoxical engagement of human and divine activity in the total work of salvation—a concept that recurs elsewhere in Philippians (notably 3:7–14).

Any talk of coordinate human and divine work with reference to salvation, however, raises once again our initial difficulty: Is not such a concept subversive of Paul's fundamental doctrine of grace? Part of the answer, of course, lies in the expression used above, "the *total* work of salvation." It is conceded by all parties in the discussion that the term *salvation* (or its cognate verb) need not be restricted, as it normally is in contemporary evangelical language, to the initial act of conversion ("Have you been saved?") or to the status of being in a right relationship with God ("Are you saved?"). It is of course true that, according to Paul, the initiative for salvation comes from God, that our justification (the *establishment* of a right relationship) does not flow from our righteous conduct, for God "justifies the ungodly" (Rom. 4:5). Moreover, once a right relationship has been established, we can in no way "add" to that status by our conduct.

But the biblical concept of salvation is not thus restricted to justification; more commonly what is in view includes God's redemptive work in its totality. Thus, while in a very important sense we have already been saved (Eph. 2:5, 8; Titus 3:5), in another sense we are yet to be saved (Rom. 5:9–10; 1 Cor. 3:15; 5:5; 2 Tim. 4:18). Calvin rightly claims "that *salvation* is taken to mean the entire course of our calling, and that this term includes all things by which God accomplishes that perfection, to which He has determined us by His free election." Because salvation in its entire scope necessarily includes the manifestation of righteousness in our lives, it follows that our activity is integral to the process of salvation; we can never afford to forget the juxtaposition between v. 9 ("not of works") and v. 10 ("for good works") in Ephesians 2. In the particular context of Philippians 2, the outworkings of the believer's *personal* salvation take the form of *corporate* obligations within the Christian community: the duty of seeking the good of others.

It may still be objected, however, that to place such an emphasis on human work injects an element of "legalism" into Christian theology. The proper response to this concern is to appreciate in all its fullness the tension[72] that obtains between vv. 12 and 13. Our natural impulse is to deny or resolve the tension by highlighting some aspects at the expense of others. One way of doing it, as we have seen, is to focus on the sociological element of the passage (the community's well-being) to the exclusion of the personal element.

For those who admit the soteriological thrust of the passage, the

---

72. The word *tension* can be very misleading, particularly if it is thought to reflect an element of irrationality. There is certainly no question here of finding antinomies in God's revelation, but merely of recognizing that in our finiteness and sin we are often unable to assimilate that revelation and thus feel as though we are being pulled in different directions.

tendency is to define v. 12 by means of v. 13 (or v. 13 by means of v. 12), that is, to tone down human activity by appealing to divine grace (or vice versa). One may, for example, so emphasize the truth that God does not force us to act against our will, that as a result grace is restricted to little more than spiritual aid: "God will help us along, but it's really up to us." Conversely, fear of legalism may lead us to a more or less passive understanding of sanctification: "Our responsibility is simply to rest in God's grace, to let Him work in us." The text itself, by its very juxtaposition of those two emphases, cries out loudly against any such attempts at resolution. And the point here is not merely that both the human and the divine are stressed, but that in one and the same passage we have what is perhaps the strongest biblical expression of each element.

Note first Paul's concern with *human activity*. Although several NT verses place considerable emphasis on the role of human responsibility in salvation (cf. esp. 2 Pet. 1:10, "for as long as you practice these things, you will never stumble"), none puts it so bluntly as Phil. 2:12. The very choice of the verb *katergazomai* is notable. Chrysostom explained this compound form as indicating great effort and care;[73] though the evidence speaks against seeing such a nuance in the verb itself, we should not completely overlook the fact that this ancient Greek speaker perceived the term as emphatic. Bauer's first heading, "achieve, accomplish," brings us closer to the distinctive nuance of the verb; he rightly places Phil. 2:12 under the second heading "bring about, produce, create." It is impossible to tone down the force with which Paul here points to our conscious activity in sanctification. The thought should give us pause: our salvation, which we confess to be God's from beginning to end, is here described as something that we must bring about.

For all that, our dependence on *divine activity* for sanctification is nowhere made as explicit as here. To begin with, God's work is viewed as having a causal relation to our working (γάϱ, *gar*, "for"); our activity is possible only because of divine grace. Second, the syntax is emphatic: Paul does not merely say, "God works" (*ho theos energei*) but "the one who works the working is God" (*theos . . . estin*

---

73. Οὐκ εἶπεν, Ἐϱγάζεσθε, ἀλλὰ Κατεϱγάζεσθε, τουτέστι, μετὰ πολλῆς τῆς σπουδῆς, μετὰ πολλῆς τῆς ἐπιμελείας. The juxtaposition of ἐϱγάζομαι and κατεϱγάζομαι in 2 Cor. 7:10 could be an instance of semantic neutralization, though Philip E. Hughes may be right in explaining the latter as emphatic. See *Paul's Second Epistle to the Corinthians* (NICNT; Grand Rapids: Eerdmans, 1962), p. 272n.

ho energōn . . . to energein). Third, the divine influence is said to extend not only to our activity, but to our very wills—a unique statement, though the idea is implied in other passages (e.g., John 1:13; Rom. 9:16). Calvin comments: "There are, in any action, two principal parts, the will, and the effective power. Both of these [Paul] ascribes to God; what more remains to us to glory in?" Fourth, the apostle reinforces our dependence on God's sovereignty with a concluding reference to "His good pleasure" (τῆς εὐδοκίας, *tēs eudokias*), a distinctly theological term used to describe divine grace (see Additional Notes).

The point is that, while sanctification requires conscious effort and concentration, our activity takes place, not in a legalistic spirit, with a view to gaining God's favor, but rather in a spirit of humility and thanksgiving, recognizing that without Christ we can do nothing (cf. John 15:5) and so He alone deserves the glory. Perhaps the finest interpretive summary of Phil. 2:12–13 comes from John Murray:

> God's working in us is not suspended because we work, nor our working suspended because God works. Neither is the relation strictly one of cooperation as if God did his part and we did ours so that the conjunction or coordination of both produced the required result. God works and we also work. But the relation is that because God works we work. All working out of salvation on our part is the effect of God's working in us. . . . We have here not only the explanation of all acceptable activity on our part but we also have the incentive to our willing and working. . . . The more persistently active we are in working, the more persuaded we may be that all the energizing grace and power is of God.[74]

Additional Notes

2:12 μὴ ἐν τῇ παρουσίᾳ μου μόνον ("not in my presence only"): Most translations appear to construe this clause with the preceding verb (ὑπηκούσατε, "you have obeyed"), so that the word "presence" has reference to Paul's past relationship with the Philippians (cf.

---

74. John Murray, *Redemption: Accomplished and Applied* (London: Banner of Truth, 1961), pp. 148–49. Note also Eadie's fine discussion on pp. 135–38 of his commentary and B. B. Warfield, "On the Biblical Notion of 'Renewal,'" in *Biblical and Theological Studies* (Philadelphia: Presbyterian and Reformed, 1932), pp. 351–74, esp. pp. 363–64. Aquinas, interestingly and helpfully, argues that v. 13 excludes four errors: (1) that man can be saved without God's help; (2) that free will is annulled by fate; (3) that whereas the accomplishing comes from God the choice (the willing) comes from us; and (4) that what God accomplishes He does through our merits. This last error, he adds, is excluded by the expression "for the good pleasure," because "before we get God's grace there is no good merit in us."

Schenk). This reading, reflecting an *ad sensum* construction, may be correct, but the μή (rather than οὐ) would seem to indicate a syntactical connection with the imperative κατεργάζεσθε.[75] This factor leads Hwth. (following Collange) to see a future reference, "not only in light of my anticipated coming," interpreted to mean that the Philippians were exhorted not to be motivated by fear of what Paul perhaps was going to do when he arrived (cf. 1 Cor. 4:21 and 2 Cor. 13:1–3). A future reference is indeed possible, but the text offers no shred of evidence for the idea that fear of the apostle may have been a factor in either his or the Philippians' minds (and can the nuance "in light of" for ὡς be supported with parallels?).

The syntax of this verse is indeed difficult: Codex Vaticanus, followed by other witnesses, smooths things out a little by dropping the ὡς; and Ltf.'s attempt to explain the syntax (whether he is right or wrong) serves to confirm its difficult character. It seems preferable to refrain from specifying the temporal reference in view and to see the clause as a general statement; the ὡς is best explained by the use in Rom. 9:32; 2 Cor. 2:17; Philem. 4 (references given by Ltf. and Vincent as pointing to motivation; cf. also Alford, "not as if [it were a matter to be done] in my presence only"). At any rate, it seems likely that Paul's absence had something to do with the Philippians' problems (see on 1:27 and 2:19–30).

Michael puts forth the interesting thesis that Moses' anticipation of his own death (Deut. 31:27) may have influenced Paul's words. The fact that Paul alludes to Deut. 32:5 in 2:14–15 lends credence to this view, and one is surprised that it has not been picked up by other commentators. Michael presses the allusion when he argues that Paul views his death as imminent (see on 2:17).

μετὰ φόβου καὶ τρόμου ("with fear and trembling"): In support of the sociological understanding of this verse, some commentators argue for a greatly attenuated sense, such as "with respect and reverence for each other." Appeal is made to the fact that Paul's other uses of this word combination (1 Cor. 2:3; 2 Cor. 7:15; Eph. 6:5) deal with human relations. These three instances, however, hardly suggest that Paul could not use the phrase in a Godward sense. Moreover, Pedersen's insightful treatment of these passages (and 2 Cor. 10:5–6) persuasively shows that the phrase is equivalent to having a disposi-

---

75. Pedersen ("Mit Furcht," pp. 4–5) states, without providing sufficient evidence, that such a connection is philologically improbable. All of his references (John 13:9; Gal. 4:18; 1 Pet. 5:2; *2 Clem.* 9:10) contain a nonfinite verb in the background.

tion of obedience to God in light of our weakness (ἐν ἀσθενείᾳ).[76] It is difficult to note the LXX use (esp. Exod. 15:16; Ps. 54:6 [55:5]; Isa. 19:16) and fail to appreciate the tone of solemnity that the phrase lends to Paul's command. The phrase in this context is probably intended to have the same force as 1 Cor. 10:12, "therefore let him who thinks he stands take heed lest he fall" (for other parallels with 1 Cor. 10:1–13, see below on vv. 14–16).

2:13 θεός: The Majority Text, with little early support, includes the article ὁ (the passage is missing in P[46]). The evidence for its omission is very impressive while its inclusion can be readily understood as a scribal addition. On the other hand, the accidental omission of particles is common. In either case, no substantive difference results.

ὑπὲρ τῆς εὐδοκίας ("for His good pleasure"): The fact that the Greek does not have the pronoun αὐτοῦ ("His") has led some to see here a reference to human goodwill in general (as in 1:15). This is out of the question, as Alford makes clear: "the insertion of the article where it is generally omitted from abstract nouns after a preposition, as here, necessarily brings in a reflexive sense,—to be referred to the subject of the sentence."[77] As for the use of ὑπέρ, Vincent appropriately refers to John 11:4 and Rom. 15:8. Conceptually, the phrase is roughly equivalent to εἰς δόξαν θεοῦ ("to the glory of God"), though its distinctive thrust is different. The predestinarian motif behind Paul's use of εὐδοκία is especially stressed by Pedersen, who appeals to Eph. 1:5, 9, 11 and to the focus on divine sovereignty in the parallel reference, 1 Cor. 12:11 (καθὼς βούλεται, "as He wills").[78]

2. BLAMELESS CHILDREN (2:14–16)

Translation

[Let me be more specific: Unlike the Israelites in the wilderness,] you must do everything without grumbling and quarreling. This way

---

76. Ibid., pp. 17–21, esp. p. 21 on Phil. 2:12–21 (however, Pedersen denies on p. 23 that Paul's words are a warning against a false sense of security). It is not clear how Hwth. can appeal to this article in support of his sociological understanding of the phrase.

77. Alford's comments were written to refute the view that this phrase begins a new sentence; such a construction has been adopted sporadically and has little to commend it.

78. Pedersen, "Mit Furcht," pp. 29–30. See also E. Vogt, " 'Peace among Men of God's Good Pleasure': Lk. 2:14," in *The Scrolls and the New Testament*, ed. K. Stendahl (New York: Harper & Brothers, 1957), pp. 114–17.

[my prayer will be answered:] you will *be blameless and pure, yes, children of God who live *without reproach in the midst of crooked and perverse people, among whom you shine like stars in the world by holding fast the word of life. As a result, I will have reason to glory at the day of Christ, [knowing] that I did not run [my spiritual race] in vain nor did I labor in vain.

Exegesis and Exposition

The coherence of the section 1:27–2:18 is confirmed when we note that the call to unity, which was first sounded in 1:27 and then expanded in 2:1–4, reappears here at the conclusion. But now the command is articulated in a quite different fashion. While the background of 1:27 is the conflict caused by opponents who bring suffering to the Christian community, here the setting is described in moral terms—a corrupt generation to which the Philippian Christian community provides a striking contrast. Moreover, whereas the instructions in 2:1–4 focus on the evil and danger of a selfish motivation, here Paul specifies the sin of γογγυσμῶν καὶ διαλογισμῶν (*gongysmōn kai dialogismōn*, lit. "grumblings and disputes"—see Additional Notes).

Now the noun *gongysmos* (corresponding to Hebrew *telûnāh*) and the verb (*dia*)*gongyzō* (Hebrew *lûn*) immediately call to mind the murmuring of the Israelites in the wilderness (Exod. 15:24; 16:2, 7–9, 12, et al.; note also John 6:41, 43, which has Exodus 16 as its background, and cf. Paul's explicit reference in 1 Cor. 10:10). Any doubts that this is the setting that Paul has in mind here are removed when we compare 2:15 with Deut. 32:5, LXX, where the Israelites are described as "spotted children, a crooked and perverse generation."[79] It is most interesting, and surely not a coincidence, that the other passage where Paul uses the experience of the Israelites in the wilderness as an example to motivate proper Christian behavior is 1 Cor. 10:1–13, that is, when writing to a church plagued by dissension.

It may be objected that the murmuring of the Israelites was directed at God, and that the problems in the wilderness are not described in the Bible as consisting of divisions among the people. Yet

---

79. Phil. 2:15: τέκνα θεοῦ ἄμωμα μέσον γενεᾶς σκολιᾶς καὶ διεστραμμένης. Deut. 32:5: τέκνα μώμητα γενεὰ σκολιὰ καὶ διεστραμμένη. (Cf. also Deut. 32:20 and Luke 9:41.) Curiously, Chrysostom sees some significance in the fact that Paul does not explicitly mention the Israelites as he does when writing to the Corinthians (the latter, he thinks, needed a sharper rebuke).

here precisely we may find an important clue to the nature of the Philippians' weakness. The complaining of the Israelites was indeed directed at God, but in the person of His representative Moses. Is it not likely—or even inevitable—that the disputes within the Philippian community involved complaints against the appointed leaders? And would not Paul's clear allusion to the wilderness experience alert the Philippians to the possibility that their behavior could be interpreted as quarreling with God (cf. Exod. 17:1–7)?[80] These must remain intriguing questions, because the letter gives no clear answer. We may, however, point to 2:29 (see comments there) as a possible hint that the church leaders in Philippi were not being treated with full respect.

An additional problem is raised by an apparent lack of exact correspondence between the Deut. 32:5 passage and Paul's application of that passage. In the former it is God's people who seem to be described both as children—spotted children, to be sure—and as a perverse generation, whereas Paul splits the description by applying the term τέκνα (*tekna*, "children") to God's people in Philippi and γενεά (*genea*, "generation"), apparently, to the pagan environment. An answer to this problem must consider several factors:

(1) The Greek of Deut. 32:5 is rather awkward,[81] but the most likely translation is, "They have sinned, they are not His children, they are blemished." In other words, the Israelites' status of sonship is here rejected; this is probably also the force of the Hebrew, which offers its own syntactical difficulties (see the critical commentaries). The idea then fits smoothly with the NT conception that God has shifted His redemptive work from Israel to Christian believers (Matt. 21:43; Rom. 2:28–29; 9:30–31).

(2) Paul certainly does not regard the Philippian believers as a rebellious group who can be described as "a crooked and perverse generation," yet the use of that phrase could serve as a powerful reminder of the dangers created by a disobedient life.

---

80. And does the unusual reference in 1:2 to "overseers and deacons" have anything to do with this possible problem? It should be pointed out that Bonnard, even though possibly correct in suggesting that insubordination is the problem in view, falsely excludes the God-ward reference (cf. also Hwth.). Gnilka appreciates this latter, "theological" sense, but he implies that the Philippians are guilty of complaining directly against God.

81. ἡμάρτοσαν οὐκ αὐτῷ τέκνα μώμετα. The significance of anti-Judaic polemic in the Christian use of the OT was stressed by J. Rendel Harris, "A Factor of Old Testament Influence in the New Testament," *ExpTim* 37 (1925–26): 6–11, esp. p. 8 on Phil. 2:15.

(3) The application of the second part of the phrase to the Gentile world generally (ἐν κόσμῳ, *en kosmō*) may somehow reflect the Pauline understanding of a great reversal in the affairs of Jews and Gentiles (notice, for example, Paul's use of Hos. 2:23 in Rom. 9:25, though the point here is quite different).

(4) In a singularly perceptive comment, Collange notes a possible irony in Paul's application of the phrase: because the Jewish nation has been deprived of its status of sonship, "nothing remains for Israel but to melt away into the 'perverse and straying' mass of the world's . . . humanity."

(5) But we may go a step further and see here an allusion to Paul's Judaizing opponents. In chapter 3 Paul will describe Judaizers as "dogs," a standard way of referring to Gentiles (while Gentile Christians he calls "the true circumcision"—see comments on 3:2–3); perhaps even here these opponents are not far from his mind. The Philippians' stand against their Jewish opponents must not be threatened by a type of behavior that has been characteristic of the Jewish nation throughout its history (cf. Stephen's speech in Acts 7). If this nuance is indeed present in Paul's use of Deut. 32:5 one should nevertheless avoid pressing it, for the explicit reference to the world (*en kosmō*, presumably parallel to *meson geneas*) indicates that the Judaizers are not the primary object in view.

The specific character of Paul's exhortation in v. 14 should not obscure the fact that the apostle couches his words in the context of a more general concern for the Philippians' sanctification. Both the preceding and the following context present the broad panorama of salvation within which the pointed command of v. 14 serves as a hinge. We can best appreciate the conceptual relationship between v. 14 and what follows by noticing how these verses parallel the structure of 1:9–11:

> *exhortation intended to promote unity*
>> the Philippians' love should abound (1:9; command implied)
>> the Philippians should not grumble (2:14)
>
> *statement of goal* (note *hina*): *moral perfection*
>> sincerity, blamelessness, righteousness (1:10–11a)
>> blamelessness, flawlessness, faultlessness (2:15; cf. Hwth.'s transl.)
>
> *eschatological reference*
>> at the day of Christ (1:10)
>> at the day of Christ (2:16)
>
> *ultimate purpose* (introduced with *eis*)
>> God's glory (1:11)
>> Paul's vindication (2:16)

145

Now as we saw in our discussion of 1:9–11, Paul's prayer focuses on the completion of the sanctifying process (though with the clear implication that the Philippians' spiritual progress must manifest itself in their present experience). In contrast, the exhortation of 2:14–16 takes on a certain forcefulness by focusing on the *now* of their Christian life (*meson geneas . . . en kosmō*). Yet even here Paul does not fail to set his sight, and that of his readers, on "the day of Christ."

In addition to his use of terms that indicate moral perfection (for which see Additional Notes), Paul describes the proper conduct of the Philippians with two clauses: "among whom you appear as lights in the world, holding fast the word of life" (so *NASB*).[82] Some ambiguities call for closer attention. For example, there has been some controversy whether the meaning of φαίνεσθε (*phainesthe*) is indeed "appear" (the common meaning of the middle voice) or "shine" (*NIV*; this meaning is normally represented by the active voice). That the middle can bear the sense "shine" seems confirmed by Isa. 60:2 (opp. *skotos*) and Matt. 24:27 (cf. **BAGD**). In fact, Kennedy's comments should have put an end to the controversy: "Surely the appearing of a φωστήρ, a luminary, must be, at the same time, a shining. Both interpretations really converge in this context."

If "shine" is then a proper translation, or at least a sure connotation, one can argue that ἐπέχοντες (*epechontes*) continues the metaphor, though with a new twist: the Philippians shine as they "hold out" (*NIV*) the brilliant word of life. One can just as easily argue that the rest of v. 16 suggests the idea of constancy, for which the translation "holding fast" (*NASB*; cf. *NIV* footnote, "hold on to") is more suitable; we may further support this latter sense by noting that proper moral conduct, not primarily evangelism, is the real point of the passage. (For a completely different understanding of the participle, see Additional Notes.)

One additional ambiguity is whether *phainesthe* should be taken as an indicative (so most versions) or as an imperative ("among whom you must shine"). The latter view was common among the early Fathers and is preserved by Calvin, but it seems awkward to have an imperative within a relative clause, which in turn follows a

---

82. The second clause is a participial construction that should be understood as either epexegetical (that is, explanatory of, and therefore equivalent to, the first clause) or instrumental ("you appear as lights *by holding fast* the word"). The difference between these two is not substantive. Ltf. takes the first clause as parenthetical and construes ἐπέχοντες with γένησθε, but such a move seems quite unnecessary.

purpose clause (cf. Hendriksen). Hwth. argues for the imperative on the grounds that "there would be no purpose" in Paul's "reminding the Philippians of what they are already doing." We must remember, though, that the most basic NT incentive to holy living is an emphasis on what we already are. Paul's marvelous description of believers in v. 15, even of Philippian believers who seem to be faltering, corresponds to the "you have always obeyed" of v. 12. Undoubtedly, the best commentary on Paul's words is Matt. 5:14–16, where Jesus describes His disciples as ones who *already* are "the light of the world," then proceeds with its implication for conduct: "let your light shine before men in such a way that they may see your good works, and glorify your Father who is in heaven."

Jesus' emphasis on God's glory, interestingly, corresponds to the goal expressed in Phil. 1:11 but stands in sharp contrast—or so it appears—with Phil. 2:16b, "that I may have cause to glory because I did not run in vain nor toil in vain." Particularly in view of the close structural and conceptual correspondence between 1:9–11 and 2:14–16, one must wonder how Paul can speak of his eschatological boasting as apparently on the same level with God's glory. It may be helpful to note that v. 16b contains two ideas, both of which find parallels in Paul's other letters: (1) the hope that his converts will be his grounds for glorying at the coming of Christ is found in 2 Cor. 1:14 and 1 Thess. 2:19; (2) the possibility that his work might come to nought (εἰς κενόν, *eis kenon*) occurred to him more than once, as we can see by such passages as Gal. 2:2 and 1 Thess. 3:5 (note also 1 Cor. 9:27 and 15:58). Quite likely, Paul's language reflects the promise of Isa. 65:17–25: when God creates the new heavens and the new earth, His people will rejoice (vv. 18–19) and will long enjoy the works of their toil (v. 22), for their labor will not be in vain (v. 23).[83]

Especially important is the parallel in Phil. 1:20, where the note of glorying is expressed positively with a reference to Christ's exaltation (in Paul's body, to be sure), but negatively with a reference to Paul's avoidance of shame. As noted in the comments there, "shame" means the disgrace of God's judgment, and Paul acknowledges that for him to fail in his ministry would not bring honor to God. We do not have here an exaggerated conception of Paul's self-importance. Rather, we see a man for whom "to live is Christ." His life and work were so identified with Christ, and his ministry—particularly his distinctive Gentile ministry—was such a crucial factor in the work of

---

83. LXX: τὰ ἔργα τῶν πόνων αὐτῶν παλαιωσοῦσιν . . . οἱ ἐκλεκτοί μου οὐ κοπιάσουσιν εἰς κενόν. Cf. also 49:1–4.

Christ's kingdom, that he could speak of his own boasting and of God's glory in the same breath.[84] Moreover, we should note once again in this regard the tension between God's work of grace and Paul's sense of his own responsibility. (The question whether or not Paul may have been uncertain of his ultimate future will receive attention in our discussion of 3:12.)

Additional Notes

2:14 γογγυσμῶν καὶ διαλογισμῶν: We could attempt to represent the plural with such a rendering as "outbursts of complaints and arguments" (cf. Ltf. on θυμοί in Gal. 5:20), but the Greek is not that emphatic. Though BAGD, no doubt correctly, supports the translation "disputing" for διαλογισμῶν (so *NASB;* similarly *NIV,* "arguing"), it must be noted that this meaning is rare. Older commentators suggested such renderings as "speculations," "doubtings," "hesitation"; Huther, commenting on 1 Tim. 2:8 (Meyer's series), argued plausibly for the sense of "deliberations against one's neighbors." The word is found among the papyri in the setting of judicial proceedings (see MM), but this evidence is hardly sufficient to see in the present verse, as Martin argues, a reference to litigations among Christians in pagan courts. Is it possible that Paul's use of the term reflects once more the Israelites' conduct in the wilderness? Note particularly the judicial flavor of Hebrew רִיב (*rîb,* "quarrel") in Exod. 17:2, 7.

2:15 ἵνα γένησθε: The reading ἦτε ("be," instead of γένησθε, "become") has both (proto-)Alexandrian and "Western" support.[85] This variant may be the result of assimilation to comparable passages (e.g., 1 Cor. 5:7; 2 Cor. 9:3; Eph. 5:27; 2 Tim. 3:17; and especially Phil. 1:10), but we could list even more passages in Paul that construe ἵνα with a subjunctive form of γίνομαι. Conceivably, some scribes may have thought that γίνομαι would imply that the Philippians were not yet children of God, but it would be misleading to press the force of "become" in this verb. So even though the textual decision is difficult, the difference between the two variants is not substantive. The verbs in question are certainly interchangeable in some contexts, and the parallel with 1:10 suggests that this is one such place.

---

84. This thought may be present even in 1:11 if P46 gives us the original reading—see Additional Notes on that verse.
85. The Latin versions have *sitis* and this rendering is thought to reflect the Greek ἦτε, but one must allow for the possibility that this Latin verb was seen as a translation equivalent for either Greek verb.

ἄμεμπτοι . . . ἀκέραιοι . . . ἄμωμα: Here again a sharp distinction among these words should probably be avoided. The first and last terms are particularly close. The second term, ἀκέραιοι, has a close semantic connection with εἰλικρινεῖς (used in the Phil. 1:10 parallel). One should hesitate to appeal to the etymology of ἀκέραιοι (α + κεράννυμι = "unmixed") and to conclude that, while ἄμεμπτοι "relates to the judgment of others," ἀκέραιοι "describes the intrinsic character."[86] Rather, we should here invoke the notion of stylistic reinforcement (see Introduction: Language and Style). The Majority Text, supported by "Western" MSS., reads ἀμώμητα for ἄμωμα, possibly by assimilation to the LXX of Deut. 32:5; these terms appear to be virtually complete synonyms.[87]

2:16 λόγον ζωῆς ἐπέχοντες: In addition to the interpretations discussed above, one should note the rendering of the Syriac Version, *ditaykûn lehûn bdûkat ḥayyē*, "because you are to them in place of life." Field argued that this translation is accurate, for it reflects an idiomatic use of ἐπέχω λόγον ("correspond") attested in late Greek authors.[88] In support of this view one could note that the combination λόγον ζωῆς does not occur elsewhere in Paul; further, out of the three other occurrences of λόγον in Philippians (1:14; 4:15, 17), only the first one means "word." These are not strong arguments and so Field's suggestion has been largely ignored; a careful refutation, however, would be helpful before the interpretation is completely forgotten.

3. A PERSONAL APPEAL (2:17–18)

Translation

Nevertheless, [you must not think that I regret my toil and pain:] if matters should worsen so that I will crown the sacrificial service brought about by your faith [or my sacrificial service for your faith] by being poured out as a libation, I still rejoice and share my joy with all of you. In the same way you should rejoice and share your joy with me.

---

86. So Ltf.; cf. Trench, *Synonyms*, pp. 204–9 and 318–22, and his longer essay discussing all three terms (plus ἀνέγκλητος and ἀνεπίληπτος), pp. 379–82.
87. For data on these and cognate terms see Chantraine, *Dictionnaire étymologique*, p. 730.
88. Frederick Field, *Notes on the Translation of the New Testament* (Cambridge: University Press, 1899), p. 194. Cf. Diogenes Laertius 7.155 μέσον τὴν γῆν, κέντρου λόγον ἐπέχουσαν, "the earth is in the middle answering to a centre" (LCL 2:259).

Exegesis and Exposition

Paul's reference in v. 16 to the toil of his ministry was in effect an appeal to the Philippians to consider the spiritual condition of their church as having weighty implications for his apostolic work. Was the apostle thereby manipulating the emotions of his converts by evoking feelings of guilt? Remarkably, here in v. 17 he manages to increase the intensity of that appeal (εἰ καὶ σπένδομαι, *ei kai spendomai,* "if my life should even be offered up in death"—see Additional Notes) while at the same time *encouraging* his converts: happen what may, the Philippians' faith and ministry are already grounds for rejoicing.

For some commentators (esp. Lohmeyer), v. 17 indicates Paul's fear that his death was imminent. Recently, however, other writers have argued that the idea of death is not at all present in this verse. Hwth. and Collange[89] argue that the verb *spendomai* does not have to "denote a killing." Of course not; it only denotes the pouring of a libation (normally wine, not blood) that accompanies a sacrifice. But this objection misses the point altogether, for the allusion to death is not based on the idea that the verb means a killing (or even necessarily a pouring of blood). Second Tim. 4:6 and Ign. *Rom.* 2.2 unquestionably show that the verb's cultic associations made it suitable for use with reference to martyrdom.

It is also argued that a reference to martyrdom is not compatible with the note of joy in this passage. This is a startling objection. Is there anything more characteristic of Philippians than Paul's juxtaposing of joy and adversity? Paul's words in 1:18–20 are particularly relevant here, for that passage too contains a repetition of *chairō* (v. 18), and the joy in view is not affected by the possibility of death (*eite dia zōēs eite dia thanatou,* v. 20).

In short, Paul realistically acknowledges that his apostolic toils and suffering could lead to martyrdom, but he was more than willing to "spend and be expended" for the sake of his converts (2 Cor. 12:15). Nothing in this passage (certainly not the present tense of *spendomai*—see Additional Notes) indicates that Paul in fact expected to die *soon.* Much less can we allow the vividness of Paul's metaphor to nullify the assurance reflected by the verb *pepoitha* in 1:25 and 2:24. Though he certainly seeks to avoid presumptuousness, Paul places his expectations in a positive light.

---

89. Following A. M. Denis, "La fonction apostolique et la liturgie nouvelle en Esprit. Étude thématique des metaphors paulinnienes du culte nouveau," *RSPT* 42 (1958): 617–56, esp. pp. 630ff.

The details of the metaphor present some perplexing questions, such as whether it is Paul or the Philippians who are represented as priests,[90] whether Jewish or pagan sacrifices are in view, etc. Given Paul's stylistic traits, these are probably the wrong questions to ask (cf. Kennedy); at any rate, the text gives no clear answer to them. They do have a bearing, however, on the substantive issue of whether τῇ θυσίᾳ καὶ λειτουργίᾳ τῆς πίστεως ὑμῶν (*tē̦ thysia̦ kai leitourgia̦ tēs pisteōs hymōn*, lit. "the sacrifice and service of your faith") refers to Paul's apostolic ministry or to the Philippians' good works.

The opinion that Paul has in mind his own sacrificial work can be defended by pointing to the emphasis on that ministry in this context and to the fact that in Rom. 15:16 the apostle refers to himself as *leitourgon . . . hierogounta* ("a minister . . . ministering as priest"). In this view, *pisteōs* may be an objective genitive ("on behalf of your faith, resulting in your faith"; possibly faith viewed as the thing being sacrificed—see Alford, Meyer). Just a few verses later Paul will use the term *leitourgia* in reference to the Philippians' gift (2:30; cf. also Rom. 15:27; 2 Cor. 9:12); and at the end of the epistle he will describe that gift as "an acceptable sacrifice" (*thysian dektēn*, 4:18). This evidence suggests strongly that the phrase in question refers to the participation of the Philippians in the gospel, the theme with which the epistle opened (1:5). If so, *pisteōs* is best understood as a subjective genitive, "ministry that springs from your faith" (so Ltf. and Hwth., but see Vincent).

The point is very important, for it reveals the apostle's pastoral heart in affirming the genuineness of the Philippians' Christian commitment. Exhortation they need—even rebuke—but not discouragement. Without the benefit of twentieth-century counseling techniques, Paul recognizes his readers' needs and focuses on their worth in Christ; indeed, he interprets their gift in the best possible light as a source of great and mutual joy (cf. also the comments on 1:7).

But now, if the reason for Paul's joy was the Philippians' sacrificial service, the question arises whether or not the usual understanding of the syntax is accurate. Long ago Ewald argued that the prepositional phrase (beginning with *epi*) should not be construed with what precedes (*spendomai*) but with what follows (*chairō*). The resulting translation, taking *epi* in its common causal function, makes excellent sense: "If I should be poured out, I have reason to

---

90. The latter view was propounded by Ltf., and Vincent strongly defended it: if the ungodly generation should put Paul to death, his "blood would be the libation which would be added to the Philippians' offering."

151

rejoice over your sacrificial service of faith."[91] This construction, however, is a little unnatural, because Paul does not normally place a long prepositional phrase before the verb. A stronger argument against it is that Paul is surely alluding to the cultic terminology of the LXX, where either the verb *spendō* or the noun *spondē* (or both!) may be construed with *epi* (e.g., Gen. 35:14; Exod. 30:9).

Additional Notes

2:17 ἀλλὰ εἰ καί: Strictly speaking, "if even" (though unacceptably awkward) is a more accurate rendering than "even if." The intensive καί affects what immediately follows, and so its position makes a clear difference on how one reads the conditional clause. We may say that εἰ καί focuses on the extremity of the condition, whereas καὶ εἰ stresses the unlikelihood of the condition (in the latter case, it becomes more natural to use ἐάν, as in Gal. 1:8; contrast 6:1); in English, "even if" serves both purposes. In the present case, εἰ καί serves to contrast Paul's hard labors (v. 16) with the extremity of death (it does not necessarily suggest that Paul viewed his death as probable, as Alford supposes). This observation in turn accounts for the contrastive ἀλλά: "Yes, I have labored hard, *but* even death cannot take away my joy."

σπένδομαι ("I am being poured out"): Hwth. argues that the present tense must describe "what is currently happening," for "there is no clue that points to future time." As in Matt. 5:29, the clue lies in the extremity of the condition, which shows that εἰ can be used where ἐάν is more common (BDF §372.3; Hwth.'s reference to BDF §323 is not to the point).

συγχαίρω: The rendering "congratulate" (as in Luke 1:58) was preferred by Ltf. but has not received much acceptance; it seems inappropriate in this context. Kennedy helpfully points to 1 Cor. 12:26. The expression "share my joy" may be imprecise, since the verb (to join in someone else's joy) seems to assume that the other party is already rejoicing. If we press this point, however, the imperative of v. 18 appears superfluous.

---

91. This suggestion has been picked up by several German scholars (including Haupt, Gnilka, Schenk) but completely ignored by English commentaries and versions. Chrysostom possibly understood the connection in the same way (the lemma begins with ἐπί), but his comments are ambiguous with respect to the syntax. Indeed, he links χαίρω with σπένδομαι and συγχαίρω with θυσία!

D. RESUMPTION OF PAUL'S MISSIONARY REPORT (2:19–30)

It is not immediately apparent how vv. 19–30 fit into the literary structure of Philippians as a whole. One approach to the problem is to stress the character of this passage as a typical Pauline "travelogue."[92] Among relevant features we may note, for example, Paul's desire to see the Philippians (v. 26; cf. Rom. 15:23; 1 Thess. 2:17; etc.), his intention to visit the Philippians soon (v. 24; cf. Rom. 15:28; Philem. 22; etc.), and his dispatching of an emissary in the meantime (vv. 19, 23, 25, 28; cf. Col. 4:8; 1 Thess. 3:2; etc.). Since the travelogues often come at the end of Paul's epistles, and since 3:1 is introduced with τὸ λοιπόν (to loipon, "finally"), some scholars identify vv. 19–30 as the closing of the body segment. If this approach should be accepted, one would not feel pressed to find a close connection between these verses and the preceding context.

Quite a different approach, however, is that which reminds us that the travelogue may come earlier in the body of the epistle (see esp. 1 Cor. 4:17–19), and this factor suggests a particular function for the passage *within* the body. Hwth., for example, stresses the way that Paul describes Timothy as one not motivated by selfish interests (vv. 20–22), that is, as someone who models the qualities commended in 1:27–2:18. Swift goes so far as to deny that 2:19 is "a break in the argument of the chapter: it is simply a transition to another link in the chain of reasoning that supports that argument."[93]

Still a third approach is indicated by the title I have given to this section. If we view 2:19–30 as resuming the missionary report of 1:12–26, we may be in a better position to recognize what is most distinctive in the literary structure of Philippians, namely, the prominence that Paul gives to informing the church in Philippi concerning his affairs and plans. Funk has noted that, as a travelogue, vv. 19–30

---

92. The identification of such a discrete unit was first made by Robert W. Funk in *Language, Hermeneutic, and Word of God: The Problem of Language in the New Testament and Contemporary Theology* (New York: Harper & Row, 1966), pp. 264–69; he offers a more extensive and very careful analysis in "The Apostolic *Parousia:* Form and Significance," in *Christian History and Interpretation: Studies Presented to John Knox,* ed. W. R. Farmer et al. (Cambridge: University Press, 1967), pp. 249–68.
93. Robert C. Swift, "The Theme and Structure of Philippians," *BSac* 141 (1984): 234–53, esp. p. 245. Note also R. Alan Culpepper, "Co-Workers in Suffering: Philippians 2:19–30," *RevExp* 77 (1980): 349–58, esp. p. 353, who stresses Paul's need for an example that would illustrate his teaching on the mind of Christ.

appear to be incomplete; his persuasive explanation is that the matter of Paul's presence is integral to the theme of the body and woven into it: "In this case, therefore, it seems legitimate to fill out the apostolic parousia from elsewhere in the letter" (e.g., 1:8, 19, 25–27; 2:12).[94] These factors suggest that we need neither exaggerate nor minimize the break at 2:19. This verse does begin a new thought (contra Swift); the segment 1:27–2:18, what we have called the central section of the letter, has its own coherence. We may readily admit that vv. 19–30 support the thrust of that central section while insisting that the primary purpose of these verses is to give information regarding Paul's plans. To put it differently, the apostle's report (1:12–26; 2:19–30), which brackets the central section, serves as the specific point of reference for both his exhortations and his commendations.

If we now shift our focus to the inner structure of vv. 19–30 themselves, we note two parallel sections, the first one dealing with Timothy (vv. 19–24), the second with Epaphroditus (vv. 25–30). Both sections are commendatory and both appear to discuss the same topic, namely, the sending of Timothy/Epaphroditus to Philippi for the mutual benefit of the Philippians and Paul. For all the similarities, however, more suggestive and exegetically significant is the contrast between the two paragraphs.

With regard to Timothy, Paul says (*twice*, vv. 19, 23) that he wishes to send him soon; and the commendation focuses on Timothy's devotion to, and likemindedness with, the apostle. The sending of Epaphroditus, on the other hand, is described as something "necessary" (ἀναγκαῖον, *anankaion*, v. 25); moreover, Paul emphasizes Epaphroditus's relationship to the Philippians and considers it appropriate (maybe needful) to request that this servant be given a warm and respectful welcome. Indeed, Paul ends by raising the Philippians' consciousness of their obligation to Epaphroditus (vv. 29–30).

It is almost impossible to avoid noting a certain apologetic tone in vv. 25–30, but we are left to reading between the lines. Although several reconstructions are possible, I shall argue that the Philippians, supposing that Epaphroditus could stay with Paul, had counted on a visit from Timothy. Paul's decision to send Epaphroditus in Timothy's stead requires explanation: the apostle first assures them that he does intend to fulfill their wish of seeing Timothy, then he

94. Funk, "The Apostolic *Parousia*," pp. 261–62.

makes a special effort to ensure that, in such an awkward situation, Epaphroditus will be treated with the appreciation he deserves.

1. TIMOTHY (2:19–24)

Translation

I fully expect through the *Lord Jesus to send Timothy to you soon, so that I too may find comfort once I learn how you are doing. [Do not misunderstand my decision not to send him just now:] he is genuinely concerned about your problems. I have made this decision because I have no one so close to me as he is—all others seek their own interests, not those of Jesus Christ. But *you know well his mettle: as a child would relate to his father, so he has served by my side for the furtherance of the gospel. So [you need not worry]: I expect to send him as soon as I have a clearer view of my affairs. And [besides] I am confident in the Lord that soon I myself *will come as well.

Exegesis and Exposition

The conjunction δέ (*de*, v. 19, translated "But" in *NASB*) may be viewed as merely resumptive/transitional; if so, we may render it "Now" or leave it untranslated (*NIV*). If the adversative notion is insisted upon, the contrast may be with v. 17 ("although l face some dangers, I still hope . . ."; so e.g., Meyer, Alford, Vincent) or, better, with the more general matter of Paul's absence, which is such a dominant theme in the epistle (cf. Ltf. and Hwth., though they see here a specific contrast with 2:12).

This passage, at any rate, raises the question whether the Philippians themselves had certain expectations with regard to an apostolic visit. Certainly they hoped to see Paul personally, but we may safely assume that they were not counting on it for the immediate future. Short of that, they may well have expected a visit from Timothy, whose ministry to the Philippians was so closely linked with Paul's (see Introduction: Historical Context). It seems reasonable— though admittedly speculative—to suppose that their voluntary decision to part with Epaphroditus, who could now stay with the apostle and minister to his needs, was intended to free Timothy for such a visit.

Perhaps we find in the word κἀγώ (*kagō*, "I also") a subtle indication of this background. When Paul sent an emissary, the purpose normally was that the church in question may be informed with

regard to Paul's affairs and thus receive encouragement.[95] Here in
Philippians Paul expresses the purpose conversely: "so that I too [or
even I] may be comforted when I learn of your condition" (ἵνα κἀγὼ
εὐψυχῶ γνοὺς τὰ περὶ ὑμῶν, hina kagō eupsychō gnous ta peri hymōn).
The statement takes for granted that the Philippians' benefit was the
main motive for the proposed visit by Timothy. It may well be that
the reason this point is not explicitly stated is that the Philippians
themselves had made the request. Indeed, here we may have one
important reason Philippians was written at all: Paul must respond
to their request.[96]

If this reconstruction has any merit at all, Paul's commendation
of Timothy takes on a new significance. Did the apostle need to prevent a misunderstanding, namely, that he hesitated to send Timothy
because he no longer trusted him? Then again, perhaps he feared that
the Philippians would wonder if Timothy had lost interest in them—
notice the emphasis on the fact that Timothy γνησίως . . . μεριμνήσει
(gnēsiōs . . . merimnēsei "will be genuinely concerned," v. 20). A third
factor is Paul's need of Timothy: formally, the commendation in v. 20
appears to explain why Paul wanted to send him (rather than someone else, note the gar), but in effect Timothy's fine qualities demonstrate why it was necessary (ἀναγκαῖον, anankaion, v. 25) for him to
stay with the apostle. (My translation above attempts to bring out
this point by inverting the order of the clauses.) Finally, as recent
commentators emphasize, Paul needed to send someone who could
help resolve the tensions in the Philippian community.

Our very fragmentary knowledge of the circumstances prevents
us from reaching clear-cut answers; indeed, it is quite possible that
all these factors may have been at work. In any case, Paul took this
opportunity to make some remarkable comments about Timothy.
That the emphasis lies on Timothy's great value for Paul is clear from
the way the commendation ends in v. 22: the Philippians themselves
were witnesses that Timothy "has proved himself" (NIV), particularly by serving alongside the apostle with the faithfulness and affection that one might expect from a son. This unique relationship made
Timothy's presence indispensable to Paul, a thought clearly implied

---

95. ἵνα γνῶτε τὰ περὶ ἡμῶν καὶ παρακαλέσῃ τὰς καρδίας ὑμῶν, Col. 4:8; Eph.
   6:22 (both with reference to Tychicus).
96. Note that such a background makes unnecessary the view that Paul felt
   obligated to commend Timothy because the Philippians had negative
   feelings toward him (cf. Hwth.). The point of the passage is not that Paul
   wants to send Timothy but rather that he cannot send him now.

by the comment that Timothy would leave him as soon as the apostle's own situation became clearer (v. 23).

But what was it about Paul's circumstances that made Timothy's presence so important? A common answer among commentators is that the apostle was uncertain about his judicial fate and wanted to wait until that matter was decided. Hwth. properly argues against this interpretation on the basis of v. 24. A better approach is to focus on the first part of the commendation (vv. 20–21) and to note that Timothy's worth is highlighted by contrasting him with others who were not "of like spirit" (ἰσόψυχον, *isopsychon*, see Additional Notes) and who "seek after their own interests."

Those words may have a double reference. Indirectly, they serve as an additional rebuke to selfish members of the Philippian community. More directly, they remind us of Paul's difficult circumstances, described in 1:12–17. In that passage, Paul's emphasis on the positive effects of his imprisonment should not keep us from recognizing the serious conflict and grievous adversity that he was experiencing (cf. 1:29–30). Although we are ignorant of the details, we may safely surmise that Paul's situation called for the support that only a confidant such as Timothy could provide. (In a later and even more serious predicament, at a time when Paul felt deserted and his death seemed imminent, he would write to Timothy: "Make an effort to come to me quickly" [2 Tim. 4:9].)

Paul's promise to the Philippians, then, was that Timothy would come to them as soon as possible, that is, when the apostle's circumstances became more stable (v. 23). However, lest the Philippians interpret his words in a purely negative way, as though he were in imminent danger, he reassures them, much as he had done earlier (1:23–26), by expressing forcefully (πέποιθα ἐν κυρίῳ, *pepoitha en kyriō*, "I am persuaded in the Lord," v. 24) his expectation to visit Philippi in the near future.

Additional Notes

2:19 ἐλπίζω δὲ ἐν κυρίῳ Ἰησοῦ: The verb is repeated in v. 23, while the phrase ἐν κυρίῳ is used in connection with πέποιθα in v. 24. In normal English usage, the verb *hope* implies a measure of doubt, but this is not necessarily the case with ἐλπίζω, particularly since the noun ἐλπίς takes on a charged theological nuance in the NT. Schenk, by pointing out the various linguistic parallels between v. 19 and vv. 23–24, argues for the contextual synonymy of ἐλπίζω and πέποιθα here. If there is any semantic distinction, perhaps one could argue that the former verb, in this context, indicates intention (could we

157

translate, "I expect"?). The reference to the Lord at the beginning and end of this paragraph adds solemnity to Paul's words and may be a further indication of the delicacy of the subject. (Instead of κυρίῳ, the "Western" MSS. D* F G, with scattered support, read Χριστῷ, perhaps because Paul does not use the title "the Lord Jesus" as frequently as he uses other combinations.)

2:20 ἰσόψυχον: The *NASB* rendering, "of kindred spirit," is very appropriate in that it preserves something of the vagueness of the Greek while favoring the most reasonable interpretation, namely, likemindedness *with Paul* (with probable reference to his love for the Philippians; cf. Chrysostom). Others prefer the idea, "I have no one else like him" (so *NIV*), which is possible but hardly necessary (Ltf.'s argument that otherwise ἄλλον or πλὴν τούτου would be required has little substance). Nothing in the text argues against seeing a reference to Paul, while the emphasis on the father-son relationship (v. 22) strongly supports such a reference.

ὅστις γνησίως τὰ περὶ ὑμῶν μεριμνήσει: A number of commentators, appealing to the father-son relationship mentioned in v. 22, interpret the adverb γνησίως according to its etymology, that is, with the nuance of "legitimacy," but this seems rather doubtful; the rendering "genuinely" or "sincerely" is unexceptionable. The literal translation of the future verb μεριμνήσει (as in *NASB*, "will genuinely be concerned") could mislead the modern reader; however we choose to explain the tense, a present rendering is justified (cf. *NIV*, "who takes a genuine interest").

2:21 οἱ πάντες γὰρ τὰ ἑαυτῶν ζητοῦσιν: The phrase is equivalent to τὰ ἑαυτῶν σκοποῦντες in 2:4 (see comments there). Quite remarkable is Paul's accusation that "all" (οἱ πάντες) were motivated by self-ishness. Clearly he cannot mean this in an absolute sense. At the very least, Epaphroditus must be excluded from such a group; it is also very unlikely that the brethren described in 1:14 belong in this category. A common way of restricting the statement is to say that it refers only to those who were available as possible emissaries (see especially Hendriksen's discussion). There is probably some truth in that, but it is not completely satisfactory, since Epaphroditus too served as an emissary. We need to admit that Paul uses a measure of hyperbole here (cf. Collange). Moreover, we should recall that Paul's primary concern in commending Timothy was not (as it may formally appear) to show his qualifications for such a trip but to persuade the Philippians that he was needed at the apostle's side. Epaphroditus, who did not share the intimacy of one who had labored with Paul for an extended period of time, stood in a different category altogether.

2:22 γινώσκετε: P⁴⁶ reads οἴδατε, a variant that conforms with the Pauline pattern of using the verb οἶδα with ὅτι. In this verse, however, the verb also rules a direct object (τὴν δοκιμήν), and in such cases Paul seems to prefer γινώσκω.⁹⁷

2:23 ἐξαυτῆς: The translation "immediately" (cf. *NASB*) is quite misleading, because the point is precisely that Timothy cannot be sent right away; the words "as soon as" sufficiently reproduce the idea conveyed by the whole clause.

2:24 ἐλεύσομαι: The addition of the words πρὸς ὑμᾶς has respectable textual support but looks suspicious (it smooths out the sense by completing the thought of the verb).

2. EPAPHRODITUS (2:25–30)

Translation

So I have found it necessary [not to grant your request but] to send to you Epaphroditus, my brother and co-worker and fellow soldier, who is also your emissary [sent as] a minister for my need. [I have made this decision] because he has been *longing for all of you. He was also in distress, since you heard that he was ill. [The report was true;] indeed, he was so ill that he came close to death. But God had mercy on him—and not on him only but also on me, lest I should have grief added upon grief. I have therefore sent him with all the greater dispatch, so that you may see him again and rejoice and I for my part may be relieved of my anxiety. So welcome him in the Lord with all joy and hold men like him in esteem, because it was for the work *of Christ that he came near death, *having risked his life so that he might do what you could not have done without him: bringing to completion your ministry to me.

Exegesis and Exposition

It has already been noted above that Paul's commendation of Epaphroditus seems to carry an apologetic overtone and that, possibly, the passage reflects a certain awkwardness: Was Epaphroditus a consolation prize, sent simply because Timothy, whom the Philippians expected, had to stay with Paul? Against this reconstruction,

---

97. Cf. Silva, "Pauline Style," p. 201.

one could argue that Paul gives quite a different reason for having "thought it necessary" to make this decision: Epaphroditus was greatly distressed about his separation from the Philippians (v. 26). But the two reasons were not mutually exclusive; rather, they coincided in demonstrating the reasonableness of Paul's decision. In any case, v. 26 focuses on the deep emotional attachment between Epaphroditus and the Philippian church, a point further stressed in v. 28—the Philippians will have cause for joy when they see him again.

Paul uses two forceful expressions in describing Epaphroditus's emotions. The linking of the verb ἐπιποθέω (*epipotheō*, "to long for") directly with the personal pronoun (contrast Rom. 1:11; 1 Thess. 3:6; 2 Tim. 1:4) is worthy of note, since Paul uses the same construction in 1:8 to describe his own feelings toward the Philippians (cf. also 2 Cor. 5:2; 9:14). Moreover, Epaphroditus's longings were accompanied by mental distress, a condition that Paul describes with an infrequent and vivid term, ἀδημονέω (*adēmoneō;* the only other NT occurrences of this verb are found in the Gethsemane pericope, Matt. 26:37; Mark 14:33).

Somewhat surprisingly, this distress is attributed to Epaphroditus's knowledge that the Philippians had heard about his illness. Once again, our ignorance of the circumstances prevents us from appreciating fully the nature of his concern. Barth suggests that Paul was seeking to interpret Epaphroditus's immature homesickness in the best possible light. Buchanan supposes that Epaphroditus was grieving because he had sent a false alarm to the Philippians and feared that they would try to send him relief.[98] Other interpretations are possible, but none certain. What seems clear is that Epaphroditus's personal need—or sense of responsibility—to return was serious. Providentially, this set of circumstances dovetailed with Paul's own need to keep Timothy at his side.

In his commendation, Paul confirms that the reports about Epaphroditus's illness were correct. Indeed (καὶ γάρ, *kai gar*, v. 27), his condition was more dangerous than the Philippians probably realized, for he nearly died. It is noteworthy that Paul makes this point thrice in vv. 27, 30: he was close (παραπλήσιον, *paraplēsion*) to death;

---

98. C. O. Buchanan, "Epaphroditus' Sickness and the Letter to the Philippians," *EvQ* 36 (1964): 157–66, esp. p. 160. Bernhard Mayer ("Paulus als Vermittler zwischen Epaphroditus und der Gemeinde von Philippi, Bemerkungen zu Phil 2, 25–30," *BZ* 31 [1987]:176–88) argues persuasively that Paul wishes to prevent a conflict between Epaphroditus and the church.

he came near (ἤγγισεν, ēngisen) death; he risked his life. One can hardly avoid the impression that Paul needed to prevent a possible misunderstanding when the Philippians saw, not Timothy (whom they had expected?), but Epaphroditus, safe and sound. Had they grieved in vain over his health? Had he been unable to fulfill his mission? Had the whole project been a fiasco?

Absolutely not. In fact, his illness was directly tied to fulfilling the Philippians' mission (v. 30). The implication seems to be that, in spite of the illness, which must have struck him during his journey, Epaphroditus pressed on at the risk of his life (cf. Introduction: Historical Context). Perhaps his condition had greatly deteriorated by the time he reached Rome, and his life hung in the balance for a while. Paul, who was already bearing some heavy burdens, must have anguished over the possibility that this work of mercy might turn into a new source of grief (v. 27).

But God showed Himself merciful and now the apostle, with joy, exalted Epaphroditus: he did what he did "for the work of Christ" (v. 30); he was not only a brother, but also Paul's "co-worker and fellow soldier" (v. 25), a description that does not necessarily refer to any previous association but may indicate just how highly Paul regarded Epaphroditus's faithfulness in fulfilling the Philippian mission. This mission he gratefully acknowledges as a priestly service (λειτουργία, leitourgia, v. 30; note leitourgos in v. 25; see comments on 2:17; 4:18), and Paul wanted to make sure that Epaphroditus was received with the honor he deserved (v. 29).

Additional Notes

2:25 ἀναγκαῖον δὲ ἡγησάμην ("But I considered it necessary"): The verb here, as well as ἔπεμψα in v. 28 (but certainly not πέμψαι in v. 25, as Martin would have it—the infinitive does not indicate past tense at all), is correctly understood by most commentators as an epistolary aorist: the action is viewed as past, according to the perspective of the recipients when they read the letter (cf. Col. 4:8; Philem. 12; BDF § 334 has some inaccuracies; cf. the fuller discussion in Rob., p. 845). If so, Epaphroditus should be viewed as the bearer of the letter. *NASB* and *NIV* attempt to convey the force of δέ with the phrase "who is also."

ὑμῶν . . . ἀπόστολον: Hwth.'s suggestion that Paul uses this word to stress Epaphroditus's equality with him seems fanciful. The very fact that Epaphroditus is described as the *Philippians'* (not Jesus Christ's) apostle makes all the difference; the nontheological sense of "envoy" (as in 2 Cor. 8:23) is surely intended. And yet, the combination of this term with λειτουργός, "[priestly] minister," is probably designed as the highest of commendations.

2:26 ἐπιποθῶν ἦν πάντας ὑμᾶς: Both the Alexandrian and the "Western" traditions are divided in their support of this reading over against the insertion of ἰδεῖν ("he was longing to see you all"). The probability that the omission is supported by P⁴⁶ and by a corrector of Sinaiticus in the original scriptorium,⁹⁹ added to the weight of the Majority Text (which is normally characterized by additions), decisively tips the scales in favor of taking the omission as original. The verb ἰδεῖν must have been added very early on the analogy of Rom. 1:11, etc.

2:28 σπουδαιοτέρως: Hwth. makes the provocative suggestion that this comparative adverb should be taken with the sense "sooner than expected" (see his translation on p. 114). Because the text does not specify the point of reference for the comparison (cf. comments on ἀναγκαιότερον in 1:24 and ὑπερύψωσεν in 2:9), Vincent's rendering commends itself: "with the greater dispatch." Vincent's understanding corresponds closely with Hwth.'s, which we may use to support the reconstruction suggested above: the Philippians did not expect to see Epaphroditus so soon—they wanted Timothy.

πάλιν: We should probably construe this adverb with ἰδόντες (against Ltf. and others). There is no contextual reason to do otherwise.

κἀγὼ ἀλυπότερος ὦ: The _NASB_ translation "less concerned" is much too weak, particularly because the allusion is to λύπην ἐπὶ λύπην in the previous verse (moreover, the addition of "about you" is gratuitous). Hwth. properly translates, "and I may be relieved of anxiety" (cf. _NIV_). Several ideas have been suggested as to why the

---

99. Both of these points are debatable. As for P⁴⁶, it appears that the scribe by mistake repeated πέμψαι πρὸς ὑμᾶς from the previous line (actually the repetition of πέμψαι cannot be ascertained). It is no doubt for this reason that NA does not list the support of P⁴⁶ for either reading. The _UBSGNT_ apparatus, however, is almost certainly correct in deducing that ἰδεῖν is omitted in this MS. More complicated is the witness of Codex Sinaiticus. A corrector, by placing a series of dots above the verb, indicated that ἰδεῖν should be omitted. But which corrector is this? _UBSGNT_, following Tischendorf, assigns this change to a late set of correctors, while NA assigns it to one of the scribes originally involved in the production of the MS. H. J. M. Milne and T. C. Skeat, in _Scribes and Correctors of the Codex Sinaiticus_ (London: British Museum, 1938), devote chapter 6 to a detailed examination of the correctors. To judge by one of the photographs in figure 15, the manner of placing the dots (such as we have at Phil. 2:26) is identified by these authors as the work of the late corrector Cᵃ. Perhaps the editors of NA have more accurate information.

sending of Epaphroditus would have had this effect on Paul. The only indication in the text itself, however, is the emotional duress that Epaphroditus was experiencing as long as he did not return to Philippi (v. 26).

2:29 ἐν κυρίῳ: According to Chrysostom, the force of these words is either "with much zeal" or "God willing."

2:30 τὸ ἔργον Χριστοῦ: It was a valid insight that led Ltf. and Lohmeyer to follow the lone authority of C in reading τὸ ἔργον by itself without a modifying genitive. The discovery of P[46], however, makes this position no longer tenable, for the three-pronged support of (τοῦ) Χριστοῦ by (proto-)Alexandrian (P[46] B 1739), "Western" (D F G Old Latin Vulg), and Byzantine witnesses is overwhelming.

παραβολευσάμενος τῇ ψυχῇ: The *KJV* reads "not regarding his life," reflecting the Majority Text variant παραβουλευσάμενος, but ancient testimony is decisively against it. Harrington C. Lees claimed to find further support for the verb παραβολεύομαι, which appears to have had gambling connotations, in the "striking" correspondence it provides with the meaning of the name Epaphroditus: "charming," because blessed by the goddess of fortune, Aphrodite, therefore "fortunate, lucky."[100] That Paul intended such a pun is possible but very unlikely. The only support Lees gives for his understanding of this name is that Sulla, in celebration of his political triumphs, adopted it as a translation of Felix, "fortunate," but even this incident had nothing to do with gambling.[101] Moreover, the verb παραβολεύομαι and the more common adjective παράβολος and verb παραβάλλομαι seldom if ever are used with explicit reference to gambling; the metaphorical senses of "risk, peril, venture," etc., are dominant.

ἵνα ἀναπληρώσῃ τὸ ὑμῶν ὑστέρημα τῆς πρός με λειτουργίας: The *NASB* renders "to complete what was deficient in your service to me," but this translation suggests, quite misleadingly, that Paul is being critical of the Philippians. (That the word ὑστέρημα need not imply a negative judgment is clear from Col. 1:24, "I complete *what is lacking* in Christ's afflictions.") Possibly we have here an allusion to the fact that, previously, they had lacked opportunity to minister to the apostle (see comments on 4:10).

An interesting parallel is 1 Cor. 16:17–18, where Paul exhorts the Corinthians to "acknowledge" (that is, show appreciation for) three

---

100. Harrington C. Lees, in the column "Entre nous," *ExpTim* 37 (1925–26): 46.
101. See Appian *The Civil Wars* 1.97 (LCL, *Appian's Roman History* 3:179); more fully Plutarch *Sulla* 34 (LCL, *Plutarch's Lives* 4:433–34).

representatives from the church at Corinth who, in coming to visit him, had made possible what the church set out to do (τὸ ὑμέτερον ὑστέρημα οὗτοι ἀνεπλήρωσαν). Whatever the precise import of this reference, Paul's use of the word ὑστέρημα was intended to remind the Corinthians of their dependence on, and debt owed to, these emissaries. We find a similar concern here in Phil. 2:30, except that the "lack" is specifically identified with reference to the Philippians' contribution; they could not have fulfilled their good work without Epaphroditus's devotion to it.

Interestingly, *1 Clem.* 38:2 uses the same expression in a different sense: the poor man should thank God that He has provided a rich man "through whom his lack might be supplied" (δι᾽ οὗ ἀναπληρωθῇ αὐτοῦ τὸ ὑστέρημα). This reference suggests that it might have seemed natural for Paul to speak about his own lack being supplied by Epaphroditus and the Philippians (as in 2 Cor. 11:9, τὸ ὑστέρημά μου προσανεπλήρωσαν), but he prefers to focus on the advantage that accrues *to the giver* (see further on 4:17).

4
Doctrinal Polemics (3:1–4:1)

Chapter 3 of Philippians is without dispute a singularly powerful passage—a foundational building block for theology and a true classic of Christian spirituality. But what is its place in the structure of the letter as a whole? This question, rather basic for the proper interpretation of the passage, admits of no easy answers. In the view of many scholars, the shift in tone and content is inexplicably abrupt, suggesting that 3:2–4:1 constitutes a separate document that has been interpolated by a later redactor.[1] This position finds literary support in the τὸ λοιπόν (*to loipon*, "finally") of 3:1, which appears to introduce the concluding section of the letter; indeed, skipping from 3:1 to 4:4 (or even to 4:2) results in a rather smooth reading. As Schmithals puts it: "Verses 3:1 and 4:4 fit together so exactly that upon sober reflection one must come to the conclusion that a later hand has pulled the two verses apart."[2]

---

1. According to E. J. Goodspeed (*An Introduction to the New Testament* [Chicago: U. of Chicago, 1937], pp. 90–91), "there is between 3:1 and 3:2 a break so harsh as to defy explanation. In 3:1 all is serene. . . . But in the next verse he breaks out against the Judaizers with an intensity unsurpassed even in Galatians." For the argument that modern scholarship has exaggerated the apostle's change of tone see B. S. MacKay, "Further Thoughts on Philippians," *NTS* 7 (1960–61): 161–70, esp. pp. 163–64.
2. Walter Schmithals, *Paul & the Gnostics* (Nashville: Abingdon, 1972), p. 72.

The main difficulty with this analysis is that the very arguments used to support it speak against the probability that a redactor is responsible for the text as it stands. If it is difficult to believe that Paul would have written in such an abrupt manner, it is even more difficult to accept that a later editor would have been so inept as to disturb a supposed original passage that fitted together "exactly." Why should he have *created* the abruptness when it was completely unnecessary for him to do so? Why not introduce the extraneous material at a less awkward point (e.g., after 1:30 or 2:18)?

The question of the epistle's integrity lies on the boundary between textual and literary criticism.[3] From a text-critical perspective we should note, first, that there is no manuscript evidence supporting the view that chapter 3 is an interpolation. In other words, this view must be regarded as a *conjectural emendation*. Second, the principle of transcriptional probability speaks against such an emendation, for the "harder" (but not impossible) reading is the text as we have it. In other words, we cannot find a persuasive motive that would induce some later editor or copyist to create this stylistic difficulty.

But the theory also fails from the perspective of literary criticism. It has often been noted that chapter 3 contains some significant parallels with the rest of the epistle, such as the *structural* similarities between 2:6–11 and 3:7–10 (see below), the pointed references to the cross in 2:8 and 3:18, and the concept of citizenship in 1:27 and 3:20. This last example is strengthened when we note the likelihood that the two verses bracket a major section by means of a literary *inclusio* (*politeuesthe . . . stēkete* in 1:27 and *politeuma . . . stēkete* in 3:20; 4:1).[4]

The case against the integrity of Philippians, therefore, is not nearly as strong as is often suggested. And yet, we must not minimize

---

3. Cf. in this regard Harry Gamble, Jr., *The Textual History of the Letter to the Romans: A Study in Textual and Literary Criticism* (SD 42; Grand Rapids: Eerdmans, 1977), which includes a brief discussion of Philippians on pp. 143–44.
4. See the Introduction: Literary Integrity, particularly the reference to Garland's persuasive article on "The Composition and Literary Unity of Philippians." One need not, however, accept Garland's explanation of the function of chapter 3 to appreciate the force of his overall argumentation. Specifically, I am not convinced that "the digression in 3:1–21 is a deliberate rhetorical device intended by Paul to affect his audience prior to the direct, emotional appeal in 4:2" (p. 173). On the other hand, his article as a whole decisively places the burden of proof where it belongs: on the side of those who claim that the letter as we have it does not hang together as a literary unit.

the abruptness at the beginning of chapter 3. To say, for example, that (*to*) *loipon* does not necessarily introduce the concluding section of an epistle is technically correct (cf. 1 Cor. 7:29; 1 Thess. 4:1). But in this passage we have a combination of features that requires explanation. To begin with, the phrase is followed by ἀδελφοί μου, χαίρετε ἐν κυρίῳ (*adelphoi mou, chairete en kyriō,* "my brothers, rejoice in the Lord"), which closely parallels 2 Cor. 13:11 (*loipon, adelphoi, chairete*).[5] Moreover, this phrase occurs right after the travelogue, which normally comes toward the end of the letter (but see above, introduction to 2:19–30). We should admit, at the very least, that there is a slight anomaly here—this feature may be one more evidence of the ease with which Paul adapts literary conventions.

On the other hand, we may leave open the possibility that Paul had indeed intended to bring the letter to an end at this point and that for some reason decided against it. Does not the second part of 3:1 suggest that the apostle had been weighing in his mind the advantages and disadvantages of repeating material (τὰ αὐτὰ γράφειν, *ta auta graphein,* "to write the same things") that he had previously communicated to the Philippians?[6] It is perhaps not too farfetched to speculate that Paul stopped writing or dictating after the words *chairete en kyriō;* by the time he returned to the document he had decided he must include a doctrinal discussion, just to be safe (ἀσφαλές, *asphales*). We may be grateful he did.

This doctrinal section admits of a threefold division. Verses 1–6

---

5. Garland ("Composition," p. 149) argues that the verb in 2 Cor. 13:11 simply means "good-bye," whereas here in Philippians (where it is joined to ἐν κυρίῳ) it must retain the meaning "rejoice." But this argument drives too sharp a wedge between the two senses. The fact that in 2 Cor. 13:11 χαίρετε is followed by other imperatives surely indicates that the meaning "rejoice" is not absent even there. Conversely, the fact that "rejoice" is the predominant thought in Philippians hardly excludes the nuance of farewell.

6. This suggestion, I think, satisfactorily answers Schmithals' complaint (*Paul & the Gnostics,* p. 72) that anyone changing so abruptly the tone and content of the letter would give a reason for the change (e.g., "I have just had news of such-and-such"). My explanation, insofar as it arises from 3:1*b*, is therefore not purely imaginary. (Cf. Gunther's discussion in *Paul,* p. 87.) I readily admit, to be sure, its speculative character, but it should be noted that one need only present *plausible* (not necessarily probative) explanations for the only attested form of the text we have. At any rate, one of the great mysteries of modern scholarship is how a proponent of radical and unverifiable conjectures can think of objecting to, and indeed deriding, any attempts to account for the text by means of "psychological speculations."

set the context for the polemics by pointing out the Judaizing threat. Over against this heresy, Paul summarizes the distinctives of his theology in vv. 7–11. The rest of the chapter may be viewed as Paul's attempt to apply these theological concerns to the Philippian situation.

A. JUDAIZERS AS THE CONTEXT FOR THEOLOGY (3:1–6)

The heading chosen for this section is intended not only as a description of Paul's approach in this letter, but as a reminder that the apostle regularly gives expression to his theology in response to false teaching and that the Judaizing groups constituted the main front of Pauline opposition. Even the epistle to the Romans, which appears to many a calmly reasoned dissertation, must surely be understood as a set of answers to the kinds of objections the Judaizers had been advancing for years against Paul's gospel of justification by grace through faith. (The subsequent history of the Christian church, we may add, illustrates in detail how God's people come to a clearer understanding of the truth when they are confronted with error.) In this particular passage Paul launches an attack on the Judaizers (vv. 2–3), and that leads to an apparent boasting of his "spiritual credentials" prior to his conversion (vv. 4–6).

1. PAUL ON THE OFFENSIVE (3:1–3)

Translation

Finally, my brothers, rejoice in the Lord. [There is a matter, however, about which I must remind you.] Writing to you again about the same things is certainly not troublesome for me, while for you it is a safeguard. [So I do not mind repeating:] keep your watch for those [who claim to be spiritually pure but are unclean] dogs, whose works [are not good as they proclaim but rather] evil, whose [ritual practices must be characterized as] mutilation. [Yes, their insistence on fleshly circumcision is a perversion,] for we [believers in Jesus] are the [true people of God], circumcised in the heart—we who worship *by the Spirit of God and place our boast in Christ Jesus while placing no confidence in the flesh.

Exegesis and Exposition

The strong words of v. 2 are reminiscent of Paul's language in portions of 2 Corinthians (e.g., 11:13–15) and especially Galatians (1:8–9; 5:12; 6:12–13). In both of those letters the objects of Paul's attack were not unconverted Jews but rather false teachers who identified themselves with the broad Christian community; the same appears to be true here in Philippians. Hwth. follows the view that the opponents were non-Christian Jews, but this is highly unlikely, because it has not been characteristic of Jewish people to pressure Gentiles to be circumcised. Moreover, as we shall see, the view that the Philippians' opponents were Judaizers (Jewish Christians who wanted Gentile Christians to become Jews in practice) fits very well the contents of chapter 3 as a whole. In any case, Paul warns the Philippians to be on guard (βλέπετε, *blepete*—see Additional Notes) against these dangerous opponents.

To appreciate the force of v. 2, we need to realize that Paul's language is not accurately described with such terms as "insulting" or "abusive." Paul has carefully chosen his terms to achieve intense irony, not merely to use derogatory speech. The very first item clearly illustrates our problem, for the pejorative sense of the English *dog* is normally applied insultingly to people considered worthless and vulgar. For the Jews, however, the term had a distinctly religious sense: it referred to the Gentiles, those people who, being outside the covenant community, were considered ritually unclean. When Jesus drew a comparison between the Syro-Phoenician woman and dogs (Mark 7:27), the woman recognized the analogy not as a vulgar insult but as a religious statement. Paul, therefore, is making a startling point: the great reversal brought in by Christ means that it is the Judaizers who must be regarded as Gentiles (cf. the comments on 2:15–16).

This theme is further developed with the next two descriptions. The phrase τοὺς κακοὺς ἐργάτας (*tous kakous ergatas*) does not merely indicate "people who do bad things" or "sinners." The phrase is surely meant to refute the Judaizers' claims that they were doing the works of the law (*erga nomou*; cf. Gal. 3:10; 5:3; 6:13). Genuine good works are done only by true believers (2 Cor. 9:8; Eph. 2:10; Col. 1:10). The Judaizers were earthly-minded false brothers, whose teaching led to the works of the flesh (Gal. 2:4; 5:13–21; Phil. 3:18–19). In this way too they were spiritual Gentiles.

The third phrase is a scathing description. These Judaizers, the apostle argues in effect, do not deserve to be called "the circumcision"[7] but rather "the mutilation" (κατατομή, *katatomē*). For the sake of clarity, the *NASB* translates "the false circumcision," but Paul

---

7. Paul can use the term περιτομή of Jews generally without the pejorative nuance (Gal. 2:7–9; Col. 4:11).

intends more than that. When Jewish rituals are practiced in a spirit that contradicts the message of the gospel, these rituals lose their true significance and become no better than pagan practices. For the Gentile Christians of Galatia, the adoption of Jewish ceremonies was tantamount to becoming enslaved all over again to their pre-Christian rituals (Gal. 4:9). Moreover, Paul's reference to mutilation in Gal. 5:12 may be, among other things, an allusion to barbaric pagan customs. Here in Philippians Paul takes the Judaizers' greatest source of pride and interprets it as the surest sign that they have no share among God's people.

Continuing this line of thought, Paul draws the antithesis sharply by affirming that Christian believers have now become the true Jews: "it is we who are the circumcision" (v. 3, with the pronoun ἡμεῖς, *hēmeis*, in an emphatic position). This conception is exceedingly important for Paul, who was often accused of rejecting the OT message (cf. Acts 21:21). The epistle to the Romans in particular is intended to answer that charge by arguing that the gospel, far from opposing the OT, fulfills it.[8] Similarly, chapter 3 of Galatians is devoted to proving that those who are united to Christ through faith are the true seed of Abraham (see esp. vv. 7, 29; cf. also 6:16, "the Israel of God," though the significance of this phrase is disputed). In accordance with this basic Pauline conception, the polemic of Philippians 3 begins with an unequivocal assertion of the great spiritual reversal: Judaizers are the new Gentiles, while Christian believers have become the true Jews.[9]

Worthy of note is the way in which Phil. 3:3 describes the distinctive qualities of the true people of God. While any of several descriptions would be valid, Paul chooses in this passage to call attention to three features, two of them positive and the last one negative. First, Paul identifies God's people as those "who worship in [*or* by] the Spirit of God." Whatever the differences between Pauline and Johannine theology, one can hardly deny that this phrase is conceptually equivalent to John 4:23–24 (true worshipers worship God "in the Spirit and in truth"). In neither passage, however, is the point being made that true worship is inner rather than external (so Hwth.

---

8. The gospel was promised by the prophets (Rom. 1:2); it was witnessed by, and establishes, the law (3:21, 31); circumcision of the heart, not of the flesh, makes one a Jew (2:28–29); Abraham's true children are those who, circumcised or not, follow the footsteps of his faith (4:11–12).

9. Cf. the full discussion by Ridderbos, *Paul*, chap. 8, and most recently Anthony Tyrrell Hanson, *The Paradox of the Cross in the Thought of St Paul* (JSNTSup 17; Sheffield: JSOT, 1987), pp. 89–97.

et al.). The reference is surely to the eschatological significance of the Holy Spirit's outpouring. The coming of Christ, in other words, has ushered in the new age of salvation, and the Holy Spirit is the sign of this redemption.[10] Those who belong to Christ are part of the new order (2 Cor. 5:17); they have the Spirit and are thus able to offer worship that is pleasing to God (Rom. 8:8–9; 12:1).

In the second place, God's people "glory in Christ Jesus." The real force of this phrase can best be appreciated by contrasting it with the third descriptive clause, "put no confidence in the flesh." Although the verbs "to glory" (καυχάομαι, *kauchaomai*) and "to have confidence" (πέποιθα, *pepoitha*) are not precisely synonymous, they may nevertheless be said to occupy the same semantic field when Paul uses them to point out the object of faith. To believe in Jesus Christ is to put one's confidence in Him; but if Jesus Christ is our grounds for confidence, He is therefore also our grounds for joyful pride and for exultant boasting. (Similarly Calvin; cf. also my comments on 1:26.)

The exact opposite of this attitude is that which places confidence in the flesh (σάρξ, *sarx*), that is, in oneself, in one's natural achievements. "For in the term 'flesh' he includes everything external in man that he could glory in, as will appear from the context; or, to express it briefly, he calls 'flesh' everything that is outside Christ" (Calvin). Hwth., however, is also right in suggesting that "Paul seems to cast at least a passing glance at the rite of circumcision" (p. 127; cf. Gal. 6:12–13). The circumcision of the flesh, as preached by the Judaizers, became for Paul the symbol of a total mindset that is opposed to the Spirit and leads to death (Rom. 8:5–8; Gal. 5:16–21).

Additional Notes

3:1 τὰ αὐτὰ γράφειν ("to write the same things"): This clause is often taken as a reference to Paul's "repeated appeals to joy" (Hwth.), whereas Martin prefers to link it with the preceding passage ("the same things" that Epaphroditus will describe when he delivers the epistle). The difficulty with the first interpretation is in trying to explain why an appeal to joy should be described as something "safe" to do (Hwth.'s attempt seems forced). As for Martin's view, nothing in the text indicates that Epaphroditus was commissioned to deliver a message. As suggested in the comments above, it seems better to link τὰ αὐτά with the passage that follows. On the reasonable assumption that Paul had on previous occasions expounded his theology to the Philippians, he expresses a mild apology for going

---

10. Cf. Ridderbos, *Paul*, sections 11, 12, 38 and passim.

over familiar ground. (Cf. in this regard Gal. 5:21, καθὼς προεῖπον, and possibly 1:9, ὡς προειρήκαμεν.)

3:2 βλέπετε (lit. "see"): The threefold repetition of this verb, the use of alliteration (κυνάς, κακούς, κατατομήν), the studied irony of the passage, and several other features make this section a striking example of Paul's rhetorical power (see Hwth., p. 123).

Kilpatrick argues that βλέπω, when used with the accusative, nowhere clearly means "beware of" (that nuance, he claims, resides in the accompanying preposition ἀπό or the particle μή); that the simple meaning "consider, take note" is preferable here; and that therefore the connection of this verse "with what has gone before is not as abrupt as is usually assumed."[11] In the references listed by him where the verb is followed by a μή clause, however, that clause simply completes the thought partially expressed by the verb (if the thought is made explicit by a direct object, such a clause is unnecessary). The English "watch the fire" usually implies a warning, such as "lest it burn up the house." Schenk (who refers to Lohmeyer and BDR §149) rightly sees no difficulty in taking the imperative as a warning.

The present imperative is often (but inconsistently) used with reference to action already in progress. Even though the rendering "keep/continue watching" must be regarded as an overtranslation, I have adopted something comparable in my paraphrase because the context does indicate that Paul is repeating a warning he had previously addressed to the Philippians.

τοὺς κακοὺς ἐργάτας: By linking this phrase to the parallel in 2 Cor. 11:13 (ἐργάται δόλιοι, "deceitful workers"), Koester sees here a reference to missionaries whom Paul regarded as malicious laborers.[12]

3:3 οἱ πνεύματι θεοῦ λατρεύοντες ("who worship by the Spirit of God"): This reading is attested by all the major textual families, and its grammatical difficulty (it has no expressed object) suggests originality. The reading θεῷ is easier ("who worship God in the Spirit") and therefore suspect, particularly because its external support is

---

11. G. D. Kilpatrick, "βλέπετε Philippians 3₂," *In Memoriam Paul Kahle*, ed. M. Black and G. Fohrer (BZAW 103; Berlin: Topelmann, 1968), pp. 146–48. He is followed by Caird, Hwth., and esp. Garland ("Composition," pp. 165–66), who argues that no external opponents are in view and that the words reflect no anger.

12. H. Koester, "The Purpose of the Polemic of a Pauline Fragment (Philippians III)," *NTS* 8 (1961–62): 317–32, esp. p. 320. Note the sharp critique of Koester's thesis by Schmithals, *Paul & the Gnostics*, pp. 118–20.

inferior. The omission of the noun in P⁴⁶ is tantalizing, but this reading is best explained as another instance of carelessness by the scribe (see Introduction: Textual History).

2. MOCK BOASTING (3:4–6)

Translation

[Do not misunderstand my words:] I myself have plenty of reasons to place confidence in the flesh. Indeed, if anyone else thinks he has reason to place confidence in the flesh, I have much more: circumcised [in strict accordance with the law] on the eighth day, a pure Israelite, from the tribe of Benjamin—[in short,] a Hebrew of the Hebrews. Moreover, I was a Pharisee with regard to the interpretation of the law, I proved my zeal by persecuting the church, [and I was so scrupulous] with regard to the righteousness set forth in our Jewish law that I was never found to be at fault.

Exegesis and Exposition

Starting a new paragraph with v. 4 may appear strange. As far as the syntax is concerned, the first clause of that verse (lit. "though I myself have confidence even in the flesh") is joined, though somewhat loosely, to v. 3. Conceptually, this division can be justified, since v. 4*a* in effect introduces Paul's "boasting" in vv. 4*b*-6. The quotation marks are needed around this word because the apostle will quickly proceed to tell us that the virtues enumerated here constitute a spiritual liability (vv. 7–8).

Why then mention them at all? In a remarkable passage, 2 Cor. 11:16–12:11, Paul felt compelled by the circumstances in Corinth to point out his apostolic credentials, but his poignant hesitations in that passage confirm that he reckoned any such defense to be mere foolishness (2 Cor. 12:7, "I have become a fool; you yourselves compelled me"). The situation in Philippi, though in some respects markedly different from what Paul faced in Corinth, may have been partially analogous. The Judaizers who threatened the Philippian community no doubt appealed to their impressive Jewish credentials in support of their message. With considerable reluctance, and not for purely rhetorical effect, Paul felt pressured to remind the Philippians that his own background was second to none.

There is, however, an important difference between the two passages. In 2 Corinthians Paul's object is to demonstrate his apostolicity (rather than his Jewishness) in the face of personal attack. Here in Philippians the listing of credentials has a more direct theological purpose—to serve as a foil for his exposition of the Christian message in vv. 7–11.

As most commentators have pointed out, the seven clauses of vv. 5–6 naturally fall into two groups: the first four items describe privileges that Paul acquired simply by virtue of his birth, while the last three focus on voluntary choices of his own. (Moreover, the second group of clauses is marked by the syntactical parallelism of the repeated *kata*.) Most of the items are self-explanatory, and Ltf. emphasizes the logical progression characterizing the first four: (1) circumcision on the eighth day sets Paul apart from pagans and from groups that may have performed circumcision in an invalid way; (2) the claim to being "of the nation of Israel" distinguishes him from proselytes, that is, from converts to Judaism, sometimes perceived as "second-class"; (3) because even a true Israelite might belong to a disreputable tribe, Paul also points out his Benjamite descent (cf. Hwth.); (4) finally, his family could not be accused of having adopted Hellenistic ways—he was "a Hebrew of Hebrews" (see Additional Notes).

As an adult, Paul continues, he chose a religious life-style that left no doubt with regard to his commitments. Significantly, the matters he brings up in this context parallel clearly his claims in Gal. 1:13–14, where the Judaizing opposition forms the backdrop for Paul's comments (though in that passage the precise point is different). Here in Philippians he first indicates that the particular approach he chose for his interpretation of the law was that of the Pharisees. This perspective, which emphasized the "ancestral traditions" (Gal. 1:14; this phrase corresponds to the rabbinic Oral Law), was widely perceived as the one most faithful to Scripture; the Judaizers, at any rate, could not have asked for anything more impressive. (Cf. Acts 22:3; 23:6; 26:5; see also the Additional Note on v. 6.)

In the second place, Paul proves the sincerity and intensity of his prior religious commitment by using "an expression of intense irony, condemning while he seems to exalt his former self: '. . . I persecuted, imprisoned, slew these infatuated Christians; this was my great claim to God's favor'" (Ltf.). The language in Gal. 1:13 is more forceful: "I used to persecute intensely the church of God and tried to destroy it."

The last clause in v. 6 has caused a great deal of discussion: lit. "according to the righteousness which is in the law having become faultless." Paul can hardly be claiming that he was sinless—or even that prior to his conversion he thought he was sinless. Such a concept was quite foreign to Jewish theology; moreover, no reasonable reading of Rom. 7:5–11 is consistent with it. But having said that, some exegetical questions remain. What is "the righteousness which is in the law" (δικαιοσύνην τὴν ἐν νόμῳ, *dikaiosynēn tēn en nomǭ*)? And how do we define "faultless" (ἄμεμπτος, *amemptos*)? Moreover, does this expression tell us anything about Paul's sense of guilt in connection with his conversion?

Let us consider this last question at once. In an article that has had considerable influence during the past two decades, Krister Stendahl argued that "in Protestant Christianity . . . the Pauline awareness of sin has been interpreted in the light of Luther's struggle with his conscience," whereas in fact "it is exactly at that point that we can discern the most drastic difference between Luther and Paul." A major piece of evidence for Stendahl is Phil. 3:6 where, he claims, "Paul speaks about his subjective conscience."[13]

But Stendahl's interpretation of this verse, I am convinced, is exactly wrong. Paul's statement is in fact quite irrelevant to the question regarding his conscience. The apostle is countering the Judaizers' claims by showing his *credentials;* all of the items listed are accessible, objectively verifiable claims. It would be almost pointless to introduce a subjective, and therefore greatly biased, judgment at the very end. The point is rather that anyone interested could have "checked the record" and found that Paul had never been charged with transgressing the law. Consequently, no one could argue that his conversion to Christianity was attributable to prior failure in his Jewish life-style.

If we recognize this factor, our other two questions can be answered much more easily. The word "faultless" does not at all reflect any illusion regarding sinlessness; rather, it must be viewed as a fairly standard way of expressing exemplary conformity to the way of life prescribed by the OT. One thinks particularly of Zacharias and Elizabeth, who are described as "walking in all the commandments and requirements of the Lord without fault [*amemptoi*]" (Luke 1:6).

We could use the word *external* to characterize the obedience in view, but unfortunately that term has come to suggest mere formality or even hypocrisy. Such a negative connotation is certainly not in view either in Luke 1:6 or in Phil. 3:6. Yet in both cases the

---

13. Krister Stendahl, "The Apostle Paul and the Introspective Conscience of the West," *HTR* 56 (1963): 199–215, esp. pp. 200–201. For an important critique of Stendahl's position see John M. Espy, "Paul's 'Robust Conscience' Re-examined," *NTS* 31 (1985): 161–88, esp. p. 166; Paul was faultless "in the quantifiable Pharisaic sense."

obedience is external in the sense that it is the only kind that can be observed by human beings and thus verified. "Paul, then, was in the judgment of men holy and free from all blame" (so Calvin, who distinguishes between literal and spiritual righteousness). Accordingly, "the righteousness which is in the law" describes an *observable* standard of conduct, that is, the righteous way of life prescribed by the OT. This peculiar form of expression anticipates the deeper issue that the apostle is about to discuss: Is such a way of life identical with the righteousness that God requires? The answer will be given in v. 9.

It must be added that when the apostle speaks about the law, he has in mind not the law in a historical vacuum but rather the law as it was understood and used in first-century Judaism. Calvin goes so far as to say: "Paul uses the word 'law' loosely for the teaching of religion, however much corrupted it was at that time, as Christianity is today in the Papacy." Without drawing the distinction that sharply, we must recognize that Paul had just spoken in v. 5 of his prior commitment to Pharisaism as providing the proper understanding of the law. To accept such an interpretation could easily lead to a false sense of spiritual achievement, for in some important respects rabbinic exegesis relaxed the divine standard.[14] Poignantly, the "rich young ruler" of the synoptics (Mark 10:17–27) exemplifies what inevitably happens when God's requirements are brought down to our level: a frightful unawareness that our own efforts are quite inadequate to win God's favor.

Additional Notes

3:4 καίπεϱ: According to Hwth., the clause introduced by this particle begins a new sentence and Paul does not complete it: "Although I have good reasons for putting confidence in myself. . . ." Hwth. then supplies the ellipsis with the additional words, "I will not do so." There seems to be little reason, however, to depart from the common punctuation: a comma at the end of v. 3 with a period at the middle of v. 4, so that the participial clause in question is viewed as dependent on the main clause of v. 3.

3:5 Ἑβϱαῖος ἐξ Ἑβϱαίων: This phrase appears to have a climactic intent and thus could be understood in the sense of "pure-blooded"; certainly a denial that he had any mixed ancestry would fit in well with the previous items, which focus on qualities related to his birth.

---

14. Cf. my article, "The Place of Historical Reconstruction in New Testament Criticism," in *Hermeneutics, Authority, and Canon*, ed. D. A. Carson and J. W. Woodbridge (Grand Rapids: Zondervan, 1986), pp. 109–33.

Most writers, however, see in this phrase a reflection of the Hebrew/Hellenist distinction (cf. Acts 6:1). "Hellenistic Judaism" normally designates Jews of the Dispersion (living outside Palestine) who adopted Greek as their language and whose way of life reflected their non-Jewish surroundings. This generalization can be very misleading, because many Hellenistic Jews were distinguished by their orthodoxy (while numerous Palestinian Jews were thoroughly Hellenized). Having been born and reared in Tarsus, however, Paul might have been suspect in this regard, and so here he makes it clear that his family upbringing was irreproachable.

3:6 δικαιοσύνην τὴν ἐν νόμῳ: This phrase is only one of several Pauline remarks about the Torah that have caused considerable controversy. Implicit here (and explicit elsewhere) is a "criticism" of the Torah that is difficult to reconcile with Paul's positive remarks in other passages. If Paul's negative comments refer to the OT law without qualifications, we face an unbearable tension within the pages of Scripture. In an attempt to escape this dilemma, some writers have argued that νόμος for Paul can be shorthand for Jewish legalism. Though this interpretation contains a measure of truth, it seems exegetically improbable, and the theological inferences drawn from it are disturbing.[15] As pointed out in the exposition above, Paul surely has in mind the OT law (not first-century Judaism as a distinct entity), but just as surely his negative remarks *reflect* the way that law was handled by his Jewish opponents.[16]

γενόμενος: *"having carried it so far . . .* that human judgment finds *nothing in me to blame in this respect!"* (Meyer).

B. THE ESSENCE OF PAULINE THEOLOGY (3:7–11)

Having made clear in vv. 4–6 that he had not been a failure in Judaism, the apostle now proceeds to give an account of his conver-

---

15. The theory in question has been forcefully propounded by Daniel P. Fuller, *Gospel and Law: Contrast or Continuum* (Grand Rapids: Eerdmans, 1980), pp. 87–88. Cf. also Kenneth L. Barker, "False Dichotomies between the Testaments," *JETS* 25 (1982): 3–16, esp. pp. 9–10. For a critique, see the review of Fuller by Douglas J. Moo in *TrinJ* 3 NS (1982): 99–103.

16. See esp. Ridderbos, *Paul*, p. 154; for a different perspective see the fine article by Douglas J. Moo, " 'Law,' 'Works of the Law,' and Legalism in Paul," *WTJ* 45 (1983): 73–100. The number of publications dealing with this question has become an uncontrollable torrent, but Moo has provided a helpful review in "Paul and the Law in the Last Ten Years," *SJT* 40 (1987): 287–307.

sion. In vv. 7–8 he explains that he came to view his previous successes as spiritual bankruptcy. This assessment leads to a succinct description of his doctrine of justification (v. 9), his experience of sanctification (v. 10), and his hope of glorification (v. 11). The cogency of this summary—to say nothing of its impact on the reader—is what warrants the heading for this section.

Paul, no doubt, would have been the first to protest that the gospel he proclaimed is too rich to be reduced to a few sentences. But if such a feat could be accomplished, the passage before us would be it. Profoundly theological yet intensely personal, these verses ban any attempts to characterize the gospel as *either* doctrine or life. Although we have here doctrinal teaching, the reader is hardly aware of the abstractions involved, so naturally and effectively does Paul allow that teaching to flow out of his spiritual experience.

A further indication of the character of this passage is the way it appears to echo 2:5–11. The sequence of privilege-death-exaltation suggests such a connection, and this is confirmed by explicit verbal parallels: *hēgeomai* (2:6; 3:7–8), *morphē* (2:7; *symmorphizō* 3:10), *heuriskō* (2:7; 3:9), *kyrios* (2:11; 3:8). When one further considers that the Christ-hymn itself blends crucial theological concepts with acute practical concerns, a clearer picture develops regarding the function of 3:7–11 in the argument of the letter. The enemies of the cross (3:18) pose a practical threat to a weakened Christian community that is already in danger of becoming schismatic. Paul's prescription is doctrine: understand the content and character of your faith, he says, and you will stop being intimidated by the barking of your opponents.

1. SPIRITUAL BANKRUPTCY (3:7–8)

Translation

*[Nevertheless,] whatever category of virtues used to be my assets, these very things I have learned to consider a loss for the sake of Christ. *Let me be clearer: I continue to consider everything [achieved in the flesh] to be a loss for the sake of the incomparable value of knowing Christ Jesus my Lord. It is for His sake that I have willingly sustained the loss of all things—indeed I consider them no better than dung so that I may gain Christ.

Exegesis and Exposition

It has become common in recent biblical scholarship, when referring to Paul's Damascus experience, to emphasize its character as a call (cf. Gal. 1:15) and to tone down the element of conversion.[17] It is true of course that Paul understood his experience as a divine calling; and it is also true that he did not view his new commitment as an abandonment of the God of Israel. But Phil. 3:7–8 leaves no doubt that Paul's submission to Christ constituted a conversion in its deepest sense. These verses repeatedly set a negative evaluation of his prior way of life against a positive description of his new experience:

The Old Life	*The New Life*
these I have reckoned a loss	for Christ
I reckon all things loss	for the value of knowing Christ
I have lost all things	for whom [i.e., for Christ]
I reckon them dung	that I may gain Christ

If we focus on the items under the left column, we notice a significant progression of thought; clearly, Paul expresses with increasing intensity his sense of dissatisfaction with those things that had previously been most important to him. For example, the direct object in v. 7, ἅτινα (*hatina*, "whatever things," reinforced with ταῦτα, *tauta*, "these things"), becomes πάντα (*panta*, "all things") in v. 8. We need not absolutize the meaning of *panta* to appreciate its full force. The thrust of the word is clearly established by the context: everything on which Paul might place his fleshly confidence. Because v. 8 begins with a very emphatic combination of five particles,[18] it is clear that Paul intends to reiterate his point in the most forceful terms possible.

One can also detect a note of progression in the shift from the perfect tense ἥγημαι (*hēgēmai*, "I have considered," v. 7) to the present ἡγοῦμαι (*hēgoumai*, "I consider," used twice in v. 8). To be sure, the perfect tense itself is hardly devoid of reference to the present,[19] but given the clear contrast between vv. 7 and 8, Paul appears to be exploiting the distinction: "Don't think I regret my decision—even now I continue to regard every one of those virtues as nothing." Schenk notes the lexical connection with 2:3 and with the various

---

17. Cf. Helmut Koester, *Introduction to the New Testament.* Hermeneia: Foundations and Facets. 2 vols. (Philadelphia: Fortress, 1982), 2:100.
18. ἀλλά, μεν, οὖν, γε, καί, though καί is omitted by some MSS.
19. Cf. BDF § 340–42. K. L. McKay, "On the Perfect and Other Aspects in New Testament Greek," *NovT* 23 (1981): 289–329, summarizes the use of the perfect by saying that it "normally describes a state as either present . . . or timeless" (p. 296). Understandably, Meyer denies that Paul intends a contrast in the tenses here. On the other hand, Schenk views Paul's use of the present as an emphatic transition complementing the perfect.

occurrences of _phroneō;_ Paul is speaking about a deep-seated resolution and frame of mind.

In addition, we have the most striking progression of all in the change from the noun ζημία (_zēmia,_ "loss," vv. 7 and 8a) to the verb ζημιόω (_zēmioō,_ passive "to suffer damage," v. 8b) to the potent noun σκύβαλα (_skybala,_ "refuse, waste," v. 8c). Most commentators point out, rightly, that the term _zēmia_ itself is rather emphatic; apparently drawing on commercial terminology (but see Additional Notes), Paul tells us that he now regards his previous "assets" (κέρδη, _kerdē_) not merely as without worth but as positively damaging, as spiritual "liabilities." "In the process of reevaluation [Paul] perceived with horror that the things he had hitherto viewed as benefiting him had in reality been working to destroy him because they were blinding him to his need for the real righteousness which God required" (Hwth.).

And yet the apostle goes even further: what he once regarded highly he now finds revolting. There is no need to downplay the meaning of _skybala_ with such equivalents as "rubbish" (_NASB, NIV_); while such a meaning is attested (cf. Sir. 27:4—the Greek term could be used of various kinds of filth), a specific reference to _excrement_ is not uncommon and the _KJV_ rendering "dung" is both appropriate and probable.[20] One must be careful, however, not to conclude that Paul regarded Jewishness in itself as revolting; his sense of identity with his people, as well as passages like Rom. 3:1–2; 9:1–5, make clear that he continued to appreciate the great value of his heritage.

It was, therefore, not the heritage as such that he revolted against, but the viewing of that heritage as a human right or achievement, thus obscuring one's need for full dependence on God's grace. It is difficult not to see here an allusion to Isa. 64:6: "all our righteous deeds are like filthy rags." Moreover, there is some evidence that the ancients understood _skybalon_ as deriving from _to tois kyni ballomenon,_ "that which is thrown to the dogs."[21] Since popular ety-

---

20. Chrysostom, without any awareness of controversy, takes the word to mean "manure," though he argues that the description need not be taken in an exclusively negative sense: "But as the dung was useful in its former state [the chaff], so that we gather it together with the wheat, and had there been no dung, there would have been no wheat, thus too it is with the Law." Schenk accepts the reference to excrement yet thinks that Paul's point has nothing to do with revulsion but rather worthlessness (cf. English slang _crap_).
21. See esp. Ltf., p. 149. On the role of popular etymology cf. Silva, _Biblical Words,_ p. 50.

mologies play a significant role in the use of language, and because Paul had earlier (v. 2) referred to his opponents as "dogs," we may have here a veiled reference to the Judaizers.

If we now refer back to the chart represented above and focus on the right column, we notice a comparable progression of thought, especially in the three phrases where the name of Christ is expressly mentioned. The first one (v. 7) is simply διὰ τὸν Χριστόν (*dia ton Christon*, "for the sake of Christ"), but in v. 8 it is expanded to "for the sake of the incomparable value of knowing Christ Jesus my Lord."[22] The significance of this idea for Pauline theology will be discussed in connection with v. 10. One should note here, nevertheless, the forcefulness of Paul's language. Ltf. points out a similar expression used by Paul in 2 Cor. 3:10 where the apostle speaks of the glory of the old covenant as being no glory at all in comparison with the ministry of righteousness. Knowing Christ overshadows anything else that might have been considered a gain. Paul had no regrets about having forsaken the source of his earlier pride, for nothing could compare with the knowledge of his Lord.

Finally, Paul expresses the purpose of his conversion with the clause ἵνα Χριστόν κερδήσω (*hina Christon kerdēsō*, "in order that I may gain Christ"). Considering the vocabulary of vv. 7–8 as a whole, it seems reasonable to find here an echo of Jesus' words, "What profit will a man have if he gains [*kerdēsē*] the whole world and suffers the loss [*zēmiōthē*] of his life?" (Matt. 16:26 and parallels). That question in turn is closely related to the parables of the hidden treasure and of the pearl (Matt. 13:44–46); the protagonist in each of these parables "sells all he has" for the sake of a priceless possession. Whether Paul was familiar with these sayings—and if so, whether he alluded to them deliberately—cannot be demonstrated. In any case, Paul's own experience constitutes a dramatic illustration of the truth taught by our Lord. Paul recognized the radical antithesis between his former way of life and the new hope offered to him; it was either one or the other. What was required was not a mere adjustment or the incorporation of an additional element—only a total conversion would be adequate. And Paul gladly forfeited his personal achievements to obtain the pearl of great price.

---

22. That Χριστοῦ ᾽Ιησοῦ is an objective genitive (as opposed to the subjective genitive, "Christ's knowing," with "me" as the implied object) is confirmed by v. 10, τοῦ γνῶναι αὐτόν.

Additional Notes

3:7 ἀλλά: The conjunction is omitted by some early Alexandrian
and "Western" witnesses (P⁴⁶, the original hand of Sinaiticus, A, G,
etc.). The verse seems to cry out for a transitional particle,²³ but this
very fact may have led scribes to add the conjunction. Hwth. argues
that the lack of a conjunction serves to stress the radicalness of Paul's
change of outlook. On the other hand, P⁴⁶ is characterized by omissions of this sort (see Introduction: Textual History); moreover, the
corrector of Sinaiticus who added the conjunction belonged to the
original scriptorium, and one must allow for the possibility that he
corrected the MS. on the basis of the master-copy. Since the reading
of these two MSS. thus becomes suspect, the weight of B, D, and the
vast majority of witnesses takes on considerable importance. A firm
decision seems impossible, and the *UBSGNT* editors are wise in including the conjunction within brackets. (Cf. also the omission of καί
in v. 8.)

κέρδη ... ζημίαν ("gain ... loss"): That these terms could be
used in the context of business practices is clear; what is not so clear
is whether or not such a connotation was normally present when the
terms were used in more general contexts (the corresponding English
terms, for instance, can often be viewed as dead metaphors). In support of the view that Paul is indeed exploiting the metaphor is the
repeated use of commercial terms in 4:14–15 (see comments there).
Meyer sees some significance in the shift from plural to singular:
"This *one* disadvantage he has seen in *everything* of which he is
speaking."

διὰ τὸν Χριστόν: Hwth. objects to the rendering "for the sake of
Christ" (*NASB, NIV*, etc.) because it suggests that Christ benefited by
Paul's decision. Such an inference is completely unnecessary, however, because "for the sake of" (like διά with the accusative in Greek)
may indicate the goal of one's actions, as in Plato, *Republic* 524c: the
mind contemplates the great and the small distinctly διὰ τὴν
σαφήνειαν, "for the sake of clarity" (where there is of course no reference to benefiting the object of the preposition). Paul's threefold use
of διά in vv. 7–8 indicates the reason for which he has counted his
former benefits as nothing. It was with a view to gaining Christ that
he changed his way of thinking; the last clause of v. 8 (ἵνα κερδήσω
Χριστόν) unambiguously makes explicit the thought of the previous
clause (cf. Ltf.)

---

23. Indeed, Gnilka says that the "ἀλλά setz den Wendepunkt."

3:8 ἀλλὰ μενοῦνγε καί (paraphrased above with "Let me be clearer"): It is not easy to reproduce the force of the Greek. The combination μεν οὖν itself "presents a considerable diversity of usage."[24] Thrall argues persuasively that the basic combination ἀλλὰ καί (and ἀλλά γε καί in Luke 24:21) is progressive; the addition of μενοῦνγε must therefore be seen as an emphatic reinforcement. This conclusion affects the text-critical question of whether or not the καί is original. This conjunction, like ἀλλά in v. 7, is omitted by P[46] (the document is defective at this point, but there is clearly no room for the conjunction), by the original hand of Sinaiticus, and by the later Alexandrian witnesses 33 and 1739. We must follow Thrall in her judgment that the omission "is obviously an attempt [but not necessarily deliberate?] to simplify what appears at first sight to be an extremely cumbersome group of particles."[25] She properly refers to the ἀλλὰ καί of 1:18 as a close parallel. As we noted in that verse, however, Paul did not merely introduce an additional element; he needed to explain his response to adversity. Similarly in 3:8 the transition may be viewed as explanatory or even mildly corrective: "Do not infer from what I have just said that my decision was limited or temporary—there is much more to it." (The *GNB* rendering—"Not only those things; I reckon everything as complete loss"—overemphasizes the shift from ἅτινα to πάντα, but this understanding is supported by Meyer.)

τῆς γνώσεως Χριστοῦ Ἰησοῦ: A good deal of scholarly discussion has focused on the meaning of γνῶσις in Paul, particularly the question of whether the term should be understood within the context of Hellenistic religions or not. The BAGD gloss, "personal acquaintance with," is generally accepted by scholars, regardless of their position on that debate.

2. SPIRITUAL WEALTH (3:9–11)

Translation

[What do I mean by "gaining" Christ? I want] to be found in union with Him, [that is, I want] to have not my own righteousness,

---

24. J. D. Denniston, *Greek Particles.* 2d ed. (Oxford: Clarendon, 1954), p. 470. For μεν γε and μεν γοῦν see pp. 159–61. For Demosthenes's use of corrective μεν οὖν see p. 479.
25. Margaret F. Thrall, *Greek Particles in the New Testament: Linguistic and Exegetical Studies* (NTTS 3; Grand Rapids: Eerdmans, 1962), pp. 11–16, esp. p. 15.

which comes from the law, but the righteousness that comes through faith in Christ, God's own righteousness based on faith. [My goal then is] to know Him, namely, [to experience] the power [that was manifested in and that arises from] His resurrection, and * to participate in His sufferings by being molded in accordance with His death—hoping that I may yet reach the resurrection * from the dead.

Exegesis and Exposition

It is somewhat artificial to break up 3:7–11 at the end of v. 8, particularly because the last words of v. 8 begin a purpose (*hina*) clause that is continued without grammatical interruption in v. 9. Conceptually, however, there is something to be gained by distinguishing these two subsections. As we have seen, vv. 7–8 may be viewed as consisting of four clauses, each of which points out both what Paul has lost and what he stands to gain. The emphasis clearly falls on the negative side: the apostle is intent on asserting that his previous achievements had yielded spiritual bankruptcy. On the other hand, vv. 9–11 focus exclusively on the positive side. The gains to which he had alluded in the previous verses are here expanded in considerable detail. It is perhaps not too farfetched to view the initial καί (*kai,* "and") of v. 9 as epexegetic of the last clause in v. 8: Paul is about to explain what it means to gain Christ.

A striking feature of this passage is the way it reflects a distinction among the three basic categories present in the application of salvation: justification (righteousness through faith, v. 9), sanctification (experiencing the power of Christ's resurrection as well as participating in His sufferings, v. 10), and glorification (bodily resurrection, v. 11). Some will no doubt object that this threefold classification is an artificial construct deriving from systematic theology and that it should not be imposed upon Paul's teaching. We may readily agree that in the apostle's writings these terms have a broader use than they have in modern dogmatics, that several other terms serve to highlight various aspects of salvation (calling, forgiveness, reconciliation, adoption, etc.), and that an exclusive preoccupation with the major loci of systematic theology could distort the Pauline teaching.

On the other hand, one could argue (from this very passage) that the categories of systematic theology themselves derive from Scripture. As may be expected of any scholarly discipline, of course, theological terms are given a more restricted or specialized meaning than they often have in the biblical text.[26] Actually, however, it is the

---

26. Cf. the exposition of 2:6–8, esp. n. 32.

Pauline corpus that has provided most of the material for a systematic doctrine of salvation. And in spite of many modern claims to the contrary, there is a basic consistency between Paul's teaching and the classic soteriological formulations, as the following exegesis will seek to demonstrate.

a. *Justification* (v. 9). It is possible that the long participial clause of v. 9 is structured in the form of a chiasm (cf. Schenk):

> *mē echōn*
>   *emēn*
>   *dikaiosynēn*
>   *tēn ek nomou*
>   *alla tēn dia pisteōs Christou*
>   *tēn ek theou*
>   *dikaiosynēn*
>   *epi tē̦ pistei*

> not having
>   my
>   righteousness
>   the one out of the law
>   but the one through faith in Christ
>   the one out of God
>   righteousness
>   upon faith

The central thrust of this verse finds expression in the clause τὴν ἐκ θεοῦ δικαιοσύνην (*tēn ek theou dikaiosynēn* "the righteousness [that comes] from God"). The shorter expression *dikaiosynē theou* provides the keynote to the epistle to the Romans (1:17; 3:5, 21ff.; and passim). Some contemporary scholars have argued that the classic Protestant conception of a righteousness imputed to the believer by God has little to do with Paul's concern. Instead, we are told, the phrase refers to a divine attribute: God's own faithfulness and power in preserving his creation.[27] Such a meaning, however, is out of the question here

---

27. This conception was articulated very forcefully by E. Käsemann in the early 1960s and is summarized in his *Commentary on Romans* (Grand Rapids: Eerdmans, 1980), pp. 24ff. The most persuasive argument for this view is Richard B. Hays, "Psalm 143 and the Logic of Romans 3," *JBL* 99 (1980): 107–15, though he makes no attempt to account for the connection between δικαιοσύνη θεοῦ and Paul's use of the verb δικαιόω. Elsewhere (see *New Testament Questions of Today* [Philadelphia: Fortress, 1969], p. 169) Käsemann himself seems to acknowledge the distinct force of Phil. 3:9. Should not the unambiguous reference in this passage provide a dominant perspective for the interpretation of the ambiguous construction in Romans?

in Phil. 3:9. Not only (1) the presence of _ek_, but also (2) the contrast with "a righteousness of my own derived from the Law," (3) the conception that God's righteousness is something we may have (ἔχων, _echōn_), and (4) the clear concern of the passage with personal salvation—all of these factors support conclusively the traditional interpretation.

It is very important to note the explicit opposition between the righteousness that comes from God (_ek theou_) and that which comes from the law (_ek nomou_). Clearly, Paul conceives of the two as mutually exclusive. Why does he? As has often been pointed out, there is a close relationship between the concepts of righteousness and life in Paul's writings (cf. Rom. 1:17; Gal. 3:11); one could almost define the one in terms of the other. But since the law cannot give life (Gal. 3:21), then any "righteousness" proceeding from the law is worthless.[28]

Moreover, Phil. 3:9 gives a pejorative description of such a righteousness by calling it ἐμήν (_emēn_, "mine," that is, of the flesh, vv. 3–4); therefore our own righteousness is mutually exclusive of God's.[29] In short, Paul has given up his own efforts toward becoming righteous through the works of the law. Instead, he now looks outside himself for the righteousness that only God, the righteous judge, can grant—a righteousness that is received διὰ πίστεως Χριστοῦ (_dia pisteōs Christou_, "through faith in Christ"), or ἐπὶ τῇ πίστει (_epi te pistei_, "on the basis of faith").

The translation "through faith in Christ" here and elsewhere in Paul has been disputed from time to time, and in recent years there has been a flurry of publications arguing against it. In particular it

---

28. For quite a different conception, cf. E. P. Sanders, _Paul, the Law, and the Jewish People_ (Philadelphia: Fortress, 1983), esp. p. 140. After drawing a comparison between 2 Cor. 3:10 and Phil. 3:9, Sanders argues that the distinction between the two righteousnesses of which Paul speaks is not one "between merit and grace, but between two dispensations. . . . It is this concrete fact of _Heilsgeschichte_ . . . not the abstract superiority of grace to merit" that renders the righteousness of the law worthless and the righteousness of God valid. (Cf. also Heiki Räisänen, "Paul's Conversion and the Development of His View of the Law," _NTS_ 33 [1987]: 404–19, esp. p. 410.) It is unfortunate that Sanders conceives of the two frameworks—_Heilsgeschichte_ on the one hand and the significance of grace on the other—as either/or propositions. Paul is not concerned about purely chronological differences but about the difference in _character_ between the two ages: the age of the flesh (= self-confidence and sin) and the age of the Spirit (promise and salvation).
29. Cf. Rom. 10:3, τοῦ θεοῦ opposite ἰδίαν, esp. in view of the whole context, 9:30–10:4.

has been pointed out that every other Pauline use of *pistis* with the genitive is certainly to be understood as a subjective genitive; note, for example, "the faithfulness of God" (Rom. 3:3) and "the faith of Abraham" (Rom. 4:12).[30] Now it is certainly possible, in principle, that Paul could have used the expression *pistis Iēsou Christou* in reference to Jesus' own faith/faithfulness; it is also true that Jesus' obedience plays a central role in Paul's theology (Rom. 5:18–19, and cf. comments on Phil. 2:8). This interpretation, however, faces the insuperable linguistic objection that Paul never speaks unambiguously of Jesus as faithful (e.g., *Iēsous pistos estin*) or believing (*episteusen Iēsous*), while he certainly speaks of individuals believing in Christ. Ambiguous grammatical forms should be interpreted in the light of unambiguous ones, and the very repetition of Gal. 2:16 ("faith in Christ" twice; "we believe in Christ Jesus" once) supports the traditional understanding.[31]

In short, then, Paul asserts that true righteousness is obtained by abandoning one's own efforts and exercising faith. As Rom. 9:30–10:4 makes perfectly clear, Paul understands faith as the opposite of "seeking to establish" one's own righteousness; in that sense, works and faith are indeed incompatible. This perspective is confirmed by the Philippians passage, where *pistis* takes on a specific nuance through its opposition with those things that Paul, as he has already told us in the previous verses, had renounced. It would therefore not

---

30. Cf. especially Richard B. Hays, *The Faith of Jesus Christ: An Investigation of the Narrative Substructure of Galatians 3:1–4:11* (SBLDS 56; Chico, Calif.: Scholars Press, 1983), pp. 158–67. At a 1983 conference in Tlayacapan, Mexico, in which both of us participated, I had the opportunity to express my reservations concerning this view. Hays's response to my oral criticisms may be found in *Conflict and Context: Hermeneutics in the Americas*, ed. M. L. Branson and C. R. Padilla (Grand Rapids: Eerdmans, 1986), pp. 274–80.

31. When we are faced with a linguistic unit whose meaning is uncertain, that meaning should be preferred that adds least to the total meaning of the passage. (On this principle of "maximal redundancy," see Silva, *Biblical Words*, pp. 153–56.) Scholars who object to the traditional interpretation of Gal. 2:16 (also 3:22 and Rom. 3:22) on the grounds that it would be redundant operate with an unjustifiably negative understanding of the role played by redundancy in communication. (Hays, for example [*The Faith of Jesus Christ*, p. 184 n. 80], acknowledges that Paul uses redundancy elsewhere, but adds that his "writing would benefit from the judicious application of a red pencil.") It should also be noted that objective genitive constructions sound "unnatural" to us (cf. ibid., p. 162), and that fact may lead us to assume, falsely, that an alternate interpretation is preferable.

be farfetched to define faith as "the act of counting as loss all those things that may be conceived as grounds for self-confidence before God."

Before leaving v. 9, we must note the striking expression Paul uses to introduce and describe his doctrine of justification: "that I may be found in Him" (εὑρεθῶ ἐν αὐτῷ, *heurethō en autō*). One could hardly ask for clearer proof that Paul's doctrine is no mere abstract speculation. This phrase alone would confirm Ltf.'s well-known comment that Philippians presents the apostle's true view of the gospel as "a Person and a Life" (see Introduction: Exegetical History).

The use of the verb *heuriskō* perhaps reflects our Lord's words in Matt. 16:24–26 (though this verb is not found in the parallels, Mark, 8:34ff. and Luke 9:23ff.): whoever is willing to lose his own life—as Paul was ready to abandon a set of attitudes and practices that had constituted his very existence—for Jesus' sake (*heneken emou;* cf. Paul's use of *dia* in vv. 7–8) will truly find his life, which is now hidden in Christ, who is our life (Col. 3:3–4). It would be difficult to demonstrate that this is the actual source of Paul's language, but the comparison with Jesus' saying suggests a certain elegance in the apostle's use of what may be a deliberate mixed metaphor, that is, the shift from "I lost everything" to "I was found" (rather than "I found something else"). Surely, a simple identification between "to be found" and "to be justified" (Bonnard, Martin) is not satisfactory, much less the view that the verb here is synonymous with "to be" (Schenk).

In any case, Paul's use of the passive *heurethō* in this passage may have a special nuance, approaching the sense of "turn out, appear, be shown," probably in imitation of the Hebrew *mṣ'* (Nif.).[32] Jesus, through His humiliation, appeared in our human form (2:7) and thus identified Himself with us so that we might "be completely united with him." The words in quotations are the rendering of 3:9 by *GNB;* this is certainly an overtranslation, but it is impossible to deny that Paul's central concern with the doctrine of union with Christ is present here (cf. *NBE,* "incorporarme a él"). But if that is so, it reinforces the view that the forensic or judicial strand cannot be made the all-embracing focus of Paul's theology. "Not justification by faith but union with the resurrected Christ by faith (of which union, to be sure,

---

32. So BAGD s.v. εὑρίσκω 2. (end), though the references there show that this usage is attested in nonbiblical Hellenistic sources. Cf. also Preisker in *TDNT* 2:769 and his references to *m. Yebam.* 4.1–2 as a parallel to Matt. 1:18.

the justifying aspect stands out most prominently) is the central motif of Paul's applied soteriology."[33]

b. *Sanctification* (v. 10). Grammatically, this verse is best understood as a second purpose clause introduced by the genitive articular infinitive τοῦ γνῶναι (*tou gnōnai*, "that I may know"). This construction parallels the *hina* clause that begins at the end of v. 8 and continues through v. 9 (however, see Additional Notes). This infinitive rules three objects: αὐτόν (*auton*, "Him"), δύναμιν (*dynamin*, "power"), and κοινωνίαν (*koinōnian*, "fellowship"). A literal rendering suggests three distinct goals: Christ Himself, *and* the power of His resurrection, *and* the fellowship of His sufferings (cf. *NASB*, similarly *NIV*). But the first *kai* can plausibly be understood as epexegetic: to know Christ *means* to experience His resurrection and to share in His sufferings.

This verse should probably be viewed as an expansion of the earlier phrase in v. 8, "the incomparable value of knowing Christ Jesus my Lord." Already in the introduction to this letter (1:9–11; recall the terms *epignōsis, aisthēsis*, and *dokimazō*) the apostle had alerted his readers to the significant role played by knowledge, particularly as it bears on the doctrine of sanctification. More fundamental, however, is the personal element intrinsic to that knowledge, and here in 3:10 Paul appears to define *knowing Christ* as the believer's experiencing of Christ's own death and resurrection. Paul's teaching on this subject is unusually rich, with many interweaving ideas contributing to a coherent whole. Consider, for example, the way in which the following three passages help to elucidate each other:

Phil. 3:10 "to know [*gnōnai*] . . . the power [*dynamin*] of His
resurrection [*anastaseōs*]"
Rom. 6:4 "Christ was raised [*ēgerthē*] from the dead through the glory
[*doxēs*] of the Father"
2 Cor. 4:6 "the light of the knowledge [*gnōseōs*] of the glory [*doxēs*] of
God in the face of Jesus Christ"

Without minimizing the differences among these passages, we can profit by identifying some common threads. Thus, for example, although 2 Cor. 4:6 does not explicitly mention the resurrection, the

---

33. R. B. Gaffin, Jr., *The Centrality of the Resurrection: A Study in Paul's Soteriology* (Grand Rapids: Baker, 1978), p. 132. Cf. also John Murray, *Redemption: Accomplished and Applied* (London: Banner of Truth, 1961), p. 161: union with Christ "is not simply a step in the application of redemption; when viewed, according to the teaching of Scripture, in its broader aspects it underlies every step of the application of redemption."

other two references make clear that this event is indeed what Paul has in view.[34] Similarly, even though the Romans passage does not use "knowledge" vocabulary in reference to our relationship with Christ, we are justified in relating the concept of knowing Christ with that of being baptized into union with Him (Rom. 6:3).

Most significant for our purposes, however, is the way that Rom. 6:1–11 and 2 Cor. 3:4–4:6 aid us in our understanding of Phil. 3:10. The Romans passage, of course, is a *locus classicus* on the doctrine of sanctification. Arguing against those who would infer (from the message of justification through faith apart from works) that Paul's teaching leads to complacency in sin, the apostle insists, in the most forceful way possible, that those whom God justifies He also sanctifies. Our identification with the risen Lord means that we must "walk in newness of life" (Rom. 6:4). Thus, when Paul in Philippians speaks about experiencing the power of Christ's resurrection, he has in mind our spiritual transformation into the image of Christ—a transformation that takes place as we behold His glory (2 Cor. 3:18).

Growth and transformation, however, are not to be had without pain. Paul had earlier (1:27–30) reminded the Philippians of the struggle, conflict, and suffering that characterize the Christian citizen. He had also underlined (2:6–11) the shameful death to which their own Lord had submitted Himself. But now, in one of his most poignant statements, Paul speaks of his goal to experience a share in the sufferings of Christ and to be formed after the manner of Christ's death.

There is a profound mystery in these words. The parallels with Rom. 6:1–11 ("we who died to sin," "baptized into His death," "buried with Him," etc.) make it clear that Paul is not thinking primarily of his physical death.[35] Precisely what is involved in Paul's doctrine of the believer's dying with Christ has been hotly debated. Ridderbos has argued persuasively that Paul has in mind "the participation of the church in the death and burial of Christ in the one-time, redemptive-historical sense of the word."[36] When Christ died, His peo-

---

34. More particularly, Paul may well be referring to Christ's resurrection appearance on the road to Damascus. See especially Seyoon Kim, *The Origin of Paul's Gospel* (Grand Rapids: Eerdmans, 1982), pp. 5–8 and passim.
35. We may admit, however, that because Paul proceeds in v. 11 to speak of his future resurrection, the thought of his physical death may lurk in the background. At any rate, it is doubtful that this clause reflects Paul's anticipation of martyrdom (so Meyer, Lohmeyer, and others).
36. Ridderbos, *Paul*, p. 206, though it hardly seems necessary to deny a refer-

ple, whom He represented, died with Him—His death became theirs. This identification or union with Christ is *appropriated by the believer through baptism*, but there is also a sense in which that death is reenacted in the spiritual experience of conversion and sanctification.

The participation of believers in Christ's death includes not only their definitive breach with sin (the main concern of Romans 6) but also those sufferings they undergo by virtue of their union with Christ. This latter idea seems to be the concern of Phil. 3:10 (but note Hwth.'s objections). The connection between the apostle's suffering and the Lord's passion surfaces in Col. 1:24 and is prominent in 2 Cor. 4:10–12. This latter passage (which admittedly is not an exact parallel to Phil. 3:10) is significant in that Paul describes his own sufferings as a "carrying about in our body the death [*nekrōsin*] of Jesus. . . . For we who live are always being delivered over to death [*thanaton*] for Jesus' sake. . . . So death [*thanatos*] works in us" (cf. also 1:9).

Believers who do not experience the perils to which Paul refers need not think they have been left out (cf. the exposition of 1:29–30). Their baptism represents a deeply traumatic experience; nothing less than the terrifying picture of Christ's death does justice to the seriousness of that experience. To be sure, they have been infused with new life, but there is a sense in which they continue to bear the death of their Lord—in their spiritual disappointments and frustrations, in their struggles with the prince of darkness. The stinging reality of Christian suffering is our reminder that we have been united with Christ. More than that, it is the very *means* God uses to transform us into the image of His Son.

c. *Glorification* (v. 11). Syntactically, v. 11 sustains a loose relationship with v. 10 and may appear to be something of an afterthought. There is, however, a very close conceptual relation between the end of v. 10 and the concern of v. 11: the latter statement sets forth the goal that gives meaning to Paul's sufferings. The idea is expressed most clearly in Rom. 8:17, "we suffer with Him so that we may also be glorified with Him" (*sympaschomen hina kai syndoxasthōmen;* cf. also 2 Tim. 2:11–12). Although some have suggested that here in v. 11 Paul does not have in view the physical resurrection

---

ence to individual conversion. For the latter concept note John Murray's article "Definitive Sanctification" (orig. 1967) in *Collected Writings of John Murray.* 4 vols. (Edinburgh: Banner of Truth, 1976–82), 2:277–84, esp. p. 279: for the believer "there is a once-for-all definitive and irrevocable breach with the realm in which sin reigns."

(cf. Hendriksen), it is difficult to see how his phrasing (τὴν ἐξα-νάστασιν τὴν ἐκ νεκρῶν, *tēn exanastasin tēn ek nekrōn*) could mean anything else. Of course, Paul looks forward to the resurrection not merely because he is interested in a new body. The resurrection represents perfection at every level of his existence, and so it is mentioned here as the culmination of his spiritual pilgrimage.

A serious problem is raised, however, by the apparent tentativeness of Paul's language, εἴ πως καταντήσω (*ei pōs katantēsō*, lit. "if somehow I may reach"—the idea is obscured by the *NASB*, "in order that I may attain"). Because Paul elsewhere speaks with great assurance about his future hope (e.g., Rom. 8:30–31; 2 Tim. 1:12), it might seem legitimate to look for a way of interpreting these words that removes the element of doubt. One could argue, for example, that Paul's tentativeness "is not in reference to the reality of his resurrection . . . but in regard to the way in which it will be his" (so Martin, who thinks the possibility of martyrdom is in view; cf. also Motyer). Unfortunately, I can find no evidence to support this interpretation. True, the word "somehow" is a common English equivalent for *pōs*, but the semantic area common to these two words is that of indefiniteness (see below), not means or method.

The most common solution is to see in the expression not at all a note of "uncertainty but rather humble expectation and modest self-confidence" (Müller). This interpretation contains an important element of truth, as we shall see, but it seems a mistake to deny the note of doubt or uncertainty. The adverb *pōs* (enclitic) serves as an indefinite modal particle; it often adds a slight nuance that cannot be easily reproduced. The specific combination *ei/ean pōs* commonly designates uncertainty (cf. LSJ), and this is surely the case in the NT. The *NIV*, for example, translates Acts 27:12: "the majority decided we should sail on, hoping to reach Phoenix."[37]

It is always important, in this connection, to distinguish between the firm, unmovable *object* of our hope and our *subjective* apprehension of it. The apostle Paul, in spite of his maturity, and though writing under inspiration, was neither omniscient nor sinless. This

---

37. εἴ πως δύναιντο [optative] καταντήσαντες εἰς Φοίνικα (note the parallel with Phil. 3:11, καταντήσω εἰς). Cf. also Rom. 1:10; 11:14; and esp. Ign. *Smyrn.* 4.1, προσεύχεσθε ὑπὲρ αὐτῶν, ἐάν πως μετανοήσωσιν, ὅπερ δύσκολον, "pray for them, if perchance they may repent, difficult though that be" (LCL 1:254). Chrysostom certainly interpreted the construction in Phil. 3:11 as expressing uncertainty: "he dared not openly assert it" (οὐδὲ ἐθάρρησεν ἀποφήνασθαι).

passage is not the only place where he expresses a note of self-distrust (cf. esp. 1 Cor. 9:27); moreover, his concern to strengthen Christian assurance is always balanced by a desire to prevent presumptuousness (1 Cor. 10:12; Gal. 4:19–20). In the very nature of the case, any warnings against complacency and a presumptuous spirit are susceptible to misinterpretation. Indeed, someone unfamiliar with the apostle's teaching could deduce, from Phil. 3:10–11, that Paul perceived he was in the process of earning the resurrection by his willingness to suffer. Of course, such an interpretation would undermine the perfectly clear thrust of vv. 7–9; yet it serves to remind us of the way in which this epistle repeatedly juxtaposes divine grace with personal responsibility (see esp. on 2:12–13).

Calvin is quite correct that Paul wants to impress upon us the difficulties, struggles, and hindrances that attend the believer's life. The apostle would remind us that even he "must watch and pray continually to abide in the fellowship of Christ's suffering . . . for only in that way the glorification with Christ . . . will be attained" (Müller). While we ought not, therefore, to minimize the note of self-distrust present in this verse, it would be unjust to generalize from it and deduce that Paul did not enjoy assurance of salvation. Too many other passages, as well as the whole tenor of his teaching, make clear that he did—and that he expected his readers to share in that assurance.

We may still ask, however, why Paul's striking expression should occur in this particular passage. The only reasonable answer, as others have suggested, is that Paul is already anticipating what he will stress in vv. 12–14. It is apparent that some perfectionist tendencies were present in the Philippian community. The apostle wants to give no encouragement to that, but perhaps he senses that the glowing descriptions of vv. 8–10 could be misused. Accordingly, the subsequent verses qualify his previous remarks to prevent a perfectionist interpretation. In that light, v. 11 can be seen as a transitional statement: although it brings the previous passage to a culmination, it also anticipates the qualifying remarks that follow.

Additional Notes

3:9 καὶ εὑρεθῶ ἐν αὐτῷ: Appealing to 2 Cor. 5:3, Hwth. argues that the verb here means "to be found when surprised by death." This suggestion in effect injects into the verb the general meaning of the context in 2 Cor. 5:3. Hwth., however, also refers to an old note in which Moffatt appeals to Epictetus in support of an "eschatological meaning" for εὑρεθῆναι.[38] The parallels are indeed striking, and Paul's own reference to death in v. 10 may seem to lend some support to this interpretation. Against it is the unlikelihood that Paul would have viewed union with Christ and "having God's righteousness" as future, rather than present, blessings. Yet could one argue that this present/future distinction represents a false dichotomy? While Paul argues emphatically that the believer has already been justified (e.g., 1 Cor. 6:11), he can also speak of justification on the last day (Rom. 2:12–13). Gnilka argues that Phil. 3:9 refers to a communion with Christ that endures to the end, and so what is in view is neither the present only nor the end-time only ("vielmehr sind beide als spannungsvolle Einheit gesehen"). In spite of these considerations, it seems much preferable to understand εὑρεθῶ along the lines suggested in the exposition above.

ἐπὶ τῇ πίστει: "*on the ground of faith* (Acts iii. 16), added at the end with solemn emphasis" (Meyer; cf. also his comments regarding the syntactical relationship between vv. 9 and 10).

3:10 On the grounds that "no one can participate in His resurrection, who has not first participated in His death," Ltf. argues that the thought expressed by κοινωνίαν παθημάτων αὐτοῦ logically precedes τὴν δύναμιν τῆς ἀναστάσεως αὐτοῦ. This analysis suggests a chiastic arrangement:

A   the power of His resurrection
  B   and the fellowship of His sufferings
  B' being conformed to His death
A' if somehow I may reach the resurrection from the dead

Although there is some plausibility in this argument, it appears to suggest that the first phrase has future reference and therefore does not describe the believer's present sanctification—an unacceptable deduction in the light of Rom. 6:1–11.

[τὴν] κοινωνίαν [τὴν] παθημάτων αὐτοῦ: Both definite articles are missing in a strong group of witnesses that include P[46], the original hand of Sinaiticus, and Vaticanus. Hwth. believes that later scribes added the article to mark κοινωνίαν "as a totally separate entity exactly parallel with" δύναμιν (p. 129); later he states that these words are "to be taken closely with the first phrase" because δύναμιν and κοινωνίαν share the same definite article (p. 144; the reasoning

---

38. James Moffatt, "Found in Him," *ExpTim* 24 (1912–13): 46; his references to Epictetus are *Discourses* 3.5.9 and 4.10.11–12.

seems circular). It should be noted that the corrector of Sinaiticus who added the articles belonged to the original scriptorium, a factor that basically neutralizes the value of the MS. to decide this question (if anything, it suggests that the master copy did have the articles). Moreover, the scribe of P[46] is notorious for his omissions (see Introduction: Textual History). The decision is difficult (cf. also on ἀλλά, v. 7). Even if we omit τήν, however, it is pressing the grammar to say, on the basis of that omission, that "the power of the resurrected Christ and the fellowship of his sufferings are not to be thought of as two totally separate experiences, but as alternate aspects of the same experience" (Hwth., p. 144).

3:11 τὴν ἐξανάστασιν τὴν ἐκ νεκρῶν: The fact that this is the only attested occurrence of the compound ἐξανάστασις has created more discussion than it probably deserves. The strong tendency in Hellenistic times to "strengthen" verbs in this way, plus the possibility that Paul may have, consciously or unconsciously, looked for stylistic variety (after using the simple form in v. 10), adequately account for its use. Meyer, who believes the two forms should not be distinguished, suggests that the compound "is to be explained solely from the more vividly imaginative view of the event which the apostle has before him" (i.e., ἐπὶ τῆς γῆς).

The majority of MSS. read τῶν νεκρῶν instead of τὴν ἐκ νεκρῶν. The preposition, however, is attested by all major Alexandrian witnesses (except the Bohairic version) and by most "Western" witnesses. Ltf. points out that the absence of the preposition would suggest a reference to the general resurrection (as in 1 Cor. 15:42), but I find it difficult to sustain that the preposition would be required if the author wanted to refer specifically to "the resurrection of Christ and of those who rise with Christ."

C. PRACTICAL THEOLOGY (3:12–16)

The function of this passage in its larger context is not immediately clear. Even though v. 12 must surely be viewed as correcting any false interpretations of Paul's words,[39] one may ask whether the reference is only to the immediately preceding verse or to some other element(s) in vv. 9–11. The answer to that question may be colored by one's identification of the opponents in view. Although it is fairly clear that vv. 12–16 (with vv. 18–19) reflect a polemic against some

---

39. Cf. BDF §495.3 on *epidiorthosis*.

group in Philippi, opinions differ markedly regarding the character of the group.

Ltf., for example, believes that the Judaizers are no longer in view; rather, v. 18 indicates the presence of individuals "who professed the Apostle's doctrine but did not follow his example" (p. 70). In vv. 12–16, "though St Paul speaks of himself, his language seems really to be directed against the antinomian spirit, which in its rebound from Jewish formalism perverted liberty into license" (p. 151, where he refers to Rom. 6:1). The idea that libertines are in view has been taken to an extreme by Schmithals, who denies that even the earlier part of the chapter was directed against Judaizers, and who argues that the polemic throughout the chapter is directed against a well-defined group of antinomians—an organized missionary movement composed of Jewish Christian Gnostics (as in 2 Cor. 11:13).[40]

Accepting the connection between Paul's opponents and some early form of Gnosticism, H. Koester nevertheless denies that they were libertinists. On the contrary, "they were Christian missionaries of Jewish origin" who preached "a doctrine of perfection based upon the Law and the continuation of Jewish practices." They believed

> that a complete fulfilment of the Law was possible—they had achieved it already and could boast about it!—and brought about the possession of the eschatological promises in full, that is, the Spirit and spiritual experiences of such heavenly gifts as resurrection and freedom from suffering and death.[41]

For his part, Klijn denies the Gnostic connection altogether and returns to Lohmeyer's identification of the opponents as non-Christian Jews (cf. also Hwth.); like Koester, Klijn believes that the whole chapter attacks the view that perfection can be "attained by strict observance of the law." On the other hand, Gunther, who has identified eighteen different hypotheses among modern scholars, prefers to see a united Judaizing (= Jewish *Christian*) group of opponents reflected throughout the letter.[42]

---

40. Schmithals, *Paul & the Gnostics*, pp. 82–115.
41. Koester, "Purpose," p. 331. The similarities and differences between Schmithals and Koester are clearly laid out by Joseph B. Tyson, "Paul's Opponents at Philippi," *Perspectives in Religious Studies* 3 (1976): 82–95.
42. A. F. J. Klijn, "Paul's Opponents in Philippians iii," *NovT* 7 (1964): 278–84, esp. pp. 281–82. John J. Gunther, *St. Paul's Opponents and Their Background: A Study of Apocalyptic and Jewish Sectarian Teachings* (NovT Supp 35; Leiden: Brill, 1973), pp. 2, 98, and passim. Gunther's argumentation is not always persuasive, and his theory may appear extreme and reductionistic (it certainly requires further nuancing). In the end, however, it may prove capable of explaining the greatest amount of data with the least number of difficulties.

Rejecting all attempts to see a single front in the Philippian opposition, Jewett has written two penetrating articles that canvas the entire debate.[43] His conclusions, reminiscent of Ltf., are that 3:2 refers to Jewish Christian missionaries, while the enemies reflected in 3:18–19

> were (a) former members of the Pauline congregation in Philippi who had been expelled during his visit there, who (b) denied the saving efficacy of the cross, (c) indulged and boasted in libertinistic behavior in the areas of food and sex, and (d) believed that in their exalted self consciousness they had already obtained final salvation.

In sorting out the various viewpoints we must note that perfectionism and antinomianism are not mutually exclusive principles. Very probably, the heresy to which 1 John is addressed consisted of individuals who reckoned themselves to have achieved spiritual perfection, yet perfection of such a sort that encouraged wrongful behavior. And for an example of the "compatibility" between an emphasis on the fulfillment of the Jewish law and a less than commendable life-style, we need only think of the churches in Galatia; those Christians had capitulated to Judaistic (legalistic) forces, yet Gal. 5:13–26 makes clear that this move had not prevented antinomian behavior in their midst. In other words, even if Phil. 3:19 describes libertinistic behavior (a debatable point; see the exegesis of that verse), one should not conclude hastily that the enemies thus characterized adopted a different theological position from that of the "mutilators" mentioned in 3:2.

Another preliminary observation is this: recent writers who prefer to view a single front of opposition to Paul have in my opinion the better argument, but this thesis too needs to be qualified by the text itself, which seems to make a clear distinction between error that is external to the Philippian church (3:2) and error that is found within the congregation (3:15–16). The latter, to be sure, may well reflect some kind of influence from the outside, but one cannot deny that the admonition of v. 15 ("Let us have this frame of mind") is addressed to a different group of people from those who are described as "dogs" in v. 2. If so, vv. 15–16 throw some light on the question of Philippian

---

43. Robert Jewett, "The Epistolary Thanksgiving and the Integrity of Philippians," *NovT* 12 (1970): 40–53 (this article says almost nothing about the thanksgiving), and "Conflicting Movements in the Early Church as Reflected in Philippians," ibid., pp. 362–90. The quotation is taken from the second article, p. 382. On p. 386 Jewett acknowledges that, if his theory is correct, it is puzzling that the Philippians could be attracted to two opposing tendencies; his solution (that both groups appealed to a desire for perfection, p. 387) strikes me as lame.

disunity. Perhaps the disunity was the result of some members having a sense of spiritual superiority. In any case, even this conclusion leaves open the question whether or not vv. 18–19 refer to an altogether different group; we must postpone a decision, however, until we can discuss those verses in detail.

For the moment, we must appreciate the *practical* force of Paul's words in vv. 12–16. Might the doctrinal character of the previous section (vv. 9–11) be perceived as abstract and thus irrelevant? Conversely, might its personal and upbeat tone appear out of touch with the hard realities of daily existence? To counteract any misunderstandings, the apostle moves immediately to acknowledge his sense of personal frustration and yet to affirm that the theology he has just delineated wells up in hope (vv. 12–14). He then appeals to the Philippians themselves (vv. 15–16) to bring their behavior in line with their doctrinal commitment if they wish to grow in their spiritual knowledge.

1. FRUSTRATION AND HOPE (3:12–14)

Translation

[You should deduce from my words that] it is not as though I have already attained my goal *[or have already received God's final verdict of justification] or have already been perfected. Rather, I am pursuing the goal with the hope of reaching it—after all, I have already been reached by Christ *[Jesus]. Yes, brothers, even I do not *[yet] reckon to have reached my goal. But one thing [is certain]: forgetting whatever is behind me and exerting myself [to reach] what is ahead, I am pursuing the goal [on which I've set my eyes] in order to win the prize promised by God's heavenly call, [which came to me] through Christ Jesus [or God's heavenly call. (And I exert this effort) by virtue of my union with Christ Jesus].

Exegesis and Exposition

The statement of v. 12 ought not to be interpreted apart from vv. 13–14, particularly in view of the parallelism between these two sections:

A (12a)	I have not attained [*lambanō*]	
B (12b)		I pursue [*diōkō*] that I may reach [*katalambanō*]
A' (13a)	I do not reckon to have reached [*katalambanō*]	
B' (13b-14)		I pursue [*diōkō*] toward the goal

The first set (A-A') consists of negative statements; here Paul makes clear what he is not claiming. These negatives help to correct any

198

false impression that may arise from vv. 9–11. The second set (B-B') consists of affirmations; because he does not yet possess all he expects, he presses on with confidence and determination.

If we focus first on the negative clauses, we are immediately impressed by the variety of terms Paul uses here to express one basic concept: λαμβάνω (*lambanō*, "take, obtain, receive"), τελειόω (*teleioō*, passive "be finished, accomplished, perfected"), καταλαμβάνω (*katalambanō*, "attain, grasp, seize"). Whatever semantic distinctions we may be able to discover (here or elsewhere) among these verbs, we must give greater weight to the simple fact that all three have the same referent in view, namely, the attainment of Paul's ultimate goal.

The precise force of *katalambanō* (a matter of some debate) must be gauged by the fact that in v. 12*b* it occurs in (syntagmatic) opposition to *diōkō*. This linking of the two verbs is rather common in Greek literature generally. Herodotus, for example, quotes a Persian as saying with reference to the Greeks: "They must be *pursued* till they be *overtaken*."[44] In 1 Cor. 9:24–25 Paul, using explicit athletic imagery, opposes the verb *trechō* ("run") to both *lambanō* and *katalambanō*. And in Rom. 9:30–31 the apostle, speaking of righteousness, opposes *diōkō* to both *katalambanō* and *phthanō* (cf. the use of this last verb in Phil. 3:16).

All of this evidence casts doubt on the view (e.g., Martin, Hwth.) that here in Philippians 3 the verb *katalambanō* is used of intellectual apprehension, as with the English "grasp." And yet there is surely a conceptual link between Paul's expressions in these verses and the goal of spiritual knowledge. Not only has Paul already formulated his aim as that of knowing Christ (v. 9), but the contrast between the active and passive voices of the verb in v. 12*b* finds an intriguing parallel in 1 Cor. 13:12, "but then I shall know even as I have been known."[45]

A remaining question, however, is the problem of identifying the

---

44. διωκτέοι εἰσὶ ἐς ὃ καταλαμφθέντες, 9.58 (LCL 4:231). Other literal uses of the combination are found in Diodorus Siculus, 17.73.3 (LCL 8:327, of Alexander's pursuit of Darius—ἐπιδιώκω is used) and Exod. 15:9, LXX (of the Egyptians' desire to overtake the Israelites). A metaphorical use (the pursuit of happiness) is found in Lucian, *Hermotimus* 77: "that which very many good and far swifter men have pursued before you and failed to reach" (LCL 6:404, διώκοντες οὐ κατέλαβον). In Sir. 27:8 we are told, "If you pursue justice, you will attain it" (ἐὰν διώκῃς τὸ δίκαιον καταλήμψῃ; cf. also 11:10).

45. τότε δὲ ἐπιγνώσομαι καθὼς καὶ ἐπεγνώσθην.

direct object of (kata)lambanō. Because the object is not expressed in Greek, this issue has received considerable attention—too much attention, in fact. Commentators appear to forget that the omission of a direct object (especially if that object could be expressed with a pronoun) is rather normal in Greek, though almost never permissible in English. Particularly fanciful is the view that Paul omitted the object deliberately as a polemic against the perfectionists' claim that they had attained everything.[46] A Greek writer will not sense any need to express the direct object if that object has just been mentioned. In this particular case the object is undoubtedly tēn exanastasin ("the resurrection," v. 11).

It must be emphasized, however, that the resurrection stands here not as an isolated event, but as the culmination of the Christian hope. This hope, in turn, had previously been expressed in terms of "knowing Christ" (v. 10). That the Person of Christ Himself stands in the background of Paul's comments is confirmed by v. 12b, where the inverse relationship involves Christ's seizing of Paul (cf. Dibelius and BAGD). Moreover, because the figure of the race has already been invoked, Paul's language also anticipates v. 14, τὸ βραβεῖον (to brabeion, "the goal").[47]

These remarks should not be taken to mean that all of the nouns mentioned or implied in the context (Christon, brabeion, ta panta) serve as the grammatical object of (kata)lambanō. Linguistically, the implied object is simply tēn exanastasin, but because of the theological implications of the resurrection, Paul's thought in this passage encompasses a great deal more: the ultimate spiritual redemption of our body (Rom. 8:23), when all things shall be freely given to us (Rom. 8:32).

But Paul uses still another concept to describe his goal, namely, perfection. We must remind ourselves once again that Paul is here stressing what he did not possess. Clearly implied in these comments is a sense of frustration; the reality of his present existence did not conform totally to the purposes expressed in vv. 9–11. The admission

---

46. So Schmithals (Paul & the Gnostics, p. 97), building on earlier comments by Ewald and others; this view has been adopted, among others, by Collange, Gnilka, and Jewett (in both of the articles mentioned above, n. 43).

47. Cf. esp. Meyer, who unfortunately excludes the related ideas, specifically ἐξανάστασιν. Toward the end of his eleventh homily Chrysostom identifies the object of ἔλαβον as τὸ βραβεῖον, but a sentence later he asks, Τί ἐστιν, Εἰ καταλάβω; Ὅπερ πρότερον ἔλεγον, Εἰ καταντήσω τὴν ἐξανάστασιν τὴν ἐκ νεκρῶν. τὴν αὐτοῦ, φησὶν, ἀνάστασιν εἰ καταλάβω.

of failure is also suggested by his need to forget what was behind (v. 13*b*). In short, Paul was not perfect, though he longed for perfection.

The verb *teleioō* occurs nowhere else in Paul's letters, though the noun *telos* and the adjective *teleios* occur with some frequency (thirteen times and seven times, respectively). This set of terms can be used, in a relative sense, of present experience, as in 1 Cor. 14:20, "in your thinking be mature [*teleioi*]," and possibly in this very passage (v. 15, but see comments below). Such a use may involve more than moral growth; it possibly reflects Paul's conviction that God's eschatological promises are a present reality for believers.[48] The "future-eschatological" sense, however, is also clearly established, as in 1 Cor. 1:8; 13:10 (disputed by some); 15:24; Eph. 4:13. In the present context, this is the only acceptable meaning; to be perfected consists of attaining the last and ultimate goal, blamelessness at the Day of Christ (Phil. 1:10—see comments there).

We may then direct our attention to vv. 12*b* and 13*b*-14, where Paul, having already expressed his disclaimer, tells us what he did claim: he was in hot pursuit! I have already commented on certain aspects of these clauses and so it is not necessary to dwell on them, but a few exegetical questions still need attention. Note first that Paul's purpose in pursuing is expressed with εἰ καὶ καταλάβω (*ei kai katalabō*, lit. "if I may even seize," "whether I may indeed seize"). The construction reflects the same element of self-distrust that Paul had brought out in v. 11.

A second, and interesting, question is the force of ἐφ' ᾧ (*eph' hǭ*) in v. 12*b*. The traditional interpretation takes this construction as indicating aim or purpose, in which case the clause acts in effect as the object of the verb *katalabō*: "if that I may apprehend that for which also I am apprehended of Christ Jesus" (so *KJV*, similarly *NASB*, *NIV*). This view is preferred by some writers and can be supported grammatically.[49] Against it, however, is the omission of the direct object with *elabon* (v. 12*a*) and with *kateilēphenai* (v. 13*a*), which suggests that *katalabō* too is used absolutely. Moreover, the construction *eph' hǭ* is clearly used as a causal expression by Paul in Rom. 5:12 and 2 Cor. 5:4 and makes very good sense here: "I hope to reach it inasmuch as I myself have already been reached by Christ."[50]

---

48. Cf. esp. 1 Cor. 10:11. For a broader discussion see my article, "Perfection and Eschatology in Hebrews," *WTJ* 39 (1976–77): 60–71.
49. Cf. Rob., p. 605.
50. Cf. also my paraphrase above. The English idiom *after all* in this context has a mild causal sense insofar as it introduces a reason for Paul's action;

In any case, the clause as a whole provides an unexpected twist to the argument. Stylistically powerful, the statement in effect balances off Paul's self-distrust with the confidence that is grounded in Christ's work of grace. We do not exaggerate to see in v. 12 one of Paul's most significant soteriological formulations. The verse makes a strong theological point regarding the tension between human agency and divine sovereignty, but the point is made within the framework of a personal confession regarding the Christian experience—a marvelous verse indeed.

Paul then expands the idea in vv. 13b–14, where in the first place human effort is emphasized by the development of the race metaphor: I do not look back at my failures or successes; I strain forward with all determination so that I can win the prize. Yet all of this exertion and mental absorption take place in response to God's upward calling (τῆς ἄνω κλήσεως, *tēs anō klēseōs*); the notion of the divine call, more than any other, signals Paul's conscious dependence on God's grace (cf. Gal. 1:6, 15).

Precisely because the term *klēsis* has such a theologically charged nuance for Paul, one must question Collange's view (followed by Hwth.) that the expression is used after the analogy of the Greek games, in which, *after* each event, a herald announced the name of the winner. No evidence has been put forth that this noun (or the verb *kaleō*) was used in that context. If anything, the call for Paul comes at the *beginning* of the race, and the prize *to which*[51] we are called may be described in various ways, such as conformity to Christ (Rom. 8:29–30), fellowship with Christ (1 Cor. 1:9), the peace of Christ (Col. 3:15), sanctification (1 Thess. 4:7), salvation through sanctification (2 Thess. 2:13–14), eternal life (1 Tim. 6:12). The "prize," clearly, is the culmination of the whole work of salvation—with all its implications—to which God has called us. That is the great hope that sustained Paul, even in the midst of discouragement and frustration.

---

in addition to that, however, the idiom is often "used as a sentence modifier to emphasize something to be taken in consideration" (*Webster's Ninth New Collegiate Dictionary* [Springfield, Mass.: Merriam-Webster, 1983], p. 630). My paraphrase, therefore, brings out the possible force of ἐφ' ᾧ as a rhetorical correction; see John Bligh, *Galatians in Greek: A Structural Analysis of St. Paul's Epistle to the Galatians, with Notes on the Greek* (Detroit: U. of Detroit, 1966), p. 166. Cf. also my comments on 4:10.

51. Taking κλήσεως as a subjective genitive (cf. Meyer): the prize announced or promised by the call. There is thus no need to take the noun as a genitive of apposition.

But what is the force of the last phrase, "in Christ Jesus"? On the surface, the simplest and most natural construction is with the immediately preceding phrase: God's call is mediated through Christ (Schenk adds that this formal phrase constitutes an abbreviated repetition of the last clause of v. 12, "I was reached by Christ Jesus"). Meyer argues that the expression should be construed with the main verb, *diōkō*, and that it "is emphatically placed at the end as that which regulates all his efforts." Aside from Weiss, modern scholars have paid no attention to this view, but the weight of Chrysostom and other Greek fathers should not be dismissed lightly.[52] I have thus included above an alternate translation that incorporates this understanding of the syntax.

Additional Notes

3:12 ἔλαβον . . . τετελείωμαι: Rob. (p. 901) explains the tense variation by saying that the aorist "denies the sufficiency of Paul's past achievements" while the perfect "denies it as a present reality." This distinction might be more appropriate when describing the difference between the *English* simple past tense (which may imply the possibility of intervening events) and the English perfect (which does not).[53] Precisely because the Greek aorist is not equivalent to the English simple past in this respect, we can frequently use the English perfect to translate the aorist (cf. Rom. 3:23). We could easily argue that ἔλαβον here should be rendered with a perfect (so *NASB*, *NIV*).

The most striking textual variant of P[46] in Philippians is found at this point. After ἔλαβον, this MS. adds ἤ ἤδη δεδικαίωμαι ("or have already been justified"). This variant is not unique to P[46]; the inser-

---

52. Though the Fathers were not addressing the grammatical issue, the above inference seems to be the clear implication of their comments. Chrysostom: Ὅρα τὸν εὐγνώμονα [his humility]. Ἐν Χριστῷ Ἰησοῦ τοῦτο ποιῶ, φησίν. Similarly, Theophylact refers to the help Christ gives and defines the phrase thus: τουτέστι, διὰ τῆς ἐκείνου συνεργείας (the English translation of Meyer's commentary incorrectly refers to Theodoret rather than Theophylact in support of this view). Finally, Oecumenius paraphrases: ἐν Χριστῷ γὰρ, φησί, τρέχω. Even though it may be that the last two Fathers were influenced by Chrysostom in their comments, we should still take cognizance of the fact that, as native Greek speakers, they sensed no difficulty in construing the expression with the relatively distant main verb. Incidentally, we need not dismiss the traditional interpretation on the grounds that it "yields a superfluous and self-obvious definition of the κλῆσις [sic] already so accurately defined" (so Meyer).
53. On the use of the English perfect, cf. Bernard Comrie, *Aspect* (Cambridge Textbooks in Linguistics; Cambridge University Press, 1976), pp. 52ff.

tion is found in the "Western" tradition as well (esp. D* and some Old Latin MSS.; F and G have διϰαίωμαι; the addition was also known to Irenaeus and Ambrosiaster). It is very difficult to account for this reading as an insertion, and the usual explanations are not weighty, e.g., that a copyist added it thinking that otherwise "the Divine side of sanctification was left too much out of sight" (Kennedy), or that the addition was made by analogy with 1 Cor. 4:4 (Gnilka and others), or that it would compensate for the lack of a direct object (Hwth.). One is also unimpressed by the argument that the addition "destroys the balance of the four-part structure of the sentence" (so Metzger—omitting the clause destroys a five-part structure, if I may be facetious). Given the Pauline emphasis on justification as something already experienced by the believer (Rom. 5:1 etc.), why would it occur to any scribe to introduce this apparently un-Pauline idea?

On the other hand, it is relatively easy to explain the omission of the clause if it is original; it was either omitted deliberately because of its apparent theological difficulty, or it was omitted accidentally because of the repetition of ἢ ἤδη (homoeoarcton). In favor of its originality, one should notice the resulting paronomasia with διώϰω.[54] If the clause is original, it would be an interesting example of a future-eschatological use of the verb (cf. Rom. 2:13), but the external evidence is so strongly in favor of the omission that the originality of the clause remains doubtful at best.

ἐφ᾿ ᾧ ϰαί ϰατελήμφθην: The force of the ϰαί is not easily reproduced. *NIV* does not try, while the "also" of *NASB* is rather unclear. Schenk is probably correct that the adverb focuses on the past event as the basis for Paul's hope.[55] My paraphrase attempts to represent this general idea with the addition of "already."

3:13 οὐ: The textual tradition is deeply divided between this reading and οὔπω. The decision is immaterial, since the context injects the nuance "not yet" to the simple οὐ. This very point suggests that the original was indeed οὐ and that scribes semi-consciously altered it in accordance with the context. Perhaps we see this process in operation in Chrysostom's homilies. The lemma says οὐ but the

---

54. So Enrique López, "En torno a Fil 3, 12," *EstBib* 34 (1975): 121–23, though his interpretation of the syntax ("I do not, on account of being received, consider myself justified") is not credible.
55. "Das adverbiale ϰαί weiste darauf zurück, dass Pl diesen Akt der Vergangenheit schon nannte, dass er also Voraussetzung für das ist, was ihn gegenwärtig und künftig bestimmt" (Schenk, p. 308).

commentary repeatedly says οὐδέπω, even when he appears to be quoting directly (Εἰ δὲ λέγει . . . Οὐδέπω λογίζομαι κατειλημφθῆναι . . .). The usual analysis of this kind of discrepancy—that the commentary gives us Chrysostom's text but that the lemma has been altered by later copyists—is probably wrong in this particular case.

3:14 κατὰ σκοπόν: Since the related verb σκοπέω is used in v. 17 (it had earlier been used in 2:4), and since it appears to have a semantic connection with φρονέω (note vv. 15–16 and see Introduction: Distinctive Teaching), it is possible that Paul intends a wordplay here. My paraphrase ("on which I have set my eyes") is an awkward attempt to alert the reader to this possible connection. Cf. Schenk, p. 258.

2. GROWTH THROUGH OBEDIENCE (3:15–16)

Translation

Therefore, [listen to me,] any [of you who consider yourselves] perfect: we should all have this frame of mind [I have described]. And if you have the wrong frame of mind [*or* if you continue to have disagreements] on some particular point, God will reveal to you even that fact. However, [be clear on this point: if we wish to grow spiritually,] we must conduct ourselves in a manner that is consistent with [the level of growth] to which God has brought us*.

Exegesis and Exposition

These two short verses present a variety of textual and exegetical problems. The section consists of three sentences, each of which contains two clauses:

(1) as many as are perfect   let us think this
(2) if you think differently   God will reveal this also to you
(3) only to what we have attained   by the same we should walk

Now the first sentence creates no serious difficulties. The word τέλειοι (*teleioi*, "perfect") may be a straightforward reference to spiritual maturity, or more probably it may reflect, by a touch of irony, the group of believers whose error Paul is addressing (cf. 1 Cor. 8:1 and Rom. 15:1; and see Ltf.). In any case, Paul is simply exhorting the Philippian church to share the humble perspective (φρονῶμεν, *phronōmen*) to which he has just given expression.

The third sentence is more difficult, partly because the style is very condensed, partly because of the textual variants found in the MSS. It is clear, however, that the two problems are related; the difficult syntax led to scribal corrections, such as "let us walk by the same rule, let us mind the same thing" (so *KJV* and the majority of MSS.; see Additional Notes). Paul's point, however, is very clear: the Philippians must behave in a manner consistent with what truth they have already received. Ltf. appropriately refers to John 7:17, where our Lord regards submissiveness to God's will as a condition for greater knowledge. Growth comes through obedience.

It is the second sentence, however, that has proved especially baffling. As Martin puts it, Paul gives the impression of "saying that agreement with his teaching is a matter of indifference and that those who dispute his statements are entitled to their views." Hwth., following Beare, argues that Paul is acknowledging his inability to change the Philippians' *attitude* by apostolic command. This suggestion does not really solve our problem, however. For the Philippians to have resisted a change in their attitude would have been tantamount to rejection of the apostle's authoritative teaching.

Meyer cannot be too far from the truth when he comments that someone could "have in general the same frame of mind which Paul has represented in himself, and to which he has summoned his readers; but at the same time an isolated concrete case (τι) may occur, which a man cannot fit into the φρονεῖν in question, and regarding which he is of opinion that he ought to be differently minded." Such an individual, he continues, would be morally inconsistent, lacking the discernment for which the apostle prayed at the beginning of the letter.

Perhaps we should also consider the possibility that the statement in question is a reference, not so much to disagreement with what Paul has just said, but to the more general disputes that the congregation has experienced. Certainly Paul's frequent use of *phroneō* throughout the letter consistently speaks of the need for greater unity among the Philippians. More specifically, the *touto phronōmen* of v. 15 probably corresponds to the *touto phroneite* of 2:5. If so, Paul is not precisely asking for agreement with his statements in the preceding verses (that point would go without saying!) but rather reiterating the great theme of the epistle—an appeal to humility for the sake of the congregation's unity. To that exhortation Paul adds the comment: "But if there continue to be some conflicts among you, I trust that God will soon bring unanimity in your midst."

Additional Notes

3:15 ἑτέρως: This adverbial form occurs only here in the NT and only once in Epictetus, ἂν δ' ἑτέρως χωρήσῃ, "But if the plan goes the other way," that is, if it fails (*Discourses* 2.16.16; LCL 1:327). A strong negative nuance is also present in Josephus, in the course of his criticizing undependable historians: "each of these writers, in giving his divergent account of the same incidents [εἰ ταὐτὰ γράφειαν ἑτέρως], hoped thereby to be thought the most veracious of all" (*Against Apion* 1.26; LCL, p. 173). LSJ has a specific acceptation, *otherwise than should be, badly, wrongly,* under which Phil. 3:15 is included; hence my paraphrase above, "if you have the wrong frame of mind."

3:16 ἐφθάσαμεν: According to Schenk, this verb is equivalent to κατελήμφθην in v. 12.

τῷ αὐτῷ στοιχεῖν: This is the preferred critical reading; it is both shorter and more difficult, and thus it accounts for the Majority reading, which adds the words κανόνι, τό αὐτὸ φρονεῖν (with some variations in the textual tradition). If the longer reading (in any of its forms) were regarded as original, there would be no reasonable explanation for the origin of the shorter reading (cf. Metzger).

3. PATTERNS OF BEHAVIOR (3:17–19)

Translation

Brothers, be united in imitating me and also watch those whose conduct conforms to the pattern you have in us. [I need to stress this point] because [you are faced with] many whose conduct—well, I have often told you about them and now I repeat with tears in my eyes, that *they are enemies of what the cross of Christ [stands for. These people who think they have arrived]—their true destination is destruction. [Though they claim to serve God] they worship their visceral impulses, while that in which they glory will prove to be their disgrace. In short, their frame of mind [is not that which we should have in Christ Jesus but] is molded by earthly things.

Exegesis and Exposition

So as to reinforce his exhortation, Paul contrasts two dramatically opposed patterns of behavior, his own and that of the enemies of the cross. The apostle elsewhere appeals to believers to imitate him (e.g., 1 Cor. 4:16; 11:1; 2 Thess. 3:7–9), but this particular passage carries a special force by virtue of what he has just conceded in vv. 12–14. Paul asks the Philippians to follow his example, not because he has achieved perfection, but because he is struggling in the same race that they are running (cf. 1:30).[56] Quite naturally, therefore, he

---

56. Cf. David Stanley, "Imitation in Paul's Letters: Its Significance for His Relationship to Jesus and to His Own Christian Foundations," in *From Jesus to Paul* (see above, chap. 3, n. 22), pp. 127–41, esp. pp. 137–38. He

identifies himself with them by the use of an affectionate and humble term, "brothers."

Moreover, Paul adds, there are others whom the Philippians can observe and use as examples. The strong word σκοπεῖτε (*skopeite*, "notice, consider, look out for, keep one's eyes on") may be an echo of the apostle's prior reference to "the goal" (*skopos;* see comments on v. 14) or even of his command that the Philippians look out for the interests of others. At any rate, it is worthwhile noticing this continued emphasis on the concentration and singleness of purpose that are required of believers as they seek to grow in sanctification.

The imperative *skopeite* may also reflect a contrast with the *blepete* of v. 2;[57] considering the Judaizers, or watching out for them, must not prevent the Philippians from keeping their eyes on the positive examples that God has provided for them. Whether or not Paul intended a link between vv. 2 and 17, he certainly saw the need for pointing out to the Philippians that there is *a pattern that they must avoid* (vv. 18–19). Unfortunately, the identification of the group whom Paul labels as "the enemies of the cross" is plagued with difficulties.

The apparent force of v. 19 is that it refers to immoral and licentious people. The phrase ὧν ὁ θεὸς ἡ κοιλία (*hōn ho theos hē koilia*, lit. "whose god is their belly") can be naturally understood as a reference to gluttony, with perhaps a broader allusion to their sensuousness and self-centeredness. (In Rom. 16:17–18 Paul speaks of those who cause divisions and who instead of serving Christ serve "their own belly," *tē heautōn koilia*.) The following phrase, καὶ ἡ δόξα ἐν τῇ αἰσχύνῃ αὐτῶν (*kai hē doxa en tē aischynē autōn,* "their glory is in their shame"), would then appear to describe sexual immorality, whereas the last clause, οἱ τὰ ἐπίγεια φρονοῦντες (*hoi ta epigeia phronountes,* "who set their minds on earthly things"), could be viewed as a more general reference to their worldliness.

A large majority of commentators[58] have found this interpreta-

---

concludes on p. 141: "Paul's singular use of imitation and example is the result of his radical insight into the Gospel as the communication of God's saving power in Christ and his total awareness of human impotence vis-à-vis that divine power." Paradoxically, then, what may appear to us immodest or even arrogant in Paul's injunction probably reflects his true humility as one thoroughly dependent on God's grace.
57. This connection was already suggested by Chrysostom. Note also Schenk, p. 258. Interestingly, Paul uses σκοπεῖτε with the negative sense in the otherwise parallel passage Rom. 16:18.
58. See the list in Hendriksen, p. 158 n. 179; cf. also above the introduction to section C in this chapter.

tion persuasive, though they differ among themselves as to the theological background of these "enemies." There are, however, some serious obstacles to this interpretation. First, such a sudden concern with antinomianism seems quite out of character in this letter. Up to this point there has been no hint that moral laxness was a problem—actual or only threatened—in the Philippian community, and nothing in what follows points in that direction either (unless one would wish to argue that 4:8 reflects a comparable concern). When more than one plausible interpretation faces the interpreter, preference should normally be given to the one that reinforces, rather than "disturbs," the thrust of a passage.[59] If the reference is to libertines, they appear to come from nowhere and to go nowhere.

Second, it seems rather unusual that Paul would describe antinomians as enemies of the cross. The apostle's emphasis on the message of the cross serves as part of his polemic *against a Jewish understanding* of salvation (cf. 1 Cor. 1:23; Gal. 3:1; 5:11; 6:12–14). And because the term "dogs" is used in the Psalms with reference to the *enemies* of God's people, one must wonder if the people being described here do not belong to the same group mentioned in v. 2.

But is it possible to understand the details of vv. 18–19 as a reference to Judaizers? According to some interpreters, the word *koilia* should be viewed as an allusion to Jewish concerns over food regulations (cf. the use of the term in Mark 7:19). Indeed, the parallel reference in Rom. 16:18 may reflect the Jewish-Gentile food controversies that Paul addresses in Rom. 14. There is however no real evidence for such a lexical meaning, and the context of Philippians 3 nowhere prepares us for it.

On the other hand, one should not quickly assume that *koilia* must refer to sensual appetites either. The more appropriate word to use in this connection would be *gastēr* (cf. the references given by Meyer and Lohmeyer). The noun *koilia* designates the lower cavity of the body.[60] Because the viscera were perceived as the seat of one's driving forces, this term had a close relation with *kardia* ("heart"). In a negative context such as this one, however, *koilia* might naturally symbolize fleshly impulses. There is much to be said, therefore, for

---

59. Cf. Silva, *Biblical Words*, pp. 153–56.
60. For this point and what follows, cf. esp. Schenk (pp. 286–87), who thinks that Paul may be referring, among other things, to the lower digestive system (and specifically the anus; he refers to Mark 7:19), which would suggest a wordplay with σκύβαλα in v. 8. However, he places even greater stress on Sir. 51:21, "My heart [ἡ κοιλία μου] was stirred to seek her [i.e. wisdom]," and argues that the group in view were wisdom-teachers.

the view (adopted by Gnilka and others) that this term is a strong expression roughly equivalent to *sarx* ("flesh"). If so, the reference is not to a specific kind of misconduct—whether licentiousness or legalism—but to a frame of mind that is opposed to the *pneuma* ("Spirit") and that may manifest itself in a variety of ways.

The word *aischynē* too has been interpreted with specific reference to Jewish practices. According to this interpretation, the term alludes to the sexual organs and thus indirectly to circumcision. If so, the phrase of which it is a part may be viewed as sarcasm. What these Judaizers boast about (circumcision) is in fact a source of shame. Here too, however, we are faced with a lack of lexical evidence to support such a use.

It seems more likely that the word refers neither to immoral behavior nor to circumcision but should rather be viewed in light of 1:20, where the cognate verb *aischynomai* is contrasted with the passive of *megalynō* ("magnify, glorify"), just as here the noun is contrasted with *doxa*. If so, the noun speaks of the objective disgrace that falls on those who come under divine judgment and is thus roughly synonymous with ἀπώλεια (*apōleia*, "destruction"), at the beginning of 3:19). Whatever these individuals consider their ground for glorying will turn out to be their destruction.

The clause in question, incidentally, is a clear allusion to Hos. 4:7. In v. 6 of that passage the people are said to be rejected *as priests* because of their lack of knowledge (cf. Phil. 3:8, 10), then follows this condemnation: "The more they multiplied, the more they sinned against me; I will change their glory into shame [LXX: *tēn doxan autōn eis atimian thēsomai*]." This reference to disobedient Israel parallels the allusion to Deuteronomy in Phil. 2:14–15 and thus indirectly supports the view that here in Phil. 3:17–18 Paul has the Judaizers in mind.

As for the last descriptive clause, *ta epigeia phronountes*, there is no need to take it as a reference to antinomianism. The thought as a whole is meant to contrast the *touto phroneite/phronōmen* of 2:5 and 3:15 and so could easily be understood as alluding to a spirit of selfishness and superiority. The term *epigeia* contrasts specifically with οὐρανοῖς (*ouranois*, "heaven") in 3:20 and with *anō* in v. 14. One is immediately reminded of Col. 3:2, "Set your mind [*phroneite*] on what is above [*ta anō*], not on what is on the earth [*ta epi tēs gēs*]," an exhortation that has as its background not the danger of libertinism but that of submission to human regulations (2:16–23).[61]

---

61. The significance of Col. 3:2 for the understanding of Phil. 3:19 is particularly stressed by P. C. Böttger, "Die eschatologische Existenz der Chris-

It would appear then that the descriptive clauses in 3:19 do not by themselves specify the nature of the heresy in view. Rather, they are strong characterizations of the fleshly mind and are thus applicable to a variety of situations. The only phrase that perhaps gives us more specific information is "the enemies of the cross of Christ" (v. 18), which, as we have already noted, is most naturally understood as a reference to Judaizers. This view would seem to be supported by the cogency of Paul's argumentation throughout the chapter (a point stressed by many, particularly Schenk, p. 291). Whether one accepts this identification or not, it is still possible to appreciate the force of v. 19. Insofar as the group in view represents a pattern of behavior to be shunned by the Philippians, we may argue that Paul is here characterizing an extreme manifestation of the selfishness that was already threatening the Philippian community and that was reflected in the church's lack of unity (cf. Introduction: Distinctive Teaching).[62]

It remains to be pointed out that these verses are charged with considerable emotion. The syntax of v. 18 falters (see Additional Notes), and Paul's deep concern is expressed both by a note of insistence ("I have often said and now I say") and by a mention of his tears (καὶ κλαίων, *kai klaiōn*). Though the apostle uses the verb *klaiō* elsewhere (Rom. 12:15; 1 Cor. 7:30), this is the only explicit reference to his own weeping. Several other passages, however (cf. 2 Cor. 7:2–16 and 1 Thess. 2:17–3:10), give clear witness to Paul's emotional sensitivity. His tears, as he thinks of the enemies of the cross, would seem to preclude any thought of personal vindictiveness when he states that their end is destruction.

Additional Notes

3:17 συμμιμηταί μου γίνεσθε: Some writers place considerable emphasis on the preposition συμ-, either by suggesting that Paul means, "become imitators [of Christ] with me," or by seeing here one more reference to the need for agreement in the community, "Imitate me, one and all of you together!" (so Hwth.; cf. *NEB*). The other approach is to see no significance in the preposition (cf. *GNB*). The ambiguous *NASB* rendering, "join in following my example," is a felicitous com-

---

ten. Erwägungen zu Phil 3,20," *ZNW* 60 (1969): 244–63, esp. pp. 257–58. He further remarks that doubts about the Pauline authorship of Colossians do not diminish the importance of the parallel.

62. If in spite of all these considerations one should continue to sense a reference to antinomianism in this passage, we should remind ourselves that immoral behavior has been known to coexist with Judaistic concerns (see above, introduction to section C in this chapter).

promise. Though we should resist placing undue emphasis on compounded forms, it seems plausible that the verb reflects Paul's concern with unity (thus my paraphrase). The best alternative is Meyer's view (appealing to Theophylact) that the context requires a connection between the verb and those who were already imitating Paul (subsequent clause). This position seems to be reflected in the *NIV*, "Join with others in following my example." If so, the second part of the verse may be viewed as a restatement of the first part.

καθὼς ἔχετε τύπον ἡμᾶς (lit. "even as you have us for a model"): The καθώς is probably not correlative to the preceding οὕτω but has an "argumentative" (Meyer) or even mildly causal function (as in 1:7; cf. BAGD *s.v.* 3.). The ἡμᾶς may be deliberately vague, but I can see no persuasive reason to deny that the reference is to Paul (contra Meyer).

3:18 πολλοί: One should not deduce that a large number is meant. The word probably has a rhetorical force (cf. Schenk, p. 284).

γάρ: Strictly speaking, this verse does not state the reason for the command of v. 17 but rather for the (unstated) fact that such a command is necessary (note my paraphrase).

περιπατοῦσιν: As Ltf. points out, one expects after this verb a qualifying adverb or phrase. Instead, the syntax is interrupted, a relative clause is introduced ("of whom I often told you"), the relative clause itself is syntactically "unfinished" (one expects it to be followed by ὅτι), the qualifying idea is then expressed by a noun phrase awkwardly attached to the relative clause (τοὺς ἐχθρούς . . .), and a description of the heretics' "walk" finally appears in v. 19 in the form of two more relative clauses plus an "abrupt nominative occurring without any grammatical connexions and expressing amazement" (Ltf.). Not surprisingly, the scribe of P⁴⁶ attempted to touch up the syntax by inserting βλέπετε (in analogy with v. 2) before τοὺς ἐχθρούς, with the resulting meaning: ". . . of whom I often told you, and now tell you even weeping, 'Beware of the enemies of the cross of Christ.'"

3:19 τέλος: My paraphrase tries to reflect Paul's possible word-play with τέλειοι in v. 15 (cf. Schenk, p. 286).

καὶ ἡ δόξα ἐν τῇ αἰσχύνῃ αὐτῶν (lit. "and the glory in their shame"): The standard interpretation of the syntax is to take ἡ δόξα as the subject of its own clause, with ἐστίν understood: "and [whose] glory is in their shame." Hwth. objects to this analysis on the grounds that the καί links ἡ δόξα with the preceding ἡ κοιλία as a single subject. His own rendering is: "Their observance of food laws and their glorying in circumcision has become their god." (Hwth. believes that non-Christian Jews are the opponents attacked throughout the chapter.) This analysis seems to me artificial and possibly even solecistic.

4. HEAVENLY CITIZENSHIP (3:20–4:1)

Translation

[So you must reject this earthly behavior and instead follow our example,] because the commonwealth that rules our conduct is in heaven, from where we also eagerly await our Savior, the Lord Jesus Christ. It is He who will transform our humble bodies *in conformity with His glorious body by the power with which He is able even to subdue all things to Himself. Therefore, my beloved and longed-for brothers, you who are the source of my joy and boasting, it is thus [by fixing your eyes on this great hope] that you must stand firm in the Lord, *beloved.

Exegesis and Exposition

The connection between this passage and the preceding statement (vv. 18–19) is not immediately clear; this ambiguity may be responsible for the substitution of *gar* ("for") with *de* ("but, now") in several early citations and other witnesses. Some modern commentators (e.g., Hwth.) stress the difficulty and argue that vv. 20–21 were originally composed in a different context. Because these verses share some interesting features with 2:5–11,[63] and because one can detect a mild (certainly unstructured) rhythm here, some scholars have argued that this passage may have been (part of) an early church hymn. Not many have been persuaded, however, and the standard editions of the Greek text cautiously set these verses in regular prose format.

The supposed contextual difficulties, as a matter of fact, have been greatly exaggerated. To begin with, the conjunction *gar* is frequently used by Paul as a transitional particle, therefore one can hardly insist that it *must* introduce the cause for the immediately previous statement.[64] More important than the conjunction, at any rate, is the clear and explicit *contrast* between the last clause of v. 19 (earthly-mindedness) and the first clause of v. 20 (heavens).

Moreover, the predominant thought of this section flows out of the exhortation of v. 17. Verses 18–19, though not parenthetical, are intended to reinforce that exhortation. Because the Philippians' need to follow the right example was Paul's main concern, vv. 20–21 too

---

63. δόξα, οὐρανός, ὑπάρχω, ταπεινόω, σχῆμα, μορφόω, κύριος. See the fine article by J. Reumann, "Philippians 3.20–21—a Hymnic Fragment?" *NTS* 30 (1986): 593–609, which provides a valuable brief history of research. His own answer to the question posed by the title is a tentative yes.

64. Meyer attempts such a connection here: *"experiential proof e contrario, and that for what immediately precedes."* This analysis may be correct.

213

were meant to support the apostolic command—and what better *reason* is available than the reminder that their true citizenship is a heavenly one?

Indeed, the broader contextual appropriateness of these verses becomes clearer when we notice that they bring to a conclusion the theme opened up in 1:27; cf. especially the reoccurrence of *politeuomai* (as the noun *politeuma*, v. 20) and *stēkō* (4:1; note also *synathleō* in 4:3). If 2:6–11 is indeed an early hymn, it seems likely that here in 3:20–21 material from that hymn "has been deliberately and skilfully adapted to produce a correspondence which would suit the apostle's purpose at this stage in his argument."[65]

We should note that this climactic section of the body of the letter consists of a statement of fact (v. 20*a*), followed by an expression of hope (vv. 20*b*-21), which in turn provides the basis for reiterating (in 4:1) the exhortation of v. 17 (indeed, the ethical imperative of the whole letter). The statement of fact in v. 20*a* (note the emphatic position of ἡμῶν, *hēmōn*, "our") is intended to provide a contrast with "the enemies'" frame of mind (note v. 19, φρονοῦντες, *phronountes*, "setting the mind"). The point is then that *our attitude* is determined by the heavenly character of the commonwealth to which we belong.

Some debate has surrounded the meaning of *politeuma*; "citizenship," "colony," "homeland," "commonwealth" are some of the suggested renderings. There is much to be said for Lincoln's thesis that the particular nuance in view is active and dynamic: "the state as a constitutive force regulating its citizens." We may therefore infer that, whether or not *politeuma* should be rendered "citizenship," the idea of citizenlike behavior is dominant in Paul's thinking (see on 1:27). That kind of behavior is possible, we should add, because the believer's heavenly power is a present reality.[66]

What may appear unusual, however, is that Paul does not here draw a *direct* connection between the fact that we belong to a heavenly commonwealth and the obligations that are therefore incumbent upon us. Rather, Paul proceeds to build his case on the character

---

65. Andrew T. Lincoln, *Paradise Now and Not Yet* (SNTSMS 43; Cambridge: Cambridge U., 1981), p. 88.

66. Lincoln, *Paradise*, pp. 99, 101. The meaning "homeland" for this term has been discredited by Böttger's thorough examination ("Die eschatologische Existenz," first part of the article, with his conclusion on p. 253: "Will man bei der Exegese die philologische Basis nicht verlassen, so tut man gut daran, die in der hellenistischen Zeit am besten bezeugte »Staat« auch für Phil 3_{20} ohne jede Modifikation zu übernehmen").

of the *hope* that such a commonwealth provides. There is a real pastoral insight here, comparable to John's remark: "Everyone who places this hope [of His appearing] on Him purifies himself, just as He is pure" (1 John 3:3). Similarly Peter, after setting forth the hope of new heavens and a new earth, points out: "Therefore, beloved, since you anticipate these [promises], be diligent to be found by Him without spot or blame" (2 Pet. 3:14). Paul himself, of course, often links eschatological hope with ethical commands (Rom. 13:11–12; 1 Cor. 15:54–58; Gal. 6:9; 1 Thess. 5:4–6).

In our passage, the description of hope becomes dominant and is strongly reminiscent of both Jesus' own exaltation (2:9–11) and Paul's earlier expression of hope (3:10–11). The sense of personal frustration we noticed in 3:12–14 can still be detected in the way Paul describes our earthly existence: τὸ σῶμα τῆς ταπεινώσεως ἡμῶν (*to sōma tēs tapeinōseōs hēmōn*, "the body of our humiliation," a phrase that recalls Jesus' own humiliation, 2:8). The intensity of the apostle's hope is perhaps underlined by the use of the verb ἀπεκδέχομαι (*apekdechomai*, "await eagerly"); the term occurs repeatedly in Rom. 8:19–25, where Paul speaks of our groaning as we anticipate our redemption. Finally, even the word σωτήρ (*sōtēr*, "Savior")—rarely used by Paul, except that it occurs ten times in the pastorals—indicates that the apostle looks to the future for his *salvation*, that is, for deliverance from the miseries and frustrations of the flesh (cf. Rom. 7:24; 8:10–11; 1 Cor. 15:42–44, 50–54).

What needs stressing, however, is that the whole of v. 21 is a long relative clause that modifies κύριον Ἰησοῦν Χριστόν (*kyrion Iēsoun Christon*, "the Lord Jesus Christ"). The focus, in other words, is not some abstract hope, but the Person of Jesus Christ Himself, whom Paul is resolved to know (3:10). We await this Lord because it is He who will transform[67] our bodies, it is His glorious body that becomes the pattern for ours, and it is His sovereign power that lends certainty to our hope (on the connection between glory and resurrection, see the comments on 3:10).

The allusion to 3:10 becomes explicit with the term σύμμορφον (*symmorphon*, "having the same form," possibly recalling *morphē* in 2:6–7); those who have been conformed to His death will surely be conformed to His resurrection (cf. also Rom. 6:5). The same adjective is used in Rom. 8:28 to describe God's foreordaining of His people to be conformed to the image of His Son. In that verse *eikōn* rather than

---

67. μετασχηματίσει: is a contrast intended with σχῆμα in 2:8?

doxa is used, but in the following verse the culmination of this process is expressed with the phrase "these He also glorified" (*edoxasen*).

Special attention should be paid to the emphasis with which Paul describes the transforming power of Christ: κατὰ τὴν ἐνέργειαν τοῦ δύνασθαι αὐτὸν καὶ ὑποτάξαι αὐτῷ τὰ πάντα (*kata tēn energeian tou dynasthai auton kai hypotaxai autō ta panta*). This rather involved clause is difficult to translate. The *NASB* reads: "by the exertion of the power that He has even to subject all things to Himself." More idiomatic as well as accurate is the *NIV:* "by the power that enables him to bring everything under his control." The point, quite clearly, is that Christ's great eschatological power—that power that abolishes all earthly authority, making all enemies, even death, a footstool (1 Cor. 15:24–28; Heb. 1:13; 2:6–8)—assures the fulfillment of His promise. Nothing can thwart God's saving purposes; what He has begun He will bring to completion (Phil. 1:6).

With that marvelous assurance established, the apostolic command is surely a light and easy yoke: "stand in the Lord" (4:1). The call to perseverance, so eloquently sounded in 1:27–30, is repeated here as Paul's simple, but most basic, exhortation. Yet it is not couched in authoritarian terms but expressed with warm affection. In a way not quite paralleled elsewhere, the apostle here piles up five distinct terms of endearment—my brothers, beloved, longed-for, my joy, my crown—before uttering the command. And after the command, he repeats the term "beloved" so as to leave no doubt regarding his attitude toward them.

The terms ἀδελφοί and ἀγαπητοί (*adelphoi*, "brothers"; *agapētoi*, "beloved") are of course relatively common in Paul. The use of χαρά (*chara*, "joy") to designate believers is found in another very emotional passage, 2 Cor. 2:3, and is particularly appropriate in an epistle that stresses Christian joy. The combination of *chara* with στέφανος (*stephanos*, "crown"), however, is found only here and in 1 Thess. 2:19 (with *doxa* added in v. 20), a point worthy of special note, since these two letters were not written in close temporal proximity. It cannot be an accident that this expression occurs only in reference to Paul's beloved Macedonian believers. In addition to all this, Paul uses the term ἐπιπόθητοι (*epipothētoi*, "longed-for"), a very strong adjective found nowhere else in the NT (it is unattested earlier than Paul), though it recalls the emotional use of the cognate verb in 1:8 (see comments there).

How does one account for so high a pitch of emotion? The answer to this question may depend on whether we construe the exhortation with what precedes or with what follows. The adverb οὕτως (*houtōs*, "thus"), which introduces the exhortation, is most naturally taken as a reference back to the preceding verses, and in particular to the great hope that provides the grounds for the implicit call to Christian citizenship in 3:20 (cf. my paraphrase above). Behind this call, however, is the earlier exhortation in 3:17 (Meyer refers specifically to *typos*), and beyond that the great imperative of the letter as a whole (1:27). In light of this rich background, particularly when contrasted with the depressing behavior of the enemies of the cross, the affectionate language of 4:1 becomes understandable.

On the other hand, there is much to be said for the view that *houtōs* directs the reader to the more personal—indeed, painful—exhortation of 4:2–3. The structural connection between those verses and the present section is supported by the linking of *politeuma* (3:20), *stēkō* (4:1), and *synathleō* (4:3), the very combination found in 1:27. If so, Paul is very concerned that his motives and attitude not be misunderstood; his emotional tone reveals the spirit of profound love and admiration with which he is about to rebuke the Philippians.

Whatever the precise syntactical force of *houtōs*, however, one should not assume that a backward and a forward reference are mutually exclusive. On the contrary, the bridging or transitional function of 4:1 is very clear.[68]

Additional Notes

3:20 ἡμῶν: There is no denying the emphatic force of placing the pronoun first in the sentence, and several commentators have helpfully pointed out the parallel in 3:3. This formal parallel is insufficient evidence, however, for Lincoln's view that the term πολίτευμα had been used by Jewish Christians as part of their propaganda and that here in v. 20 Paul takes it over as a catchword.[69]

ἐξ οὗ: This singular relative pronoun agrees grammatically with πολίτευμα, a fact that appears to support the understanding of the noun as a concrete place (e.g., "homeland"). There can be no strong objection to seeing the plural οὐρανοῖς as the real antecedent; such *ad sensum* constructions are very common.[70] The understanding of

---

68. This verse is reminiscent of Gal. 5:1, about which commentators are divided as to whether it should be linked with chapter 4 or 5.
69. Lincoln, *Paradise*, p. 97. Similarly Schenk (p. 324), following Böttger ("Die eschatologische Existenz," p. 259). Reumann ("Philippians 3.20–21," p. 605) shows the unlikely character of this theory.
70. BDF §134, though the usual type is that of singular collective nouns construed as plural. Lincoln (*Paradise*, p. 99) calls attention to the sense of βασιλεία as "reign" rather than "realm."

πολίτευμα as "state" or "commonwealth" seems in any case appropriate, since it preserves, but does not emphasize, the spatial element.

3:21 σύμμορφον: The Majority Text reading is εἰς τὸ γένεσθαι αὐτὸ σύμμορφον, "in order that it might become conformed." This is a fairly obvious attempt to improve the terse syntax. The earliest Greek evidence for this reading is a seventh-century correction of D.

κατὰ τὴν ἐνέργειαν τοῦ δύνασθαι αὐτόν: Cf. BDF §400.2: "Certain passages exhibit a very loose relationship between the substantive and infinitive and tend toward the consecutive sense" ("the power so that He can").

4:1 ἀγαπητοί . . . ἀγαπητοί: The second occurrence, no doubt perceived to be redundant, was omitted by a few (mostly "Western") witnesses. The opposite tendency—toward uniformity—led to the addition of a second μου. These variants are very instructive for our assessment of both the Pauline style and scribal activity.

5
Final Concerns (4:2–23)

The exhortations that begin in v. 2 may signal that Paul has concluded the body of the letter and begun the *paraenesis* (hortatory section). This structural pattern appears most clearly in Rom. 12:1 and Gal. 5:1 (or 5:2) and is reflected elsewhere (e.g., Col. 3:1; 1 Thess. 4:1). One also finds considerable variety, however. In the case of 1 Corinthians, one could argue that the hortatory section (1 Cor. 5:1–16:12?) is longer than the "body" of the letter,[1] while 2 Corinthians appears to be missing such a section altogether. Moreover, it may be a mistake to draw too sharp a distinction between body and *paraenesis*.

Philippians is somewhat anomalous in at least two respects. Verses 2–3 of chapter 4, though undoubtedly hortatory, show a strong structural link with the body.[2] Further, vv. 10–20 seem out of place, a factor that has led many scholars, without sufficient warrant, to view that section as part of a different letter. As we shall see, it is not all that difficult to account for the position of vv. 10–20. The former question—whether vv. 2–3 should be viewed as the end of the

---

1. Cf. Calvin J. Roetzel, *The Letters of Paul: Conversations in Context* (Atlanta: John Knox, 1975), pp. 24, 28.
2. Cf. comments on v. 1. Garland ("Composition," pp. 160–61) argues forcefully that Paul "intended 1:27–4:3 to be a structural unit."

body or the beginning of the *paraenesis*—is less easily answered. As pointed out earlier, it may well be that 3:20–4:3 forms an *inclusio* with 1:27. Without necessarily denying that possibility, however, we should fully appreciate the transitional character of 4:1. And because it seems a little artificial to separate the exhortation of vv. 2–3 from those that follow, we are well advised to view 4:2–23 as the concluding section of the letter, consisting of *paraenesis* (vv. 2–9), a word of thanks (vv. 10–20), and the closing (vv. 21–23).

A. EXHORTATIONS (4:2–9)

Paraenetic material in Paul's letters often occurs as a long string of loosely related commands; good examples are Rom. 12:9ff. and 1 Thess. 5:12ff. A comparably lengthy string is absent from Philippians, though 4:4–7 perhaps reflects this pattern. Another typical approach is to list a series of virtues and/or vices, as in Rom. 1:28–32; 5:3–5; 1 Cor. 6:9–11; Gal. 5:19–24; 1 Tim. 3:2–3; 2 Tim. 3:2–5; etc. (cf. 2 Pet. 1:5–7). This pattern is clearly found in Phil. 4:8. Thirdly, and more rarely, Paul might address instructions to specific individuals as he does here in vv. 2–3 (the only other clear example is Col. 4:17).[3] These three paraenetic patterns suggest a threefold outline of the section: final call for unity (vv. 2–3); joy and anxiety (vv. 4–7); obedience and peace (vv. 8–9).

1. FINAL CALL FOR UNITY (4:2–3)

Translation

I beseech Euodia and I beseech Syntyche to adopt the same frame of mind by virtue of their union with the Lord. Moreover, I ask any of you loyal friends to be of assistance to them, for these women have struggled with me in the work of the gospel along with Clement and *with the rest of my co-workers—[you may be sure that] their names are in the Book of Life.

Exegesis and Exposition

Paul's repeated appeals for unanimity among the Philippians do not quite prepare us for his direct words in these verses. The only real

---

3. Whether or not extended ethical instruction should be viewed as a distinct type of paraenetic material (cf. Roetzel, *Letters*, p. 24) is debatable. In one sense, everything between Phil. 1:27 and 4:9 could be viewed as prolonged exhortation.

parallel to this personal exhortation (apart from the pastorals and Philemon) is, as we have just noted, Col. 4:17, where Archippus is encouraged to fulfill his ministry; the *blepete* ("take heed," "see to it") that introduces that exhortation suggests an indirect criticism. Here in Phil. 4:2–3, however, we have an express and unquestionable rebuke. It tells us a great deal about the seriousness of the Philippian problem that Paul should find it necessary to take such a step. At the same time, the apostle's directness confirms how close he felt to this church; one does not take risks of this sort unless one can depend on thick cushions of love and trust to absorb the impact of a rebuke.

Moreover, it is to the great credit of the Philippian community, and of Euodia and Syntyche in particular, that Paul considered them mature enough to be able to handle this unusual admonition. This point is worth emphasizing, because many readers tend to view Euodia and Syntyche in a negative light—troublemakers in an otherwise model church. Most likely, however, what we have here is not a personal quarrel between cantankerous old women, but rather a substantive division within the church leadership, which from the very beginning consisted largely of faithful women.[4] The evidence is too vague to help us specify the nature of their leadership (even the suggestion that they were deaconesses cannot be proved), but one must not minimize the force of Paul's description of those two women as "co-workers" (συνεργῶν, *snyergōn*, but see Additional Notes) who shared in the apostolic struggle (συνήθλησαν, *synēthlēsan*—see on 1:27, 30). They were surely mainstays of the believing Philippian community. Cf. Chrysostom: "These women seem to me to be the chief of the Church which was there."

A very interesting question is raised by the explicit mention of Clement, an individual otherwise unknown to us. Ltf. (who believed that the "true yokefellow" was a reference to Epaphroditus as bearer of the letter) interpreted the clause in question as follows: "I invite Clement also, with the rest of my fellow-labourers . . . to aid in this work of reconciliation." Hwth. correctly argues that the clause should rather be construed with the verb *synēthlēsan* ("Clement too struggled with me"), but one still wonders why Clement should be mentioned by name. It may be simply that by linking Euodia and Syntyche with a prominent leader in the community, Paul strengthens his appeal: "These are worthy women who deserve your help." Is it possible that Clement himself was somehow involved, though per-

---

4. Cf. Francis X. Malinowsky, "The Brave Women of Philippi," *BTB* 15 (1985): 60–64.

haps less directly, in the controversy? Earlier (see on 2:14) I considered the possibility that some of the Philippians may have been guilty of grumbling against their leaders. If so, the present commendation of Clement can be naturally understood as Paul's desire to reinforce his exhortation that the leaders of the church be held in high regard (cf. 2:29).

Special attention should be paid to Paul's instruction (though in the form of a request: ἐρωτῶ, *erōtō*, "I ask") that others in the church become involved in the attempt to heal the division between Euodia and Syntyche. Who the γνήσιε σύζυγε (*gnēsie syzyge*, "noble yokefellow") was has been the source of great speculation. Was it Epaphroditus? A man actually named Syzygos? Paul's wife? Many other proposals have been made, none of which can be proved or disproved. On the basis of our limited information, the most reasonable interpretation is that the appellative is in effect Paul's way of inviting the various members of the church to prove themselves loyal partners in the work of the gospel. (On Paul's use of the second person singular to address the recipients of the letter, cf. Rom. 2:1, 17; 8:2 v.l.; 9:20; 11:17ff.; 1 Cor. 14:17; 15:36; Gal. 6:1. Most of these instances, however, are negative in tone.)

The striking emphasis of this letter on corporate responsibility reaches a dramatic high point in the exhortation of v. 3. The discord between Euodia and Syntyche cannot be viewed by the congregation as a personal matter. These courageous women, whose names too were written in the Book of Life, needed the assistance of the whole church to resolve their differences; brothers and sisters must not be discouraged from intervening in the dispute simply because they are afraid of "meddling." Though Paul in this letter does not use the figure of the body with reference to the church (Rom. 12:4–5; 1 Cor. 12:12ff.; Eph. 4:15–16; Col. 2:18–19), one would be hard-pressed to find a more striking illustration of that principle than the request of Phil. 4:3.

Additional Notes

4:2 παρακαλῶ ... παρακαλῶ: This repetition of the verb is unusual. It strengthens the exhortation by addressing each woman individually. The use of παρακαλῶ rather than a harsher term (cf. ἐπιτάσσω, Philem. 8) is consonant with the tone already established in v. 1.

τὸ αὐτὸ φρονεῖν: Most translations, such as "to live in harmony" (*NASB*) or "to agree with each other" (*NIV*), though defensible, obscure the connection between this verse and 2:2, where the same phrase occurs (alongside τὸ ἓν φρονοῦντες). The expression throws light on the contrasting passage, εἴ τι ἑτέρως φρονεῖτε (3:15); indeed, Schenk (p. 271) views 4:2–3 as the concrete implementation and the elucidation of 3:15*b*.

4:3 Κλήμεντος: It is useless to speculate on the identity of this individual. Ltf. (pp. 168–71) has probably said all that can be said about this matter.

καὶ τῶν λοιπῶν συνεργῶν μου ("and the rest of my co-workers"): The variant of Codex Sinaiticus, καὶ τῶν συνεργῶν μου καὶ τῶν λοιπῶν ("and my co-workers, and the others"), should not be quickly dismissed as "scribal inadvertence" (Hwth., following Metzger). The evidence of P[16], which unfortunately cannot be read with certainty, suggests that this was an early competing variant; it appears to reflect a different understanding of Paul's words (i.e., that the women and Clement are not included under the category of "co-workers").

2. JOY AND ANXIETY (4:4–7)

Translation

Rejoice in the Lord always. [I may appear repetitious, but] I will say it once more: rejoice. Your gentleness should be apparent to everyone. [After all, remember that the coming of] the Lord is near. So let nothing worry you. Instead, in every circumstance, by prayer and entreaty, let God know, along with your [reasons for] thanksgiving, what your requests are. And by virtue of your union with Christ Jesus, God's peace, which surpasses all understanding, will stand guard over your hearts and your *thoughts.

Exegesis and Exposition

As already noted, these verses reflect a form of exhortation found near the end of some of Paul's letters, where loosely related injunctions are strung together. Having noted that feature, however, one realizes that the comparison is somewhat superficial, for here in Philippians one finds only three sets of commands: rejoice, be gentle, and relieve your anxiety through prayer. Moreover, the first imperative stands in a class of its own, partly because joy has been a recurring theme of the letter, and partly because the command to rejoice at this point is almost a farewell (cf. Ltf., Hwth.).

Most important is that the exhortations in this section are not as loosely related as may appear at first blush. Joy, a forbearing spirit, and inward peace are qualities that very much belong together, particularly in the context of the problems faced by the Philippian community. The threat posed by their opponents (1:28; 3:2, 18), their solicitous concern for the apostle in prison (1:18, 19; 4:10), the trau-

223

ma created by selfishness within the chruch—these and other problems called for pastoral guidance and exhortation of the very kind
exemplified in this passage.

Neither Paul's difficult circumstances nor the frightening dangers faced by the Philippians can be allowed to eclipse Christian joy
as the mark of faith. Clearly Paul does not have in view such superficial happiness as manifests itself only when things go well. No, it is
a rejoicing that can be had πάντοτε (*pantote*, "always"), because it
depends not on changing circumstances but on the One who does not
change: "Rejoice *in the Lord.*" And, in a manner reminiscent of 1:18,
Paul repeats the command with reference to the future: "again I will
say, rejoice!" It is as though the apostle anticipated some natural
objections—"How can we possibly rejoice given our circumstances?"—and sensed the need to reiterate the command.

The exhortation that follows in v. 5 may be viewed as reinforcing
Paul's call for believers to rejoice. Genuine Christian joy is not in-
ward-looking. It is not by concentrating on our need for happiness,
but on the needs of others, that we learn to rejoice. And so the apostle
calls the Philippians once again to look out, not "for your own interests, but also for the interests of others," and so to regard others as
"more important" than yourselves. That is the language Paul used in
2:3–4. Here in 4:5 he says, "Let your forbearing spirit [ἐπιεικές, *epi-
eikes*] be known to all men" (cf. *NASB* and BAGD). Several commentators have suggested that the word reflects an attitude of contentment with one's state, even when one has not been treated justly.
Although it would be difficult to prove that this nuance is a basic
semantic component of the word, the context of the letter as a whole
supports it. In other words, Paul expects believers to be guided by a
frame of mind that does not put priority on personal rights. Believers
whose primary concern is whether or not they are being dealt with
fairly will fail to exercise a fundamental element of Christian behavior: preferring others above themselves.

The thrust of this command is then essentially the same as that of
2:3–4. And just as in chapter 2 in which Paul followed up his exhortation with an appeal to the humility of Christ, before whom we will all
bow at the Parousia (2:5–11), so here in 4:5 Paul reinforces his command with the simple but powerful comment, ὁ κύριος ἐγγύς (*ho
kyrios engys*, "the Lord is near"). It may well be that the apostle
wants to remind us of the One who personifies the grace of *epieikeia*,[5]

---

5. Cf. 2 Cor. 10:1, παρακαλῶ ὑμᾶς διὰ τῆς πραΰτητος καὶ ἐπιεικείας τοῦ
Χριστοῦ.

and that His approaching return should awaken us to follow His example (see also Additional Notes). As Ltf. paraphrases, "To what purpose is this rivalry, this self-assertion? The end is nigh, when you will have to resign all. Bear with others now, that God may bear with you then."

The appeal to our Lord's return also becomes the basis for the third exhortation (vv. 6–7), which is expressed more fully than the other two: it includes a prohibition ("let nothing worry you"), a command ("tell God what your requests are"), specific instructions for the proper fulfillment of the command ("in everything—by prayer and entreaty—with thanksgiving"), and a comforting promise (v. 7). Paul uses four different words in reference to prayer: προσευχή (*proseuchē*, "prayer"), δέησις (*deēsis*, "prayer, petition"), εὐχαριστία (*eucharistia*, "thanksgiving"), and αἴτημα (*aitēma*, "petition, request"). This variety does not indicate an attempt to identify four discrete types of, or elements in, prayer. Apart from the occurrence of *eucharistia*—which certainly refers to the distinct aspect of thanksgiving and which appears to receive some emphasis (see Additional Notes)—the variation has a stylistic motive, reflected also in the triplet νοῦς, καρδία, νόημα (*nous, kardia, noēma*, "mind, heart, thought"), and in the fourfold repetition of πᾶς (*pas*, "all," in the forms *pantote*, v. 4; *pasin*, v. 5; *panti*, v. 6; *panta*, v. 7).

The real significance of this stylistic richness is not what it says about the theological components of prayer (or the psychological make-up of human beings) but rather about the great importance that Paul attaches to the believer's prayer life. The opposite of anxiety—indeed its relief—is the peace that only God, in answer to prayer, bestows upon His people. It is worthwhile noting that our Lord's instructions not to worry (*mē merimnate tē psychē*, Matt. 6:25 and Luke 12:22) are grounded in the assurance that God knows our needs (Matt. 6:32; Luke 12:30), and this very fact provides the theological underpinnings for effective prayer (Matt. 6:7–8; cf. in the broader context 7:7–11 and Luke 11:9–13). That the apostle is here reflecting, or even directly alluding to, Jesus' teaching seems very likely indeed.

Now Paul characterizes God's peace with the words, ἡ ὑπερέχουσα πάντα νοῦν (*hē hyperechousa panta noun*). What is the force of this description? Very common is the view that our verse parallels Eph. 3:20: God can do "beyond all things" (*hyper panta*) that "we ask or think" (*aitoumetha ē nooumen*). This understanding of Phil. 4:7 has been disputed by some important scholars. Meyer, for example, appeals to the context and argues that the point of reference (*panta noun*) is the attempt on our part to find relief through other logical *reasons*, but God's peace easily surpasses such reasons.[6] This approach could perhaps be supported by appealing to the similar expression in 3:8 (*dia to hyperechon tēs gnōseōs Christou Iēsou*), where the idea is not so much that the knowledge of Jesus transcends our understanding but that it is of surpassing value.

On the other hand, it is not at all clear that the immediate context supports Meyer's view. What the context certainly indicates is that the Philippians had plenty of reasons *to worry*, a thought that is also reflected in the next section (see comments on 4:12, 19). Moreover, the whole situational context of the letter should be brought into consideration. God's peace transcends our intellectual powers precisely because believers experience it when it is unexpected, in circumstances that make it appear impossible: Paul suffering in prison, the Philippians threatened by quarrels within and by enemies without.

That the Christians in Philippi were suffering anxiety because of opposition from outsiders (1:27) is understandable. But are we justified in relating Paul's exhortation to the lack of unanimity among the Philippians themselves? Hwth. believes that the Philippians' self-centeredness does not at all come into view here, but the command of v. 5, as we have seen, suggests otherwise. One is reminded of James 4:2: "You want something but don't get it. You kill and covet, but you cannot have what you want. You quarrel and fight. You do not have, because you do not ask God" (*NIV*).

The recipients of James's letter, no doubt, were experiencing problems far more severe than anything present in Philippi, but this obvious fact should not prevent us from noticing a common feature: the linking of anxiety (arising from lack of contentment), quarrels, and the failure to bring petition to God. That the Philippians, who knew something about poverty (2 Cor. 8:1–2), needed to learn a lesson about Christian contentment seems clear from Paul's words in

---

6. Similarly Ltf.: "surpassing every device" (though he is more tentative than Meyer). Schenk (pp. 247–48) explicitly denies that Eph. 3:20 is a good parallel and views the verb ὑπερέχω as providing the presupposition for the following φρουρέω. Motivating Schenk, however, is a concern to avoid a certain irrationalism that has sometimes been read into Paul's words. This concern is justified, but the acknowledgment that some things are beyond our comprehension can hardly be interpreted as a slide into irrationalism. Incidentally, it is clear that Chrysostom understood the phrase as a reference to that which our mind is not able to understand. Among his comments: Ὁ ῥυσάμενος ὑμᾶς οὕτως, ὡς οὐδὲ νοῦς καταλαβεῖν δύναται.

4:11, 12, 19; and surely the lack of humility among some members of the congregation (2:3–4) must have been another symptom of the same disease.

Paul's antidote is very clear: Let joy take the place of your discontent and anxiety. Look away from yourselves to the needs of your brothers, being willing to yield your rights and privileges for their sake. And as far as *your* needs are concerned, bring them all before God in an attitude of thankfulness for what He has already given you. If you do this, you will learn what true and unshakeable contentment really is.

Additional Notes

4:5 ὁ κύριος ἐγγύς: Some interpreters prefer to see in this comment a reference, not to the *temporal* nearness of the Parousia, but to the "spatial" nearness of Jesus Himself—His presence and availability. Others (e.g., Hwth.) think we have a deliberate ambiguity on Paul's part. Similar language is indeed used in a spatial sense in the LXX, but nowhere clearly in the NT, where the emphasis is on the Lord's direct presence rather than His nearness (but cf. James 4:8). Ltf. properly appeals to the parallel in James 5:8, where believers are enjoined to show patience (μακροθυμήσατε) on the grounds of the approaching return of Christ (ὅτι ἡ παρουσία τοῦ κυρίου ἤγγικεν). This parallel, incidentally, would seem to support the view that ὁ κύριος ἐγγύς should be construed with what precedes, not with what follows (cf. Meyer, but note that he wrongly attributes this construction to Chrysostom). Quite possibly this is a false question, because what precedes (gentleness) and what follows (lack of anxiety) are themselves very closely connected. Vincent (following Alford and Ellicott) believes that the clause links up with both, a plausible view that I have tried to preserve in the paraphrase.

4:6 τῇ προσευχῇ . . . τῇ δεήσει . . . τὰ αἰτήματα: As noticed earlier (see Additional Notes on 1:4), δέησις can be used either in a broad sense (equivalent to προσευχή) or with a narrower focus (equivalent to αἴτημα). The former is preferable here, which suggests that we should not look for any significant semantic distinction between προσευχή and δέησις in this context; the translation "prayer and petition" (used by several modern versions) effectively captures the slightly ambiguous sense of the Greek. Schenk (p. 246) perhaps goes too far when he says that, in spite of the repetition of the article, these two nouns form a hendiadys here.

μετὰ εὐχαριστίας: This prepositional phrase is to be construed, not with what precedes (by prayer with thanksgiving), but with what follows (present your requests with thanksgiving; cf. Meyer). If so, notice that this phrase begins a new clause and occupies an emphatic position.

4:7 ἡ εἰρήνη: The old view that this word refers to brotherly harmony, though consonant with the thrust of the whole letter, is rightly rejected by Meyer because the form of Paul's promise ("will guard your hearts") does not at all suggest this idea.

τὰ νοήματα: Some "Western" witnesses read σώματα, "bodies" (with P[16] conflating the two nouns, though the reading is doubtful). Lohmeyer raised the possibility that this variant is original and that it indicates in a unique way the holistic significance of martyrdom. If so, later scribes would have substituted the more general and colorless νοήματα. He admitted, however, that the evidence was insufficient. On the other hand, the variant should not be dismissed too quickly (regardless of one's position on the role of martyrdom in this letter). Accounting for the change from νοήματα to σώματα is rather difficult.

3. OBEDIENCE AND PEACE (4:8–9)

Translation

Finally, brothers, keep your minds on that which is true, honorable, righteous, pure, lovely, respectable—yes, on any virtue and anything *worthy of praise. Put to practice the things that you have both learned and accepted, both heard and seen exemplified in me. And the God of peace [Himself] will be with you.

Exegesis and Exposition

Although (as pointed out in the introduction to this section) Paul elsewhere exhorts believers by using lists of virtues and/or vices, the list here in 4:8 is distinctive in several respects. For one thing, it has a strong and effective rhetorical tone. Paul achieves this stylistic effect by the sixfold repetition of the relative pronoun ὅσα (*hosa*, "whatever"), followed by two conditional clauses, "if [there is] any virtue, if [there is] any praise." These last two clauses are meant to reinforce the all-encompassing character of Paul's exhortation, since no list could be complete (cf. also Gal. 5:21, *kai ta homoia toutois*, "and things like these"). It is also unusual for Paul to use the verb λογίζομαι (*logizomai*, "think, consider") with reference to a list of virtues; one might have expected to see here once again the verb *phroneō* (as in Rom. 8:5; Col. 3:2).

More important is the substance of this list, since it contains five terms that are not particularly common in the Pauline letters: σεμνός (*semnos*, "honorable, noble"; occurs in the pastorals); ἁγνός (*hagnos*, "pure"; 2 Cor. 7:11; 11:2; also in the pastorals); προσφιλής (*prosphilēs*, "lovely, winsome"; nowhere else in the NT); εὔφημος (*euphēmos*, "of good repute"; also a NT *hapax legomenon*, though the noun *euphēmia* occurs in 2 Cor. 6:8); ἀρετή (*aretē*, "excellence, virtue"; nowhere else in Paul). Moreover, the term ἔπαινος (*epainos*, "praise"), though relatively common in Paul, occurs here in an unusual passive sense ("worthy of praise"), and some writers infer that it reflects the Greek ethical use of the word with reference to the society's approval of human conduct.[7]

On the basis of these data and the fact that moral philosophers sometimes used similar lists of virtues, Hwth. (following other scholars) argues that Paul is here appealing to the Philippians' cultural background, that is, to their familiarity with current pagan morality: "You must not fail to live up to the ideals of your fellow men, which were also your ideals, before you were converted."[8] It is of course true that Paul's lists, like many other elements in his style, reflect the world in which he lived. Moreover, the note of citizenship characteristic of this letter (1:27; 3:21) may be thought to support some allusion to civic duty.

On the other hand, Paul's very use of the citizenship motif is intended to draw the Philippians' attention to their higher Christian allegiance, and that is surely the case here as well. The idea that at this point in the letter Paul descends from such heights and asks his brothers merely to act like well-behaved Greek citizens can hardly be taken seriously. Given the broad context of the epistle as a whole, the narrower context of 3:2–4:9 (see esp. Schenk, p. 270), and the immediate context of v. 9 in particular, we must understand Paul's list as representing distinctly Christian virtues (though we need not deny that many non-Christian citizens exemplify such virtues in their lives).

In v. 9 Paul intensifies the force of his exhortation in three ways. First, he changes his vocabulary: instead of repeating *logizesthe* ("consider") or a comparable verb, he says πράσσετε (*prassete*, "do, practice"). Second, he emphasizes the sound instruction the Philip-

---

7. For a different possibility, cf. Silva, "New Lexical Semitisms?" *ZNW* 69 (1978): 253–57, esp. pp. 255 and 257.

8. Cf. also H. D. Betz, *Galatians: A Commentary on Paul's Letter to the Churches in Galatia* (Hermeneia; Philadelphia: Fortress, 1979), pp. 281–83, on Gal. 5:19ff. For an older but clear summary of the material, see B. S. Easton, "New Testament Ethical Lists," *JBL* 51 (1932): 1–12.

pians have received with a fourfold reminder: "learned . . . received
. . . heard . . . seen." With such modeling before them (cf. also 1:30;
3:17) the Philippians have no excuse for improper behavior. Third,
Paul ties this exhortation to his previous promise of peace (v. 7) with
the words, "and the God of peace shall be with you." It is not only the
peace of God but the God of peace Himself who will overshadow us
with His care. Yet that promise is conditioned by the command to
lead obedient lives. Whereas vv. 6–7 call upon us to exercise faith
through prayer, vv. 8–9 draw us to a holy walk. And so the simple,
even childlike, message of the familiar hymn captures quite accurately Paul's words: "Trust and obey, for there's no other way to be
happy in Jesus, but to trust and obey."

Additional Notes

4:8 ἔπαινος: The passive sense "worthy of praise" may have been
unfamiliar to some scribes, for the "Western" textual tradition reads
ἔπαινος ἐπιστήμης ("praise of understanding"), thus preserving the
active sense of the word.

Should we attempt to differentiate among the terms in this list
beyond the vague distinctions conveyed by the English renderings
given in the exposition? Meyer is no doubt correct that the terms do
not indicate different and individual virtues; rather, "each represents
the Christian moral character generally, so that in reality the *same
thing* is described, but *according to the various aspects which commended it.*" In short, all of these qualities could be subsumed under τὰ
ἀγαθά.

4:9 ἃ καί: According to Schenk (p. 270), this first occurrence of καί
in the verse should be seen as an adversative. Such a construction
(rather unclear in any case) cannot be correct. As a coordinating
conjunction, the particle would have to be first in the sentence.

B. A WORD OF THANKS (4:10–20)

This passage, though at first blush innocuous, has been the source
of much controversy. To a number of scholars the passage seems out
of place: Why would Paul wait until the end of the epistle to thank the
Philippians? (The question becomes especially pressing if one of the
major reasons for the writing of the letter was in fact to acknowledge
receipt of the Philippians' gift.) This difficulty has led many fine
scholars to view the passage as a separate brief letter, sent by Paul
immediately after receiving the gift. The lack of any textual or historical evidence for this position, however, is a serious obstacle that can

be removed only by the most persuasive kind of internal evidence. Such evidence is not forthcoming, and thus broad segments of scholarship have resisted this partitioning of the letter. As we shall presently see, there are plausible explanations for Paul's having decided to place these words at the end of the epistle.

A second difficulty is the tone of this passage. There is a certain hesitancy in Paul's expression; indeed, the way he qualifies his thanks (see esp. vv. 11, 17) has suggested to some scholars that he was not particularly enthusiastic about the gift. Perhaps we can best make this point by paraphrasing Paul's words as they might be misunderstood by someone unkindly disposed toward the apostle:

> I am glad that at long last, after waiting all this time, you finally decided to think about me. Of course, I realize you were meaning to do it—you just could not get around to it. I hope you understand, however, that I do not really need the money. My circumstances do not bother me—I have learned to handle all kinds of situations. Nevertheless, it's a good thing you decided to send the money—I mean for *your* sake, of course, not mine. You are really the ones that profit by sending an offering.

This is of course a very unfair caricature (if only because of what it leaves out!), but it may assist us in understanding why modern readers are sometimes put off by Paul's remarks.

The way to approach this problem is to become conscious of the distance (cultural and otherwise) that separates us from the apostle. The cultural difficulty is that all of us tend to identify gratefulness with a set of conventions that we are accustomed to. If we were to visit a foreign country where people do not say "Please" to introduce a request, we would be tempted to view them as rude (and it may take us a very long time to appreciate that, perhaps, the intonation of their voice conveys in their culture the very attitude we associate with "Please"). Just because we are not likely to express thanks the way Paul does it in this passage can hardly be sufficient grounds to conclude that he was ungrateful.

In addition to this cultural problem, we need to appreciate the tensions that Paul must have felt in his present circumstances. On the one hand, he was very much in need; even here he speaks of his affliction (v. 14). In at least some respects he must have had to depend on the churches. On the other hand, Paul had a strong sense of apostolic responsibility that prevented him from asking the churches to help even though he had the "right" to do so (see esp. 1 Cor. 9:1–18; 1 Thess. 2:9). Already once, when accepting help from the Philippians, he felt as though he had robbed them (2 Cor. 11:8–9; the term "Macedonians" must refer primarily, if not exclusively, to the church in

231

Philippi), and now he is faced with the problem of acknowledging a truly sacrificial gift from a group of believers who were themselves in need.

Every minister has probably learned from experience how difficult it is to accept gifts graciously. How does one, without appearing ungrateful, discourage parishioners from spending their substance? Conversely, how does one give full, enthusiastic, and sincere thanks without suggesting that more is expected? Seen in this light, Paul's words take on new meaning; in fact, one can hardly think of a more appreciative description of the Philippians' gift than the powerful theological interpretation Paul gives to it in v. 18.

These considerations greatly minimize the problems that scholars have perceived in the placing of the passage at the end of the epistle. As already pointed out with reference to 1:5, Paul begins the letter with a clear and joyful reference to the Philippians' gift. Any further comments regarding it, however, called for a sensitive handling that was best postponed until after other matters had been taken care of.

The way Paul alternates between appreciation and qualification makes it difficult to outline the passage. For practical purposes, I shall deal with vv. 10–14 under the heading "Need and contentment," and with vv. 15–20 as Paul's "Theology of Christian giving."[9]

1. NEED AND CONTENTMENT (4:10–14)

Translation

[Have I asked you to rejoice in the Lord? You should know that] I myself rejoice greatly in the Lord because at last you have been able to make your concern for me flourish again. To be sure, [I know full well that] you have had this concern all along—you simply had no opportunity to show it. [Do not misunderstand my enthusiasm:] It is not out of a sense of deprivation that I speak, for I have learned to be content whatever my circumstances. I know how to deal with dearth and I know how to deal with abundance. I have been taught [to cope] with each and every situation: being full and hungry, experiencing plenty and shortage. I am strong enough for all these things through *the One who empowers me. Of course, [that does not mean I do not

---

9. My division is admittedly simplistic, especially when one considers Schenk's extensive—and often illuminating—discussion of the passage's "Text syntax" (pp. 29–59). On the other hand, it is difficult to avoid the impression that Schenk has overdone the analysis.

appreciate your gift!] You have truly done well to share in my affliction.

Exegesis and Exposition

The progression of thought in these verses can be viewed as follows:

(1) commendation, v. 10*a*
(2) first qualification, v. 10*b*
(3) second qualification, vv. 11–13
(4) commendation restated, v. 14

The restatement in v. 14 was made necessary by the very length of Paul's qualifications (which might leave the impression that his thanks were a mere formality). But why were the qualifications needed in the first place? In addition to the factors already treated above, we must note the specific focus of Paul's comments.

The second clause of v. 10 is introduced with the combination ἐφ' ᾧ (*eph̄ hǭ*). The literal translation "upon which" makes no sense, and this fact suggests that we are dealing with an idiomatic expression. Ltf., following in general the common interpretation in the nineteenth century, tried to preserve the literal meaning of the preposition by viewing "my wants" (a meaning implied in the clause τὸ ὑπὲρ ἐμοῦ φρονεῖν, *to hyper emou phronein*, "your caring for me") as the antecedent of the pronoun *hǭ*. The resulting meaning would be: "at length you revived your interest in me—in which [concerns] you did indeed interest yourselves."[10] The usual understanding nowadays is that the phrase has taken on a causal meaning ("for the reason that" → "for, because").[11] Because the translation "for" in 4:10 remains ambiguous, however, it has become common to use the rendering "indeed" for the more inclusive phrase *eph' hǭ kai*.

This rendering is probably the best alternative, but scholars do not usually recognize (or point out) that it injects a slight concessional force into the phrase (cf. *NEB*, "for that matter"). This idea, first proposed by Luther (in his translation *wiewohl*, "although"), has been routinely dismissed in the standard commentaries. Yet there is

---

10. The best older discussion, though unnecessarily complicated, is found in Meyer. For a recent and extensive, but not always convincing, treatment that also tries to preserve the literal meaning (φρονεῖν ἐπί = "take pride in"), cf. Norbert Baumert, "Ist Philipper 4,10 richtig übersetzt?" *TBZU* 13 (1969): 256–62.
11. This is the meaning suggested in BDF (§ 235.2) and in BAGD (p. 287) for all four passages where it occurs: Rom. 5:12; 2 Cor. 5:4; Phil. 3:12; 4:10.

some plausibility to Bligh's view (see above on 3:12) that all four NT instances may be viewed as rhetorical corrections. At any rate, Luther's sense of contextual propriety led him to a defensible rendering, even though he would have been unable to provide broader linguistic support for it.

The reason for dwelling on the thrust of *eph' hǭ* is to emphasize the function of v. 10*b* as intended to correct any false impressions arising out of v. 10*a*. The words ἤδη ποτέ (*ēdē pote*, usually rendered "finally, at last") might suggest an indirect rebuke that the Philippians had shown no concern for an extended period. The answer to this difficulty is not to struggle over the precise force of ἀνεθάλετε (*anethalete*, "you caused to grow, revived"; see Additional Notes). We should rather focus, as already suggested, on the concessional or correcting force of the second part of the verse; in other words, Paul rejoices because the Philippians *have finally had the opportunity* to demonstrate their concern, and they have used that opportunity to the fullest.

It is the second qualification, however, that occupies Paul's attention in greater detail (vv. 11–13). The very warmth of his gratefulness ("I rejoiced greatly") might suggest that he had felt discontent over his needy condition. He must therefore make clear what is the nature of true Christian contentment. But why should he be so concerned about this? Was Paul afraid that the Philippians might view him as "unspiritual"? Quite the contrary, it was for the sake of the Philippians themselves that he must deal with this subject. We must keep in mind that this passage is flanked by a reference to the Philippians' anxiety over *their* needs (4:6–7) and by a promise that God will supply those needs (4:19). The Philippians needed to hear—and to see exemplified in the apostle—that the enjoyment of material abundance is *not* the basis for contentment.

In the course of his remarks Paul uses two terms that occur nowhere else in the NT. In v. 12 he says μεμύημαι (*memyēmai*, lit., "I have been initiated"). The verb *myeō* was normally used with reference to rituals of initiation into the mystery religions, and the question arises whether or not Paul is exploiting that meaning here. Most commentators think so, with several of them (including Ltf. and Hwth.) placing considerable emphasis on it. That the word could be used in a nontechnical way is clearly attested,[12] and one may argue that Paul uses the verb here merely as a colorful stylistic variant for

---

12. Cf. *TDNT* 4:828.

ἔμαθον (*emathon*, "I learned," v. 11) and οἶδα (*oida*, "I know," v. 12 twice).[13] It would seem out of place for Paul to draw at this point a deliberate comparison with cultic initiations, though we must allow for the possibility that, given the associations of the word, Paul uses it with a touch of irony.

The other unexpected form is αὐτάρκης (*autarkēs*, v. 11), a term popular among Hellenistic philosophers to describe self-sufficiency and independence from external pressures. Here again we must distinguish between semitechnical meanings and more general usage. Paul is not concerned about his self-achievement. Although his use of this term may well reflect the broad influence of Stoicism on Greco-Roman society (otherwise clearly attested in the rest of the apostle's vocabulary), the general nuance of "contentment" is surely to be preferred in this context. Indeed, Paul makes perfectly clear in v. 13 what he means: his sense of contentment does not arise out of personal resources but comes from the one who strengthens him.

As was possibly the case with *memyētai*, however, the word may have been chosen deliberately to suggest *and therefore counteract* pagan notions. There is a sense in which Christians, precisely by recognizing their weaknesses, are able to manifest true self-sufficiency. Once again in this epistle we are perhaps being reminded of the great paradox: our dependence on God's power does not preclude our effort, and our working does not contradict the reality of grace (see on 2:12–13).

Additional Notes

4:10 ἐχάρην: Hwth. labels this verb an epistolary aorist, but that makes little sense. Surely this is a genuine past tense referring back to Epaphroditus's arrival with the gift, not a present tense viewed from the perspective of the recipients. Without leaning on the etymological connection between χαίρω and εὐχαριστέω (as Schenk does), we should recognize that this expression of joy certainly communicates thankfulness.

ἀνεθάλετε: This verb should probably be taken in a transitive sense, with τὸ ὑπὲρ ἐμοῦ φρονεῖν as its object: "you revived your care for me." Meyer, on the grounds that this resulting meaning reflects

---

13. Similarly, Schenk argues that, contextually, μεμύημαι occupies the same lexical field as the two other verbs. Apparently, he allows for no additional nuance (on the grounds that it is impossible to identify what concrete reference such a nuance would have), but perhaps we need not go that far.

insensitivity on Paul's part, prefers to take the verb intransitively (with τὸ ὑπὲρ ἐμοῦ φρονεῖν as an accusative of reference) and argues that it points to a financial resurgence experienced by the Philippians. Such a move is both unlikely and unnecessary.

φρονεῖν . . . ἐφρονεῖτε: It is impossible in an English translation to convey the clear meaning of this verse and at the same time to draw the connection with other occurrences of φρονέω in this epistle. But the connection is surely there. And it may be doubly significant that Paul, after assuring the Philippians that he had the right frame of mind toward them (1:7), and then rebuking them for not having the right frame of mind toward one another (2:2, 5; 3:15; 4:2), here at the end encourages them by recognizing a very positive trait in their attitude.

4:12 μεμύημαι: Some translations (cf. *NASB* and *NIV*) attempt to preserve the nuance discussed above with the rendering "I have learned the secret." English readers unfamiliar with the mystery religions, however, probably attach to this phrase a quite different nuance from that intended by Paul (if indeed he had a double meaning in view at all).

4:13 τῷ ἐνδυναμοῦντί με: The Majority Text, reflected in *KJV*, adds Χριστῷ at the end of this clause. Although this reading is attested as early as the fourth century (the second corrector of Codex Sinaiticus belonged to the original scriptorium), the omission has much wider and stronger attestation. Of course, the meaning is the same with either reading.

4:14 συγκοινωνήσαντες: On the significance of this verb as reflecting financial support, see the exegesis of 1:5.

2. A THEOLOGY OF CHRISTIAN GIVING (4:15–20)

Translation

*But [I am hardly surprised by your generosity:] you yourselves know, Philippians, that when the gospel first [came to you] and I left Macedonia, no church shared with me in matters of income and expenditure except you only. Why, even when I was still in Thessalonica, once and again you sent [provisions] *for my needs. [If I commend you so much] it is not because I am interested in receiving [more] gifts; what I am interested in is the proceeds that will accrue to your account. Indeed, I have received all I need and more. I am fully taken care of now that I have received from Epaphroditus what you sent—a beautiful fragrance, an acceptable sacrifice, pleasing to God. [Who can doubt] then that my God *will fully take care of all

**your needs [not merely according to what you consider necessary
but] according to His riches in glory, [which become ours] in union
with Christ Jesus! Now to our God and Father belongs the glory
forever and ever. Amen.**

Exegesis and Exposition

As if to leave no doubt regarding his appreciation for their gift,
the apostle reminds the Philippians of the unique service they have
performed from the very beginning in contributing to his ministry. It
is not clear whether this uniqueness lay in the fact that they were the
only church willing to contribute or that Paul gave to them alone the
privilege of sharing in this way. Ltf. takes the latter alternative: "You
yourselves will recollect that, though it was my rule not to receive
such contributions, I made an exception in your case." Even if Paul
did make an exception, however, it seems unlikely that he would
make a point of it in this context. Indeed, v. 16 very clearly emphasizes the Philippians' generous initiative—not the granting of apostolic privilege—when he was in need in Thessalonica.[14]

Once again, however, Paul feared that his strong commendation
may be interpreted as a request for more. Just as in v. 11 he had
introduced an important qualification with the words οὐχ ὅτι, so in v.
17 he seeks to correct any false impressions: οὐχ ὅτι ἐπιζητῶ τὸ δόμα
(*ouch hoti epizētō to doma*, "Not that I seek the gift"). This time the
apostle does not dwell on the theme of true contentment. Instead, he
gives a new and unexpected twist to the discussion by saying that
what he is really after is τὸν καρπὸν τὸν πλεονάζοντα εἰς λόγον ὑμῶν
(*ton karpon ton pleonazonta eis logon hymōn*, "the fruit that increases
to your account").

Note that the qualification in vv. 11–13 had a negative thrust.
There Paul explains that it was *not* personal contentment that accounted for his joyful outlook. On the other hand, v. 17 focuses on the
positive side: the actual grounds for Paul's joy consists in what the
gift demonstrates about the Philippians themselves. We find a comparable concern in chapter 9 of 2 Corinthians. There Paul in effect
rebukes the Corinthians for their hesitancy in contributing to the
offering for the poor in Jerusalem. He feared greatly that the church
would end up giving out of a sense of compulsion; such an offering,
inasmuch as it does not proceed from a cheerful heart, does not con-

---

14. Cf. Malinowsky ("Brave Women," p. 62): Paul accepted gifts "only from
the Philippian church because the women there would not take no for an
answer."

stitute a rich bounty (*eulogia*, v. 5), regardless of the size of the offering. Accordingly, vv. 8–15 of that chapter emphasize, not what the
contribution would mean for the Jerusalem church, but what it
would mean for the Corinthians themselves.

Here in Philippians the apostle, as if to settle once for all that he
is not requesting any further gifts (possibly implying that he will not
accept them in the future?), underlines his present satisfaction by
using three increasingly emphatic verbs in v. 18. The first verb is
ἀπέχω (*apecho*), which could be translated in the general sense of
"receive back, hold, keep" (cf. Philem. 15). Paul seems deliberately to
exploit the commercial nuance associated with the verb. In this very
passage he has already used the language of banking and business.
For example, λόγον δόσεως καὶ λήμψεως (*logon doseōs kai lēmpseōs*, lit.
"matter of giving and receiving," v. 15) is recognized by most scholars as the accounting language of debits and credits. Similarly, *ton
karpon* in v. 17 can plausibly reflect the idea of profit or even interest
credited to an account (*logon*).

Would not the readers be expected to understand *apechō* along
the same lines? Notice, moreover, that Paul does not use a past tense,
as one might anticipate if a general meaning were in view ("everything arrived safely"). The combination *apechō panta*, therefore,
could well be translated with an equivalent English business expression, such as "I am in receipt of all," or even "Paid in full!" It
would be a mistake, however, to infer that such language suggests
coldness or aloofness. On the contrary, we may well imagine a warm
Pauline smile as he dictated these words; Paul's playfulness here is
one more evidence of the closeness existing between him and the
Philippians.

The next two verbs are περισσεύω (*perisseuō*, "I abound") and
πεπλήρωμαι (*peplērōmai*, "I am amply supplied"). It may be that both
of these terms continue the business metaphor.[15] On the other hand,
the transition to a more explicitly theological interpretation of the
Philippians' gift is apparent here. The verb *perisseuō* in particular
takes on a clear eschatological nuance for Paul: believers truly experience the abundance of the Messianic age (see Additional Notes on
1:9).

One must not think, of course, that prior to this point Paul has

---

15. Cf. F. W. Danker, "Under Contract: A Form-Critical Study of Linguistic
Adaptation in Romans," in *Festschrift to Honor F. Wilbur Gingrich*, ed. E.
H. Barth and R. E. Cocroft (Leiden: Brill, 1972), pp. 91–114, esp. pp. 96,
100.

overlooked the theological implications of the offering. The expression in v. 14, καλῶς ἐποιήσατε (*kalōs epoiēsate*, "you have done well") recalls Gal. 6:9 (*to kalon poiountes mē enkakōmen*, "let us not be weary in well-doing"), a passage that also focuses on financial stewardship. Again, the phrase *logon doseōs kai lēmpseōs* in v. 15, though it may indeed suggest a banker's ledger, strongly reminds us of the language used by Paul in Rom. 15:27, where Christian Gentiles are represented as *debtors* (*opheilētai*) to the Jews for their spiritual heritage, and where moreover the Gentiles' offering is described with the verb *leitourgeō* (cf. Phil. 2:30).

Ltf. and Hwth. object to this perspective on the grounds that it destroys the business metaphor. The concern is justified, but Paul hardly expects anyone to press his figurative language.[16] Chrysostom and a long line of interpreters (including Martin, who also appeals to 1 Cor. 9:11) are most likely right in seeing here an allusion to the Pauline principle of material remuneration for spiritual blessing (cf. also Gal. 6:6). Even the phrase in v. 17, *ton karpon ton pleonazonta eis logon hymōn*, whether or not it reflects the language of banking, may allude to the theological principle that we will reap fruit that corresponds to what we have sown (a saying that appears also in the financial contexts of 2 Cor. 9:6; Gal. 6:8).

But even if one should insist on an exclusively business metaphor for vv. 15 and 17–18*a*, the latter part of v. 18 is undoubtedly and directly theological. There Paul describes the gift as ὀσμὴν εὐωδίας, θυσίαν δεκτήν, εὐάρεστον τῷ θεῷ (*osmēn euōdias, thysian dektēn, euareston tǭ theǭ*, lit. "an aroma of fragrance, an acceptable sacrifice, well-pleasing to God"). The use of such OT cultic terminology to describe Christian worship became common in the early church, in part no doubt because the OT itself recognizes that outward rituals should be but the manifestation of inward realities (this is certainly the meaning of the prophetic insistence that obedience "is better than sacrifice," 1 Sam. 15:22; cf. Ps. 51:16–17; Isa. 1:11–20; Hos. 6:6). The notion that Christian praise corresponds quite precisely to the Jewish sacrifices is made explicit in Heb. 13:15–16, that is, by the NT writer who shows the greatest interest in formulating the relation between the old and new covenants.

What makes Paul's words doubly significant is that he uses vir-

---

16. Cf. ibid., p. 96 n. 3. See Meyer on v. 15 for a convoluted discussion about who (Paul or the Philippians or both) is pictured as giving and who as receiving. Such a detailed examination of a metaphor is uncalled for.

tually identical language in Eph. 5:2 to describe Christ's sacrifice: "an offering and a sacrifice to God for an aroma of fragrance."[17] The uniqueness, and therefore inimitable character, of that self-sacrifice should not prevent us from recognizing that Jesus' humiliation— even to the point of death—does indeed provide a pattern for our behavior (cf. on Phil. 2:5–11). Similar language is also used by Paul in Rom. 12:1 with reference to sanctification more broadly conceived. It is important to note again (cf. above on 1:5–6) that contributing out of our material resources is not any less "spiritual" an activity than other aspects of the Christian experience. Indeed, it is an integral factor in the believer's sanctification.

Paul concludes by assuring the Philippians that God's own resources, "His riches in glory" (τὸ πλοῦτος αὐτοῦ ἐν δόξῃ, *to ploutos autou en doxē*, v. 19), are more than adequate to meet their needs (πληρώσει πᾶσαν χρείαν, *plērōsei pasan chreian*). Hwth. is correct in pointing to Paul's use of two terms found earlier in the passage (*plēroō*, v. 18; *chreia*, v. 16) and in insisting that v. 19 must refer to material needs. But is he correct to add that "material, physical needs are *exclusively* under discussion here" (emphasis added)? Should we view material and spiritual resources as mutually exclusive categories? While Paul does not ignore the realities of physical discomfort and suffering, his main concern is to help the Philippians find their true contentment in the peace and power of God (4:6–7, 11–13).

These considerations minimize the problem whether the original reading is the indicative *plērōsei* (interpreted as though Paul were guaranteeing that the Philippians would never be in want) or the optative *plērōsai* (indicating a wish; see the Additional Notes). Whether a prayer or a statement of fact, the words are intended to

---

17. προσφορὰν καὶ θυσίαν τῷ θεῷ εἰς ὀσμὴν εὐωδίας. The question arises whether or not Paul's language in Philippians has a deeper significance than the simply figurative. K. Weiss, "Paulus—Priester der christlicher Kultgemeinde," *TLZ* 79 (1954): 355–64, thought so, and the idea has been developed more fully by Michael Newton, *The Concept of Purity at Qumran and in the Letters of Paul* (SNTSMS 53; Cambridge: Cambridge U., 1985), pp. 60–68. According to Newton, Paul saw himself as the priest who received the gifts and offered them in a pleasing way to God: "Now that the Jerusalem Temple has been replaced as the dwelling place of God the offerings of the Christians are real enough for Paul and require certain conditions now that they are taking place in God's Temple, the Church" (p. 67). This view deserves consideration, though the evidence appears to me somewhat ambiguous.

encourage the community with the *assurance* that God can and does provide all that believers need to enjoy true contentment. How significant Paul considered this truth to be is underlined by the doxology of v. 20.

Additional Notes

4:15 δέ: The omission of this particle in P⁴⁶ and D*, if not accidental, may suggest that scribes viewed this sentence as the beginning of a new thought. Almost any division of the passage appears a little artificial.

4:16 ὅτι: With Meyer, it is best to interpret this conjunction as argumentative in character (cf. my paraphrase).

εἰς: The omission of this preposition in some important witnesses must certainly have been caused by the identical ending of the previous word, δίς.

4:17 οὐχ ὅτι ἐπιζητῶ τὸ δόμα: My paraphrase above reflects a particular understanding of the whole passage, namely, that Paul wished to discourage the Philippians from sending more gifts. This meaning is of course not inherent in the clause by itself. As Meyer points out, the presence of the article speaks against it. On the other hand, Meyer has no good reason to deny that this concern did indeed motivate Paul.

4:19 πληρώσει: The main "Western" MSS., with the strong support of such minuscules as 33 and 1739, read the aorist optative, πληρώσαι, "May my God fill all your need." One can think of no persuasive motive that would lead scribes to change the verb in *either* direction. The variation probably arose accidentally. At any rate, the value of the Alexandrian tradition, especially because it is supported here by the Majority Text, makes the indicative the preferable reading. As pointed out in the exposition, however, the note of assurance is not really diminished if the optative is original.

C. CLOSING (4:21–23)

Translation

Greet every saint in [the name of] Christ Jesus. The brothers who are with me greet you too. I also send you greetings from the whole sanctified community, in particular those who belong to Caesar's household. May the grace of the Lord Jesus Christ be with your *spirit.

Exegesis and Exposition

The final greetings in this letter conform very closely to the standardized closings in Paul's letters. Only two matters call for comment.

The mention of οἱ ἐκ τῆς Καίσαρος οἰκίας (*hoi ek tēs Kaisaros oikias*, "those of the house of Caesar," possibly a reference to the slaves) is unique in Paul, and it has played a part in the debate regarding the place from which Paul wrote Philippians. Little of significance has been said beyond Ltf.'s careful discussion (pp. 171–78). It is now acknowledged on all sides that this reference, by itself, cannot have a decisive role in solving the problem. In conjunction with other data, I would still want to argue that its occurrence here strengthens the case for a Roman imprisonment as the background to the letter.

The other matter involves Paul's benediction in v. 23. With very minor variations, such a benediction occurs in all of Paul's letters (the most distinctive ones are found in 2 Corinthians and Ephesians). One peculiarity here is the reference to the spirit of the Philippians (μετὰ τοῦ πνεύματος ὑμῶν, *meta tou pneumatos hymōn*). The same expression is found in only one other letter written by Paul to his churches, namely Galatians (but cf. 2 Timothy and Philemon). Although there are some correspondences between these two epistles, the differences are much more significant. It is thus probably misleading to look for any points of contact that might account for this common feature. Apart from the added forcefulness of the word *pneuma*, it seems unlikely that this phrase is substantively different from the simpler expression, *meth' hymōn*.

Additional Note

4:23 τοῦ πνεύματος: The textual tradition decisively supports this reading. The alternate πάντων, attested as early as the fourth century (one of the correctors of Sinaiticus), is no doubt the result of assimilation to the closings of Romans, 2 Corinthians, and 2 Thessalonians (cf. also 1 Corinthians and Ephesians). What is not so clear is why a comparable scribal change is not attested for Gal. 6:18.

Selected Index of Subjects

Index of Modern Authors
(For commentators prior
to the Reformation
see the Index of Ancient Literature)

Index of Ancient Literature

Selected Index of Scripture